D1238747

Saving Thoreau's Birthplace:
How Citizens Rallied to Bring Henry Out of the Woods
Copyright © Lucille Stott 2018

ISBN: 978-0-9996249-4-4

TMC
books
LLC
731 Tasker Hill Rd.
Conway, NH 03818
USA
www.tmcbooks.com

Saving Thoreau's Birthplace

How Citizens Rallied to Bring Henry Out of the Woods

Lucille Stott

My mother was telling to-night of the sounds she used to hear summer nights when she was young and lived on the Virginia Road—the lowing of cows, or cackling of geese, or the beating of a drum as far off as Hildreth's, but above all Joe Merriam whistling to his team, for he was an admirable whistler. Says she used to get up at midnight and go and sit on the door-step when all in the house were asleep, and she could hear nothing in the world but the ticking of the clock in the house behind her.

—Henry David Thoreau, Journal, 26 May 1857

Title page image: An 1897 drawing from memory, by Mary Wheeler, depicting Henry David Thoreau's birthplace on its original site at 215 Virginia Road.

To SANDY,
my partner in all things,
who has given the gift of Thoreau
to so many students over the years

For THE THOREAU FARM TRUST,
in celebration of its first twenty years (1998-2018)

For HENRY,
who knew the importance of beginnings:

"For it matters not how small the beginning may seem to be:
what is once done well is done forever."

—"Civil Disobedience"

Contents

ACKNOWLEDGMENTS

Fellow Mainer Stephen King wrote, "To write is human; to edit is divine." The errors in this account are all mine. Those you won't see were likely caught by one or more of the generous people who offered information, wisdom, institutional memory, readerly advice, and moral support along the way.

I am grateful to the many people who shared meeting minutes, letters, memos, documents, reports, emails, personal notes, and other primary sources that, taken together, captured the zeitgeist of the Save the Birthplace years. The following are among those whose special contributions allowed the story to come together and made it a pleasure to tell:

Doris Smith, an early inspiration as a citizen activist, lent me her journal and her encouragement.

Richard Lodge, Richard Fahlander, and Bryan Davis, my former colleagues at *The Concord Journal,* helped bring the story of Thoreau's birthplace to the public's attention, and current editor-in-chief Kathy Cordeiro who offered generous support.

Joseph Wheeler, the Thoreau Farm Trust's founding president, and his wife, Verona, our beloved muse, kept us inspired and on task in the early days—and all the days thereafter.

Molly Eberle and Nancy Grohol, the Thoreau Farm Trust's first two executive directors, provided leadership and vision during our most critical moments.

Early advocates, friends of the Thoreau Farm Trust, and current and former staff of the Town of Concord provided archival materials, historical information, and valuable reminiscences: Tom Blanding, Court Booth, Helen Bowdoin, Margaret Carroll-Bergman, the Concord Town Clerk's office, Michael Frederick, Jack Green, Michael Kellett, Al Lima, Ken Lizotte, Nancy McJennett, Anna Winter Rasmussen, Marcia Rasmussen, Sally Schnitzer, Joe Valentine, and Christopher Whelan.

Historic materials conservator Bill Finch, our gifted house detective, uncovered the hidden treasures of the birth house and paved the way for its restoration and rehabilitation, donating priceless photographs and documentation for the Thoreau Farm Trust's archives.

Historic architect Larry Sorli oversaw the restoration project, working closely with Bill Finch and offering guidance, wisdom, and a great deal of hands-on work to ensure an aesthetically pleasing, informative, and environmentally friendly result that honors the entire life of the house. He also co-authored the Historic Structure Report, which chronicles the construction project and resides in the Special Collections of the Concord Free Public Library.

Historian Anne McCarthy Forbes co-authored the Historic Structure Report and wrote the successful application to the Massachusetts Historical Commission that secured a spot for the Thoreau Birthplace on the National Register of Historic Places.

Leslie Perrin Wilson, curator of Special Collections at the Concord Free Public Library, was unfailingly generous with her time, advice, and encouragement, as was her colleague Conni Manoli.

My smart, resourceful research assistant, Bowdoin College student Emily Brown, offered help and advice through the long process of reconstructing the story.

The talented Ted Walsh, publisher and artist, lent his creative vision to the task.

Ken Krause, meticulous proofreader, paid attention to the details.

Sandy Stott, longtime writer and editor of the Thoreau Farm's blog, "The Roost," urged me to tell this story. He has been my trusted advisor, my steadfast champion, and a hardworking parking attendant and bartender at Thoreau Farm Trust events.

Lucille Stott is the former editor of *The Concord Journal* and the Appalachian Mountain Club journal *Appalachia*. She retired in 2014 from a career as an English teacher and administrator at Concord Academy in Concord, Massachusetts, and currently works as a freelance writer and editor in Brunswick, Maine. She continues her involvement with the Thoreau Farm Trust as a trustee emerita.

INTRODUCTION

I think that I love society as much as most....
I am naturally no hermit.

— H.D. Thoreau, *Walden*

This story has a happy ending. But the course of saving an under-appreciated national treasure never did run smooth, and the rescue of Henry David Thoreau's birthplace in Concord, Massachusetts, was no exception. From the day in May 1995 when James Breen Jr., the last private owner of the house and surrounding farmland, died at age 81 in the fields he had worked since he was a boy, it would take fifteen years for the historic house to be saved, restored, and revived.

During that time, partnerships would be formed and dissolved, plans would be devised and discarded, hopes would be raised and dashed, and friendships would be forged and tested. Those who remember the slow, tortuous process that led to the house's resurrection continue to shake their heads at the many starts and stops along the way. But they also acknowledge the value of having given the project the time and consideration it needed to be done right.

In the spirit of full disclosure, I want to make it clear from the outset that I am writing this story not as a detached observer but as a participant. I was closely involved with the effort to save, restore, and re-use the birthplace, first as editor and managing editor of the local newspaper, *The Concord Journal*, in the mid-1990s, and then as a faculty member at Concord Academy and a founding board member of the Thoreau Farm Trust, the nonprofit citizens' group incorporated in 1998 that shepherded the project to completion.

The work that went into that effort—and my continued connection to the house and its mission—are among the most meaningful experiences of my life, and the people I have worked with and included in this account remain among the most inspiring citizen activists I've ever encountered. As I spoke with them about the many years of advocacy and hard work, I probed not only for their recollections of events but also for their reasons for remaining so devoted to the project, even when progress was slow and success elusive.

There are so many urgent ills that need our attention and help. It is perhaps hard to understand why saving the birthplace of a man who was born in 1817 was worthy of the time, effort, and money it took to make it happen. Yet everyone who helped, whether with time, effort, or money, felt connected to something larger than themselves. When we try to articulate the reasons for our dedication, we point most often to Thoreau's significance as a poetic visionary whose continuing relevance is undeniable. We had a sense at the time that if we were willing to discard the birthplace of one of our great American original thinkers, we were excising a precious piece of our collective consciousness.

But there was something else at work on us as well. We didn't think in these terms, but looking back on the intellectual, emotional, and physical effort it took to persist in the face of repeated setbacks—and the need to rely on collaboration and cooperation to get the job done—we were joined in a fellowship of caring, for the birthplace and for each other. The practice of caring becomes a habit. Many of those involved in saving the Thoreau birthplace had developed the habit long before and had been practicing some form of community activism ever since; some of us were novices. For me, the effort to save the birthplace served as an awakening—and a reason to remain awake to the dangers of "a life without principle." To care about this house was to care about it all.

The impetus to take on this retrospective account grew out of my visit to the birthplace on July 12, 2017, during the celebration of Thoreau's 200th birthday. At most, a couple of dozen of the scores of visitors who passed through the house that day remembered, as I did, how dilapidated it once had been and the effort it took over so many years to bring it back to life. The history of the house and the details of its restoration and rehabilitation have been expertly documented by architect Larry Sorli and architectural historian Anne McCarthy Forbes. But no one had yet chronicled the citizen effort to save the house in the first place. And time was running out. Already a few of the early participants were no longer with us, and memories were fading fast.

Yet I'm not sure I would have launched the project had it not been for two additional catalysts. The first was our country's 2016 presidential election. By the time of my 2017 visit to the birth house, many Americans were feeling despair at the growing divisiveness that had begun to tear us apart as a nation and powerless to do anything about it. More than ever, at a time when our citizenship was being put to a severe test, it felt important to remind people not only of the importance of mining Thoreau's writings for solace and inspiration but also of the positive influence concerned citizens could still exert if they joined hands and hearts to make things better. The public-private partnership that saved Thoreau's birthplace is an invigorating example of what people can do for good when they care enough to seek common ground. Faced with the possible destruction of the property, we were forced to reach out across political and social divides to build a coalition of fellow advocates. If we had refused to work together, we would have failed.

The second catalyst was the 2017 publication of a new biography, *Henry David Thoreau: A Life*, by Laura Dassow Walls. A visitor to Thoreau's birthplace once left this note on the message board in the house's foyer: "I came here to meet him at last." That is precisely how I felt as I read Walls's biography, a meticulously researched, elegantly written story of the complex, multilayered man few have come to know and appreciate. Walls writes in her Preface, "Thoreau earned the devotion of friends who saw in him no saint, but something perhaps more rare: a humane being living a whole human life." That was the Thoreau we sought to represent and honor at his restored birthplace.

For those of us involved, the act of saving the house was not about preserving a historical landmark or creating a museum. A distinguished museum and several well-appointed period houses already operated in town, and no one needed another. The purpose of restoring *this* house was to honor Thoreau's intimate connection to his family and hometown and to remind people that, despite the mythology that persists in exiling him to the margins of society, most of his days were busily spent in the heart of his community. We wanted the birth house to celebrate a life force who filled forty-four years with poetry and purpose and who continues to wake us up to the need for attention and deliberation in all we do, every day.

— September 2018

:y, December 21, 1995 • 75 Cents — ⬩ ⬩ Vol. 67, No. 46 • 3 Sections, 88 Pages

E CONCORD JOURNAL

;ought to preserve Thoreau birthplace

⬩aniel
:er
\e of the group known as
\e actually been born in
\u House in town to take
e. The Old Manse and
\preserve of the author's
\nd town officials feel the
\uch a site is at the house
\ginia Road. But they fear
:lopers and the house for-

\v located at 341 Virginia
\ireen family for about 85
last May, his wife, Ruth,
\aynard, where her daugh-
\daughter, Dorothy, lives

:d in selling the 18.4-acre
\rney Nathaniel Brown of
ing at bids from develop-
\Gerry Breen.

But Doris Smith of 295 Virginia Road is spearheading a grassroots effort to buy the house and land
and preserve them for posterity. So far, she has gar-
nered a lot of vocal support — 31 people showed up
at her house a couple of weeks ago for an informational meeting — but no financial commitments, and
she is beginning to worry that a developer will snap
up the property.

HISTORICAL PERSPECTIVE - P.12

Smith said she spoke with Gerry and Ruth Breen
after James's death, when she knew Ruth would be
leaving the house. "I told them I couldn't bear to have
a developer come in and destroy history," said Smith.
"I asked, 'Would you like me to help preserve it?'
They said yes."

Since then, Smith and her supporters have put the
house up for nomination for the National Historic

See THOREAU HOUSE, page 12

The Thoreau birthplace was moved in 1878 from 215 Virginia Road to its current site at 341 Virginia Road.

The first article alerting the public to the threat to Thoreau's birthplace was published in
The Concord Journal on Dec. 21, 1995.

I

"THERE IS A THOREAU
FOR EVERYONE"

*Our woods and waters will always be different because of this man. Something of
him abides and truly 'for good' in his town. Here he was born, and within its
borders he found a wealth of beauty and interest—all that he asked—and shared it
with us all.*

—Edward Hoar, as told to Edward Emerson

When you are editor of the weekly newspaper in an iconic New
England town like Concord, Massachusetts, Thursday is come-
to-Jesus day. The papers hit the stands and mailboxes that morning,
and the phones start ringing before you arrive at your desk, not yet
fully recovered from Tuesday's late-night deadline pressure and
Wednesday's rush to print. Oily shards of salty potato chips poke up
from between your computer keys, and your abandoned coffee mug is
thick with the kind of mossy growth usually found in a petri dish.
Typically, the day's callers have been roused from their reading to
report a typo, a missing calendar item, an opinion that angered them,
or—worst-case scenario—a serious error that has eluded even your
closest scrutiny.

I had come to dread Thursdays. It would take only one legitimate
gripe to ruin my mood, and most weeks served to remind me, all too
painfully, that many eyes don't always make right work.

This account begins on one of those Thursdays, one that in the
end would redeem all the rest. On Dec. 14, 1995, a worried caller—
Doris Smith of Virginia Road—relayed a pressing concern that would
alter my life and the life of our town. Doris told me she and her
husband, George, lived next door to the farmhouse where Henry
David Thoreau was born and that if something weren't done quickly,
the house would likely be torn down.

It is difficult to venture anywhere in Concord without a reminder
that you are treading in Thoreau's footsteps. But a farm on Virginia
Road, nearly four miles from Walden Pond and well off the path that

draws scholars, students, and pilgrims to Concord by the hundreds of thousands each year? That was news to me.

Smith sounded measured and reasonable and, best of all, she was seeking help not atonement. She told me the neighboring farmhouse, which had been privately owned since it was built in the 18th century, had been put on the market by Ruth Breen and her daughters, Geraldine and Dorothy. Mrs. Breen's husband, James Jr., had recently died, reportedly while working in his field, and his wife did not feel she could manage the farm by herself.

At the time of Smith's call, things had already advanced with alarming speed. Developers had quickly shown interest in purchasing the 18-acre property for a small housing development and one had even proposed demolishing Thoreau's birth house, which had deteriorated markedly over time, unless it could be sold and moved off the property.

Not long after Doris Smith's call, the Breen family allowed me to visit the house. Ruth had moved in with Geraldine in a neighboring town, and the house had been vacant for several months. Emptied of its human presence and family furnishings, it felt weary and forlorn.

The compact, two-story house faced south, its small living room on the east side separated from the kitchen and dining area on the west side by a narrow, winding staircase that rose from the tiny foyer just inside the front door. After making my way up the rickety wooden steps to the second floor, I entered the empty bedroom, the "east chamber," where David Henry Thoreau had been born. (On graduating from Harvard College in 1837, Thoreau would reverse the order of his given names, since everyone had always called him Henry.) The original wide pine floorboards creaked in welcome, and without warning, I was overcome with emotion. I realized a little sheepishly, for I'd always thought of myself as a practical, feet-on-the-ground kind of person, that what I was feeling was awe. The poet Mallarmé believed an artist should not depict "the thing, but the effect it produces." No one would have called this little room, with its faded wallpaper, peeling window frames, and layers of dust, "awesome," but awe was the effect it produced on me, and I would find over time that I was not alone.

My surprise arose in large part because I was not, in any scholarly sense, a Thoreauvian. I had read *Walden* rather perfunctorily as a student, and had come to appreciate the beauty of Walden Pond during my almost twenty years of working and living in and near Concord. I had especially appreciated the essays "Civil Disobedience" and "Walking," and could muster some of Henry's famous axioms on demand, as could pretty much anyone in town. I believed that "[i]n Wildness is the preservation of the world" and aspired, as best I could, to "[s]implify, simplify." In my White Mountain hikes and my saunters along the familiar trails of home, Thoreau had served as an inspiration to slow down, forget peak-bagging and mileage counts, and remember that "heaven is under our feet."

But that day, in that house, something entirely new was happening to me. It was more a feeling than a thought: here was where the genius of Thoreau had been brought into the world. Everything he had accomplished, all he had written, what he still meant to so many had risen from this place. In that bedchamber, I had unexpectedly discovered a different Thoreau, the Henry with a heartbeat. This Henry belonged to his family and to the town he would later dub "the most estimable place in the world." I liked this Henry. I wanted to get to know all about him. And most of all, I wanted to help prevent him from being uprooted from the place where he had first seen the sun, his "morning star."

Later, when I set about rereading *Walden* and came across his comments about why he had built his little home at Walden Pond and why he had left it, I realized I had been having a singularly Thoreauvian moment in his birth house: As Henry said he had done at Walden, I had gone to the house because I wished to report "deliberately, to front only the essential facts." But, as it turned out, the place had more to teach me than I thought. Paraphrasing Thoreau, I've found, becomes something of a fetish. He was uncommonly adept at articulating the human condition we recognize as our own.

Over the next several years, I devoured Robert Richardson's biography of Thoreau, reread *Walden* and "Walking," dipped repeatedly into the journals, and discovered a small treasure: *Henry Thoreau As Remembered By A Young Friend*, written by Edward Emerson, son of Ralph Waldo. In the process of my education, I was privileged to join a remarkable group of local citizens who were making it their purpose to save Thoreau's birthplace from what then appeared to be imminent destruction.

Today, after years of negotiations, delays, and fundraising, the house once again rests securely on a portion of the original farm where Thoreau was born. It remains simple and unassuming, a reflection of Henry's full life as a son, brother, friend, and citizen. True to the original vision, it has become the site of lively, interactive programs for all ages, designed to highlight Thoreau's forward-thinking ideas and explore the many ways his life and work continue to urge us to action.

"Thoreau lives on because there is a Thoreau for everyone," said Leslie Perrin Wilson, curator of Special Collections at the Concord Free Public Library, to *Boston Globe* reporter James Sullivan in January 2017. "There's the Thoreau who celebrated his natural surroundings through careful observation and measurement; the man of conscience who practiced civil disobedience by refusing to pay taxes to a government that condoned slavery and prosecuted a war with Mexico that he considered unjust; the villager who enjoyed companionship far more than some of the myths handed down about him suggest. There is [also], of course, the Thoreau who heard a different drummer. And there's always room for more."

In other words, to paraphrase Mark Twain's famous cable to the newspaper that erroneously published his obituary, the death of Henry David Thoreau has been greatly exaggerated.

II

"WHY DO WE NEED THIS HOUSE?"

Every day or two, I strolled to the village to hear some of the gossip
which is incessantly going on there … and which, taken in homeopathic doses,
was really as refreshing in its way as the rustle of leaves and the peeping of frogs.
—H.D. Thoreau, *Walden*

If you visit the Thoreau birthplace today, it might be hard to imagine a time when its destruction felt imminent and saving the house was a doubtful prospect. At one point early in my involvement with the cause, as I was talking about how important I felt it was to stop the birthplace from being overrun with development and maybe even destroyed, a very smart, very prominent resident of Concord sniffed, "We can't save every tree Thoreau pissed on, you know. Why do we need this house?"

I had to admit she had a point. Thoreau wrote in the opening chapter of *Walden* that he had "traveled a good deal in Concord," and his footprints are everywhere in his hometown. You can take Walden Street or Thoreau Street from the village center to Walden Pond. Or you can head out in the other direction to the dense, trail-woven forest tract—Estabrook Woods—on the north edge of town, a favorite Thoreau haunt.

You can glimpse the site of one of the Thoreau family homes on Monument Street (now part of the Colonial Inn), stroll past the former schoolhouse on Academy Lane where he briefly taught, and admire the privately-owned Main Street home, the so-called Yellow House, in whose front room he died. You can even stop by the site of the former jailhouse—commemorated by a granite marker on Monument Square—where Thoreau spent a night in 1846 for not paying his poll tax, an experience that prompted him to write "Resistance to Civil Government," more commonly known today as "Civil Disobedience."

The Concord Free Public Library, one of the finest small libraries in the country, houses the manuscript of Thoreau's essay "Walking," the field notes he gathered, and the surveys he drew up, including one of Walden Pond. The library's Leslie Perrin Wilson has told me that visitors—even the scholars among them—often react emotionally when holding these documents, particularly the "Walking" manuscript, which originated in journal entries and lecture notes, and which contains, on page 45, the famous axiom, "In Wildness is the preservation of the world."

"To watch people respond to this is very moving," said Wilson. "I've seen them cry." Wilson added that visitors to the Thoreau collection are a diverse group, in age, background, and nationality. "Thoreau doesn't belong to the experts," she said. "He belongs to the people. I love talking to a group of high school or college students who have their breath taken away. Thoreau is truly a universal language."

A visitor interested in artifacts can find more than 250 Thoreau-related objects at the Concord Museum, which contains the world's largest collection of Thoreauviana, including his flute, his walking stick, and the desk on which he wrote "Civil Disobedience" and *Walden*.

Despite Thoreau's reluctance to become a model for others' lives, the most visited Thoreau-related place in Concord remains Walden Pond, now a state reservation. There you can walk along a well-worn trail to his house site, discovered by Roland Robbins in 1945, one hundred years after Henry built it. Many people leave a stone, often with messages attached, for the commemorative cairn, an idea originated in 1872 by Bronson Alcott and his friend Mary Newbury Adams. The little house Thoreau inhabited is no longer there, however. After Henry left it on Sept. 6, 1847, it was moved and used by local farmers and was finally destroyed for firewood and timber. The Thoreau Society, which runs the Shop at Walden Pond, has constructed a life-size replica that stands beside the entrance to the park.

One of the most beautiful walks in town is through picturesque Sleepy Hollow Cemetery, where Thoreau is buried with his family. Devotees leave tokens at his gravesite—stones, feathers, pine cones, sometimes even personal notes. Originally, Thoreau was buried in the maternal family plot in the oldest part of the cemetery. Later, in the 1870s, he and his family were moved to the section known as Author's Ridge, near the Hawthornes, the Alcotts, and the Emersons.

But in 1995, among the many places in town that celebrate Thoreau's lasting influence, there was one significant omission. Of all the famous authors associated with the town of Concord, including Louisa May Alcott, Ralph Waldo Emerson, and Nathaniel Hawthorne, Thoreau is the only one who was actually born there. For decades, visitors have been able to tour the houses where Alcott, Emerson, and Hawthorne once lived, yet until 2010 there was no family home to mark Thoreau's life as Concord's native son.

One reason for the oversight was that Thoreau lived only eight months in the house on Virginia Road where he was born. His mother, Cynthia, had spent much of her childhood and adolescence there and had recounted her love of the place to her son, who made reference to her words in his journals. When Cynthia and her husband, John, moved back to the house to farm the land, they were stymied by a long, bitter spate of punishing weather. In particular, severe climate abnormalities in 1816 led to the famous "year without a summer," which wreaked havoc on all of New England's farming communities. So within a year of Henry's birth, the young family was forced to leave. Sixty-one years after Thoreau's birth, in 1878, the house was moved eastward on the farm to make way for a newer dwelling, a practice not uncommon at the time.

Another reason for the omission, perhaps an even more significant one, was the fact that Thoreau remains best known for the two years, two months, and two days he spent living in his little house on the shore of Walden Pond. His time at the pond has become the stuff of myth and, as such, has lost much of its link to reality. One of my hopes in joining the effort to save the house where he was born— and I know my feelings were shared by others who became active in that effort—was to celebrate his largely unsung role as an active, caring member of a family and a community.

Most of Thoreau's life was, in fact, lived with and in consideration for others, including his time at Walden. One of his reasons for moving to the edge of town was to write the manuscript that became *A Week on the Concord and Merrimack*, a reflection of his deep bond with his brother, John, who died in 1842 at the age of 26. Henry was still grieving and surely wanted solitude from a family home that took in boarders—solitude to become one with nature and to write in peace. But he never staked a claim to hermithood. He welcomed regular visitors to his tiny home, ventured almost daily into town, and continued to work as a day laborer, earning $1 a day. His friend Bronson Alcott called him "the most welcome of companions, this plain countryman." ("The Forester," *Atlantic Monthly*, April 1862.)

Young Edward Emerson, son of Ralph Waldo and a profound admirer of Thoreau, noted in his 1862 eulogy at Thoreau's funeral that when Henry entered a home in Concord, he would look around for the children, whom he would regale with stories of muskrats and squirrels and of the "Homeric battle of red and black ants." His expeditions in search of huckleberries, chestnuts, and grapes were popular local outings, and he even cut down Concord's first town Christmas tree, beginning a tradition that continues to this day. Another young friend, Louisa May Alcott, wrote, "Thoreau ... used to come smiling up to his neighbors, to announce that the bluebirds had arrived, with as much interest in the fact as other men take in messages by the Atlantic cable." ("Merry's Museum," March 1869.)

Thoreau connected with other people—and other people to each other—through his fascination with the natural world. These connections were evident on May 9, 2012, at First Parish Church in Concord, when the Transcendental Council celebrated Thoreau's human relationships in a special service commemorating the funeral held there for him 150 years before, three days after he had died from tuberculosis at age 44. The moving anniversary service featured remarks captured in writing from Thoreau's friends, neighbors, and family members before and after his death. It drew more than 400 people on a beautiful Sunday afternoon.

Those who insist on seeing Thoreau as a one-dimensional figure, defined by solitude and ill humor, would have been surprised by the abundance of affection expressed by his contemporaries and the number of devoted friends who gathered around him as he lay dying. Readers at this commemorative event related story after story of warm relationships, and it was easy to imagine Thoreau captivating the young and engaging the old with vivid tales from his encounters with local flora and fauna. When a group of town children brought food to the house for the ailing Henry and were not allowed to see their great champion, Henry protested, insisting that the children be allowed inside. Sam Staples, his one-time jailor, was quoted as saying after a visit to the bedridden Henry that his friend "seemed so serene and happy," a quality that Thoreau's sister Sophia would later describe in a letter as "the power of spirit over matter."

The memorial service ended with a recitation of Louisa May Alcott's poem "Thoreau's Flute." She had proudly accepted $10 from

The Atlantic Monthly when it was published in 1863 and informed her diary that it was her "best." Her paean speaks of the strong effects Thoreau's presence exerted on those who knew him. But it also predicts his lasting influence on us all—his enduring music in our heads as we try to stay awake to each day, his forceful reminder of the need to fight for social justice, his hope that we, too, will speak a word for nature. Its second stanza has become its most widely known:

> For such as he there is no death;
> His life the eternal life commands;
> Above man's aims his nature rose:
> The wisdom of a just content
> Made one small spot a continent,
> And turned to poetry life's prose.

More recently, the masterful biography by Laura Dassow Walls, *Henry David Thoreau: A Life*, published by University of Chicago Press in 2017, succeeds in capturing the full-blooded Thoreau that we hoped his birthplace would someday evoke. Walls's portrayal of Thoreau convincingly separates the myths from the man. She shows that he was prickly and eccentric but no misanthrope; he was a daily saunterer but also a hardworking pencil maker, day laborer, and land surveyor; he never married but helped support his family, cultivated many friends, and was a favorite among Concord's children; and he was a busy, social being who never became a hermit.

"For emotional balance and sanity," writes Wall, "Thoreau needed the 'skylight' of Nature. But the very image illustrates that he lived in a richly peopled social space, tied to those around him with a network of unbreakable chains."

Walls's warm treatment of Thoreau as a man allows us to appreciate the importance he placed not just on where he stood but *with whom*—his family, his friends, and his neighbors. Here is the man who helped fugitive slaves escape, gave stirring lectures at the Lyceum, kept one chair for solitude, two for friendship, and three for society, and wrote in his journal, "There is no remedy for love but to love more."

By trying so hard to save Thoreau's birthplace in the face of skepticism at best and dismissal at worst, we hoped the simple farmhouse where it all began would expand people's understanding of the genius and visionary who found in both nature *and* human companionship a bracing way to live and a graceful way to die. It seemed not only good but necessary to honor the forty-one years, nine months, and twenty-nine days Henry David Thoreau did *not* live at Walden Pond.

III

THE HOUSE IN DANGER

In the end, our society will be defined
not only by what we create but by what we refuse to destroy.

—John Sawhill, The Nature Conservancy

I had joined *The Concord Journal* as its editor in February 1995, still using the name Daniel, which I would later change to my married name, Stott. At the time, I lived in the nearby town of Chelmsford, where I had been a reporter and editor at *The Chelmsford Independent*, another local weekly, since 1991. But I knew and loved Concord well, having taught and served as an administrator at Concord Academy from 1978 to 1990. I'd lived on its campus in the village center for five of those years, before taking a hiatus from teaching to pursue an interest in writing.

During my years living and working in Concord, my knowledge of Thoreau was limited to his time at Walden Pond, where I loved to swim, and Estabrook Woods, where I would take my daily runs. Until Doris Smith called me in December 1995, I was unaware that Thoreau had been born in a farmhouse on Virginia Road. So, as the story of its vulnerability became public, I had a great deal to learn. And the more I learned, the more I became convinced that something had to be done to save that house.

Louise Fadiman, a Concord writer and independent historian, was one of the small group of local citizens who understood how important the Breens' Virginia Road property was. Shortly before James Breen's death on May 26, 1995, she visited the house and spoke to him, gaining his permission to take photographs of the property for a book she was writing called *The Concord Experience*. She would later tell *Baltimore Sun* reporter Richard O'Mara that she had to chase Breen across his fields, but that once she caught up with him he was very pleasant. He told her she was welcome to take pictures of the house on the condition that she include in her book that the Breen family owned the property, a condition she agreed to and met.

In an article published in *The Boston Globe* ten months later, on March 24, 1996, Fadiman told *Globe* correspondent Leslie Anderson that Breen, who had never read Thoreau but understood the cultural value of the house that had been in his family since 1908, took great pride in the fact that he had "hung on" and preserved both the house and the farm, believing it was a kind of mission. For most of his life, he had slept in the very room where Thoreau was born. "Lots of people pass by," he told Fadiman. "They stop and take pictures. But the town doesn't seem to care about it.... I don't know what's going to happen when I'm gone."

As it turned out, James Breen died only a few weeks after Fadiman's visit, while out tending his fields, after farming the land all his life as did his father before him. In 1909, the 27-year-old James Sr. had bought the house and farm from a relative after emigrating from Ireland. He lived there for the rest of his life, cultivating the land, raising chickens, and even maintaining a small herd of dairy cattle. He died in 1963, leaving the house and land to James Jr., who continued to grow a variety of crops.

At the time of James Jr.'s death, the land had been cultivated for more than 300 years. The fact that he died without a will proved both harmful and fortuitous for the historic property, which was tied up in probate for more than a year. Hardy rhubarb plants continued to grow spontaneously and in great abundance behind the house, but the rest of the land lay fallow for the first time in three centuries. James's widow, Ruth, unable to maintain the house by herself, moved in with Geraldine in the neighboring town of Maynard. Another daughter, Dorothy, lived in San Diego. On the one hand, the historic house, which the Breens had not had the means to refurbish over the years, would suffer from neglect during the months that its fate remained in limbo. The roof would sag, the paint would peel, the three sheds would collapse, and the foundation would develop fissures and holes that allowed critters to enter and find a home. On the other hand, the absence of attention and modernization would ultimately bring a gleam to the eyes of historic preservationists and restoration architects, who knew that under layers of wallpaper and linoleum, they were likely to find a good deal of the original fabric of the early 18th-century structure.

The Breen family needed to sell the house and farm, which had become much too expensive and difficult for them to maintain. With buildable land scarce and property values high in upscale Concord, it would not be difficult, once the estate cleared probate. Some estimated the market value of the property to be upwards of $1.5 million, though the deteriorating house provided little of that value. Even though the site was now in the flight path of Hanscom Air Force Base, whose loud jets regularly disturbed the peace of the bucolic landscape, willing buyers would certainly be easy to find. In fact, developers wasted no time in getting in touch with the Breen family, and it became clear that Ruth and her daughters hoped to set in place a plan for selling the property that could be triggered as soon as the estate was settled.

Worried that the birth house could be destroyed and the historic farmland turned into house lots, David Stephens, a resident of nearby Philip Farm Road, gathered a handful of neighbors at his home that fall to inform them that "the Thoreau house" was going to be sold. Most of those present knew the place as the Breen house and weren't aware that Thoreau had been born there, but Stephens stressed its significance and said it should be preserved as a historic landmark. He enlisted Doris Smith, who with her husband, George, lived next door to the Virginia Road house and knew the Breens, to make some calls around town to see if she could gather support for such an effort. From that point on, Smith took the lead, but she gives abundant credit to Stephens for "starting the ball rolling," and offering advice along the way.

"Mr. and Mrs. Breen were very isolated people and kept to themselves," recalls Smith. "They never advertised that their farm was the Thoreau birthplace and were annoyed when people from everywhere, even Japan, would knock on their door and ask to see the house. I had never been inside the house until well into the effort to save it. Jim died in his field with a plant in his hand. Ruth Breen moved in with her daughter Gerry after Jim's death. I called and asked if they would allow us to try to protect the farm so it would not be lost forever. Ruth and Gerry told me they were talking to a developer but would prefer to have the property saved. They gave permission for us to go ahead."

Going ahead meant gathering interested people around her dining room table. Members of this informal group came and went throughout the next several months and comprised neighbors, local activists and educators, and Thoreau enthusiasts. Director of Planning and Land Management Al Lima was the only Concord staff member to attend, but he was from the start one of the most avid supporters of the effort and an influential advocate with fellow town officials. Other attendees came from such groups as the Thoreau Country Conservation Alliance, the Concord Historical Commission, and the Thoreau Society.

In October, Smith contacted the Massachusetts Historical Commission to inquire about the possibility of having the Thoreau birthplace listed on the National Register of Historic Places. She received a reply from R. Terrence Adams, the state's preservation planner, letting her know that the Concord Historical Commission had conducted a comprehensive inventory of the cultural resources within the town, which included the property at 341 Virginia Road. He directed her to contact the local commission to find out if its members would support recommending the property for inclusion on the National Register. If they did, she would need to forward their recommendation to the state commission with her reasons for wishing it to be designated. Once the formal recommendation had been received, he said the process of review usually took at least eighteen months.

Smith received a positive response from the Concord Historical Commission's chairman, Theodore Osgood, who apologized on behalf of the state for the "bureaucratic and time-consuming" nature of the nomination process. He said the Concord Commission had voted unanimously on Nov. 14 to recommend that the Thoreau birthplace be nominated and that such a listing would be "most appropriate." He told Smith, "Now, the ball is back in your court." She needed to forward the local commission's recommendation, along with current photographs of the property and a statement of her reasons for seeking the designation, which she did.

Not long afterward, a two-page, single-spaced letter dated Feb. 2, 1996, arrived in Smith's mailbox. In it, Michael Steinitz, the survey director for the Massachusetts Historical Commission (MHC), offered guarded encouragement for Smith to continue pursuing the nomination. But the details were daunting, and it took several paragraphs for the positive message to emerge. Steinitz used most of his ink to list the characteristics of the property that might preclude it from eligibility. Birthplaces and buildings that had been moved from their original sites were not usually considered, he said. He added that there were two other Thoreau-related Concord properties already on the list: Walden Pond and the Thoreau-Alcott House, designated in 1966 and 1976, respectively. Since Thoreau had only lived at the birthplace during the first year of his life, the site did not reflect his more "productive" years.

What kept the property in contention, he said, was the surrounding land, which remained closely associated with the 19th- and early 20th-century agricultural history of Concord. And though the house had been moved a short distance to another area of the original farm, "the alterations that took place at this time ... were typical of late 19th-century 'modernizations' of older buildings, and part of the process of configuring a farmstead complex at the new site."

Steinitz acknowledged that the site "has long been recognized among the places in Concord associated with the life of Thoreau. Soon after his death, Thoreau's birthplace, at its new Virginia Road location, was widely noted in the literature on Thoreau, and it quickly became one of the local pilgrimage sites visited by Thoreau enthusiasts." Citing "the exceptional significance of Thoreau as a literary figure and the historical recognition of 341 Virginia Road as the house in which he was born," Steinitz said the MHC staff believed the property could also be considered for listing because of its association with him, however short that association had been.

The part of the letter that gave Smith serious pause, however, arrived at the very end. The commission gave its blessing for her to "consider undertaking a National Register nomination," but felt that the documentation supporting the nomination should ideally be prepared by a professional architectural historian with solid knowledge of the National Register's criteria and guidelines. The process, said Steinitz, involved multiple steps. Once the MHC received the completed nomination, it would take two to three years for a determination to be made. So Smith and the Town of Concord were looking at many months of work and waiting if they chose to move ahead. Complicating matters at the time was the hesitancy on the part of the Breen family. The MHC would not consider a nomination that did not include the owners' consent, and the Breens, even as they favored preservation, were concerned that a listing on the National Register might deter a potential private buyer from assuming responsibility for such a publicly-valued property.

As a result of all this, further work on the nomination was delayed until a new owner of the property could be determined. But Smith had launched the effort, and her work would pay off in the end.

Another way Doris Smith and friends sought to save the property was by establishing a nonprofit fundraising organization they called the Save the Thoreau Birthplace Foundation. During its short-lived existence, the foundation raised few dollars—much of the expense of incorporating and operating it was assumed by the Smiths and a few of its other members—but it served to advance the cause through its sponsorship of events and media campaigns.

Ultimately, the outreach that had the most immediate and long-term impact on the effort to save the birthplace was Smith's decision to spread the word by enlisting the help of *The Concord Journal*. She made that call on Thursday, Dec. 14, 1995, the first day of the weekly news cycle.

It's hard to believe today that there was a time when people turned first to their local newspaper to get the word out about their concerns and opinions. *The Concord Journal* was a well-read source of local information and included editorials, columns, letters, and op-ed pieces written almost entirely by its own journalists and town residents. It was truly a go-to local resource, whose staff kept their feet on the street. We had computers and email at the time but were only just beginning to have a website presence. We still printed pages on a press and edited them by hand on drafting tables, using X-Acto knives that regularly sent editors to the first-aid station or, occasionally, to the ER. For me, that hands-on work retains a romantic aura, despite the Band-Aids.

At times, I can't help but wonder what the effects of a social media campaign would have been, if Doris Smith and her small band of amateur preservationists had been equipped with the tools to mount a full-fledged online advocacy and crowdfunding campaign. The Internet did exist in 1995, of course, and organizations were beginning to set up websites. Smith and her fellow activists had, in fact, set up their own. About the time she contacted *The Concord Journal*, Smith suggested at one of her meetings that their group put out a plea on the web page for public donations to save the birthplace. But the social media phenomenon would not take hold until a couple of years later, and such an appeal would not have had much impact. Had they possessed today's ability—and know-how—to reach a worldwide audience at the click of a "Send" button, such an appeal effort would have likely elicited an immediate flurry of responses and maybe a substantial number of donations via PayPal. Missing from it all, however, would have been the personal investment needed over the long term to meet what would develop into a complex, multilayered challenge.

In his provocative article, "Small Change: Why the Revolution Won't Be Tweeted," (*The New Yorker*, Oct. 4, 2010), Malcolm Gladwell acknowledges the capacity of Facebook and other networking sites to alert people to pressing issues and gather "Likes" and other modes of support from a distance. But, he says, "The platforms of social media are built around weak ties." What are needed when things get complicated, when vision is required, when intricate planning must be carried out, and when ongoing negotiations become necessary are strong ties that link people to each other and to the work at hand. "Social networks are effective at increasing *participation*—by lessening the level of motivation that participation requires," says Gladwell. In other words, we might send some money to a cause that catches our attention, but that's an easy, commitment-lite way to participate. What is needed to advance a complex and nuanced cause is exactly what we had at the time: people willing to put themselves on the line by using their social capital in an up-close-and-personal way, knowing they were putting it at risk for a cause that might fail. Thoreau beat all of us to this insight when he wrote in *Walden*, "The cost of a thing is the amount of what I will call life which is required to be exchanged for it, immediately or in the long run."

So, at *The Concord Journal*, we went about in what today would be considered the old-fashioned way. Once we were alerted to the story, we knew we needed to act quickly. My two reporters, Richard Fahlander and Bryan Davis, stepped up to help gather information and talk with as many involved people as they could, and our terrific editor-in-chief, Richard Lodge, gave us the go-ahead to investigate and, when we were fully informed, to take a stand.

Late December, with its holiday distractions and seasonal fatigue, is a terrible time to break a local news story meant to grab attention. But we grasped the urgency and knew there was no choice but to get the story out as quickly as possible. So the following Thursday's *Journal*—published four days before Christmas—carried a front-page story, "Move is on to save Thoreau house from development," which ran on to two jump pages.

The main story reported that several local groups believed in the value of saving the threatened birthplace, but that "these groups are either financially strapped or deep into their own preservation efforts. Though [Doris] Smith has heard nothing but support from their representatives, she has not yet gotten any one group to take a leadership role in the preservation effort."

Gerry Breen said in the article that she appreciated what Smith was trying to do. "We'd love to preserve the house," she said. "There's no other house to honor Thoreau in Concord."

Al Lima, Concord's director of Planning and Land Management, said that town officials had known for some time that the property would soon become available but believed it should be up to a "private entity" to take the lead in preserving the house and farmland. He acknowledged, however, that he believed the property to be unique and worthy of preserving. "Once the general public is fully aware of what is happening, I think there will be a lot of interest," he said.

In fact, Lima was pulling his punches. He had long held out the hope that the Breen property could be preserved, both to honor Thoreau and to celebrate the historic farmland. He had been involved in gauging the value of the property for several years, but other town officials had kept a formal distance from the issue, which limited how much public support he could express as a town staff member. Once Smith and others had engaged the public, the situation began to change. Selectman Judy Walpole and Natural Resources Director Dan Monahan agreed to be interviewed for the article and Walpole had already attended a meeting, mainly as an information-gatherer, at Doris Smith's home. She said she had recently asked Lima to gather a group of town committee members for a meeting about the property. "I would like to sit down with this group and discuss interest in the property and what role, if any, the town would be able to play," said Walpole. Still, she was quick to add that though the town would be supportive of private efforts to preserve the property, public funds were too limited for the town to take a leadership role in those efforts.

Lima said that because the land was taxed under the state's 61A farmland provision, the town would have first right of refusal once a formal offer of purchase had been signed by the sellers. He mentioned that if that were to happen, the town would have the option of assigning its right of refusal to a conservation group, such as the Trust for Public Land, which could then purchase it without the help of town funding, an option Walpole said the town would consider if its refusal right were to be triggered.

Monahan weighed in on the value of the land itself, as separate from the Thoreau birth house: "It is part of what is known as the Virginia Road Woods Natural Vegetation Area as designated on [the town's] Open Space Plan and is surrounded by land that is protected," he said.

Throughout the article, those interviewed seemed to believe that a preservation-minded savior would step forward and rescue the property once the word of potential development had been spread. Concord resident Joe Valentine, who would become an extremely active and articulate participant in the preservation effort, recalls thinking at the time that "as soon as the rest of the country found out about the current condition and plight of the very house in which Thoreau was born, the checks would pour in." Today, he acknowledges with a wry laugh, "We were, of course, very wrong about that!"

Embedded in the main article was a sidebar by Concord's resident Thoreau scholar, Tom Blanding. Quickly and expertly, Blanding had produced a succinct, eloquent history of the house, containing all the essential facts that would be addressed in the coming months, and a compelling argument for why it should be saved. Entitled "A Historical Perspective," it was the very first of many attempts over the next two years to raise awareness of the history and value of the uncommon treasure that was about to be lost, and it remains one of the best.

Despite the poor timing, the announcement of the danger to the house attracted a good deal of public attention. The following week's *Concord Journal* featured a front-page story entitled, "Thoreau house will be an issue for new year." Doris Smith reported that she had received a phone call from someone who had read the previous week's article and believed the birth house would become "a wonderful place for a writing center." But it soon became clear that this would turn out to be another of the many conversations Smith had been having over the past several months: the caller had a great idea but no money to implement it.

"A Historical Perspective"
By Thomas Blanding

Surely, O Lord, he hath not greatly erred,
Who hath so little from his birthplace stirred.
—Henry David Thoreau

Of all the classic Concord authors, Henry Thoreau is Concord's only native son. On the eve of his graduation from Harvard College he wrote, "I shall ever pride myself upon the place of my birth—may she never have cause to be ashamed of her sons."

After he had picked up his diploma, Thoreau went home again, marching all the way to a different drummer. He traveled a good deal in Concord and, more than any other Concord author, became associated with the rural aspect of the town. He was born on July 12, 1817, on his maternal grandmother's farm along the Virginia Road. Ellery Channing, his friend and first biographer, said, "It was lovely he should draw his first breath in a pure country air, out of crowded towns, amid the pleasant russet fields."

If you venture out Virginia Road today, you can still see (for now, at least) the 300-year-old farmhouse in which Thoreau first saw the light 173 years go. Standing on 18.4 acres of agricultural land—a remnant of the original 17th-century Wheeler and 18th-century Minott farm—Thoreau's birthplace seems demurely, more than defiantly, detached from the airfields and office parks which have come to surround it. Concord historian Ruth Wheeler summarizes the early history of the farm: "Most of its neighborhood belonged in the last half of the seventeenth century after the second division of Concord land to Sgt. Thomas Wheeler (1625-1704). He conveyed land 'at Verginy in Concord' to his sons John (1655-1736) and Timothy (1667-1718). Deacon John lived here (Thoreau's birthplace) and Timothy in the salt box house against Pine Hill, half a mile to the east. … Deacon John's heirs sold the farm in 1755 to Samuel Minot, a cousin who lived on the Bay Road beyond Meriam's Corner. Samuel then gave it to his son Jonas 'for love and affection.'

Captain Jonas Minott was one of the leaders of the local militia that fought the British on April 19, 1775. He died on March 20, 1813, leaving his wife Mary her widow's third of the estate. Mary Minott had had several children by her previous marriage to the Reverend Asa Dunbar. The youngest child, Cynthia, who spent her youth and early adulthood on the farm, married John Thoreau in the spring of 1812. At the time Henry was born, John was a down-on-his-luck storekeeper working the much dwindled fields of his mother-in-law's farm. In the wake of the "Year Without a Summer" or "Poverty Year," a period of extreme cold in New England, these were hard seasons for the Thoreaus, who had to sell additional acreage (and John's gold wedding ring) just to make ends meet. They gave up the Minott farm eight months after Henry's birth and moved into the village. In October 1818, the farmhouse and its thirty or so remaining acres were sold at public auction.

Henry Thoreau came to admire his grandmother's house, "built in the old substantial style," which he would later often pass on his walks. It was a sturdy salt box with a long roof sloping nearly to the ground in the rear, as Thoreau described it, "not standing but seated on its hinder parts in the attitude of strength and repose, bearing the sky on its broad shoulders like Atlas." Thoreau thought that a house acquires a new beauty as it ages and blends with the landscape. Nature finishes what the carpenter began. Thoreau's birthplace is the prototype for the venerable structure he describes in an unpublished manuscript: "There is a time when every house becomes beautiful at last, and we cease to quarrel with the original architect, when Time with his scythe and weather staining and mossy brush has come to smooth over and cover up the farmer's blunders—when the elements have repaired man's faults."

In the winter of 1878, sixteen years after Thoreau's death, his birthplace, minus part of its long rear roof, was moved a short distance down the road on runners, where it still stands, an unmarked and for the most part unremarked private residence. A plaque set up just six years ago marks the original site and a newer house built on the old foundation.

A visitor to Concord wrote in *The Bookman*, in July 1931: "I think perhaps the house in which Thoreau was born might be a good investment for the State, or for some enterprising Henry Ford. Thoreau's reputation is growing with the years, and in the end the effect of his life and works upon the history of America may not be so inconsiderable. Unless someone has done so since I was there, the birthplace of Thoreau is being used still as a farmhouse. Perhaps that is what Thoreau himself would have preferred."

The Breen family's attorney, Nathaniel Brown, told *The Journal*, "The Breens are interested in divesting themselves of the property. We are accepting bids from anyone at this point." He added that a number of offers had come in from developers but no agreement had yet been struck.

Brown, a Bedford Minute Man whose mother had used her own funds to help preserve a historic house in that neighboring town, confirmed that he and the Breens appreciated Doris Smith's efforts to gather support for preserving the property. "I am no stranger to the sensibility to old homes," he said. "Even if an offer [from a developer] were to be accepted, it is possible that the purchaser would be willing to work with local interest groups to preserve the historic structure." One option, he said, would be to separate the house from the land sale and move it to another location where it could be preserved. But this was far from an ideal option, since a move away from the original farm would greatly reduce the historic value of the house. The aged structure might not even survive such a transport.

Reaction to the preservation effort was mixed at that early stage, with naysayers and advocates debating the value of the property. But many were hearing about the Thoreau birthplace for the first time, and it would never retreat into anonymity again.

The house where Thoreau was born shown in 1878, just after it was moved to its current location.

IV

"THE MOST IMPORTANT BIRTHPLACE IN THE WHOLE OF THE LAND"

He was Concord himself in one man.

—Sophia Hawthorne, letter

One of the reasons Tom Blanding had all the facts about the Thoreau birthplace at his fingertips in December 1995 was that he had already made an effort to ensure its preservation during James Breen's lifetime and had more recently been helping Doris Smith and her neighbors as they organized for the preservation effort.

In December 1990, four and a half years before Mr. Breen died, he gave permission to members of a local nonprofit, the Thoreau Country Conservation Alliance, to partner with the Town of Concord on a feasibility study that would determine the historic value of his Virginia Road house and land and their importance to the community and the wider world. Though the property was not yet on the National Register of Historic Places, the TCCA felt strongly that it belonged there.

Blanding, a widely respected authority on Thoreau's life and works, had co-founded the Thoreau Country Conservation Alliance in 1988 with J. Walter Brain, Ed Schofield, Vidar Jorgenson, and Jack Borden, all local members of the Thoreau Society. Soft in speech and rumpled in appearance, Blanding was living a simple, unadorned life in a little house he rented from his former in-laws. It was a life inspired by Thoreau and supported very modestly by speaking fees and seminars on Thoreau and the Transcendentalists. Blanding launched the TCCA in an effort to raise awareness of threats to Thoreau-related sites, especially Walden Woods.

Walden Woods is a forested landscape of more than 2,500 acres surrounding Walden Pond in Concord and neighboring Lincoln. The land had been eyed for development since the 1950s and had always escaped unscathed. But more recent efforts to build an industrial park on a large swath of the land had brought renewed protest from local environmentalists, the Concord Historical Society, and the TCCA.

KICK-OFF MEETING
THOREAU COUNTRY
CONSERVATION ALLIANCE

7:30 p.m.
Tuesday, June 7, 1988
Alcott School, 91 Laurel Street, Concord

Come and learn about a new community-based citizens' group dedicated to protecting and restoring important natural and cultural sites associated with Henry D. Thoreau.

❦ PROGRAM ❦

Topic	Moderator	Time
Introduction to Henry Thoreau	Tom Blanding	7:30–7:40
What Is Thoreau Country?	Walter Brain	7:40–7:50
Current Threats	Vidar Jorgensen	7:50–8:00
Where Do We Go from Here?	Ed Schofield	8:00–8:10
Additional Discussion	Jack Borden	8:10–8:40

THOREAU COUNTRY CONSERVATION ALLIANCE, INC.
100 Barrett's Mill Road
Concord, Massachusetts 01742
Telephone (617) 369-5802, 860-7116

Working with the National Trust for Historic Preservation, these groups succeeded in having Walden Pond and Woods listed among America's 11 Most Endangered Places in 1990.

Shortly after I became editor of *The Concord Journal*, I heard about Blanding's work and felt I should meet him and learn about the efforts to save Walden Woods. Knowing the backstory would help me understand the ongoing debates on the issue, which were still making news from time to time.

I liked Blanding immediately. His warm welcome to his book-filled home and his quiet erudition drew me in, and I was impressed with his encyclopedic mastery of all things Thoreau. I learned that he had appeared on CNN in 1990 to spread the word about the threats to Walden Woods. Watching the program that day was Don Henley, co-founder of the Eagles rock band. An environmental activist and philanthropist, Henley had majored in English in college after developing a deep appreciation for Thoreau's writing and approach to life. Henley and Blanding were both in their early 40s at the time. Blanding had never heard of Henley—or the Eagles—so when he got a call from the famous recording artist following his CNN appearance, he didn't immediately understand the import of Henley's offer to "do what I can to help." Blanding, a "mean trumpet player," according to his friends, asked who Henley was. "I'm a musician," Henley replied. "Oh, I'm a musician, too," said Blanding, believing to have found common ground.

Ultimately, Henley's timely intervention resulted in the founding of the Walden Woods Project in 1990. It has since raised millions of dollars to preserve and maintain thousands of acres of threatened land. Four years later, the Walden Woods Project purchased the historic Higginson estate in Lincoln, a town contiguous to Concord, to serve as its permanent headquarters, known as the Thoreau Institute. The organization focuses on raising money to preserve the woods, archiving Thoreau materials (largely owned by the Thoreau Society) in a climate-controlled library, working with state agencies to protect Walden Pond, and welcoming scholars, teachers, and students for research and educational programming.

From the start, the Walden Woods Project enjoyed a high profile, thanks to Henley's local appearances and benefit performances and the support he drew from fellow celebrities. The official opening of the Thoreau Institute in 1995 was a star-studded event, with speeches by President Bill Clinton and First Lady Hillary Clinton, U.S. Senators Ted Kennedy and John Kerry, and a special performance by the Eagles. The publicity that surrounded the project and the glittering fundraising events featuring Hollywood notables and Grammy Award-winning musicians attracted many wealthy donors, which allowed the Walden Woods Project to purchase land around the pond and furnish and maintain its institute.

Along the way, the early activists from the Thoreau Country Conservation Alliance were mostly left behind. It was a tricky situation, because the financial cost of purchasing and preserving land around Walden Woods was far beyond the scope of what the small, grassroots organization could do alone. In his effort to reach out and help, Henley contacted Senator Ted Kennedy's office and spoke with one of his aides, Kathi Anderson, who became excited by the prospect of organizing and managing what would become the Walden Woods Project. Once she entered the picture, the entire effort was lifted out of the hands of the Thoreau Country Conservation Alliance and shaped into a professionally managed operation with influential political ties.

With the perspective of time, it's clear that the protection of Walden Woods benefited enormously from the help of an "angel" like Don Henley. Ultimately, though mixed feelings linger even today about the extravagant means used to preserve Walden Woods and establish a Thoreau center on a Lincoln estate, no one can deny the value of its success. Pioneers like Tom Blanding, who preferred a more grassroots approach, eventually turned their attention to other environmental and cultural causes, of which there was certainly no shortage.

One of these was the Thoreau birthplace. Like the preservation of Walden Woods, though on a much smaller scale, the saving of the birthplace was a complicated cause that involved a degree of controversy because of the short time Thoreau had lived there and its subsequent move a few hundred yards eastward on the farm.

In the early 1990s, Blanding, his friend and fellow environmental advocate J. Walter Brain, and other TCCA members understood the importance of the house where it all began, and they had a big idea. What if the house where Thoreau was born, at 341 Virginia Road, and the newer house built on its original site, at 215 Virginia Road, could be purchased by the National Park Service and joined together again by their respective farmlands? The National Park Service was already a major presence in Concord and Lincoln in the form of the Minute Man National Historical Park, the steward of the Revolutionary War sites at the North Bridge and along the Battle Road. As might be expected, the relationship between the Park Service and the town had not always been an easy one, involving a tug-of-war over property acquisition and use. But by 1990, things between the two entities had become more amicable, and Brain was hopeful that negotiations among the property owners, the Town of Concord, and the Park Service might proceed smoothly.

On Dec. 10, 1990, Brain attended a planning exercise organized by Lawrence Gall, superintendent of Minute Man National Historical Park. The exercise was meant to explore the possibility of establishing a trail system linking the parklands along the Battle Road to historical landscapes and open spaces on both public and private lands. In a letter addressed to Gall after that meeting, Brain noted that the Thoreau birthplace on Virginia Road could become "another important link" on the park's proposed trails. He said that the historic house was "in the view of many, the most important birthplace in the whole of the land, from sea to shining sea."

Brain added in his letter that he believed the Breen family, owners of the Thoreau birth house, and the Rand family, owners of the house that was built on the birthplace's original site, "appear to be willing sellers." His vision was that the open land attached to both houses would provide "an agreeable patch of countryside for the Thoreau birthplace, but [also] extend the attractive farm country of the Park lands at the Battle Road."

Copied on Brain's letter to Gall were Alan Edmond, Concord's town manager, Al Lima, its director of Planning and Land Management, and Daniel Monahan, director of its Natural Resources Department. It's interesting to note that even in this early stage of thinking about the importance of the birthplace, the farmland surrounding it was very much in the frame. From the beginning, and throughout the long effort to save, restore, and re-use the house, the property's farming tradition played a key role. To this day, supporters cite the preserving of the land as a large part of the project's appeal and eventual success in attracting advocates and funders. Even 130 years after his death, Thoreau was continuing to connect people to each other by directing their attention to what lay under their feet.

In the end, nothing ever became of the idea of joining the two properties. But interest in the house where Thoreau was born remained lively, at least among a small group of local Thoreauvians and environmentalists. In order to prove to the National Park Service and other potential candidates for protecting the birthplace that the property had both local and worldwide significance, the Town of Concord needed an official stamp of approval from certified preservationists. With the help of Blanding and Brain, the town sought to have a feasibility study of the site conducted by the Architectural Conservation Trust (ACT) for Massachusetts. The ACT, a loan fund designated for historic preservation, was planning in 1992 to conduct two to three feasibility studies of historic properties judged by their owners to be endangered. Funding for the studies would come partly from the U.S. Department of the Interior's National Park Service and would need to be matched by the town and willing private entities.

An application for the birthplace to be chosen for one of the planned feasibility studies was submitted in December 1991. The current condition of the house was characterized as needing "considerable stabilization work to prevent further deterioration," since "the owner is an older individual who cannot afford the major cost to stabilize the structure." With James Breen's health declining along with his ability to work his farmland, it was pointed out that "the property currently has no protections against inappropriate renovation or demolition. Sale of the property could result in these possibilities, or the site's eighteen acres could be developed into house lots." Even if the property were not sold in the near future, "the continued neglect of the structure will accelerate its deterioration." Mention was also made in the application of the significance of the historic farmland, which should continue to be preserved and cultivated as it had been for more than 300 years.

As part of the application, Brain wrote a detailed statement of the property's history and significance. He also described the structure as it appeared in 1991 as "a humble clapboard house," whose white paint was "faded and peeling and in need of upkeep." Its appearance, wrote Brain, seemed entirely appropriate to "Thoreau's humble lifestyle and stoic brand of philosophy."

In addition to Brain's commentary, letters of support were sent from the TCCA, the Concord Historical Commission, the Concord Historical Collaborative (comprising at that time the Concord Museum, the Emerson House, the Minute Man National Historical Park, The Old Manse, Orchard House, the Thoreau Lyceum, and the Walden Pond State Reservation), the National Park Service, the Concord Board of Selectmen, the Concord Department of Planning and Land Management, and the Walden Woods Project. All were unequivocal in their assertion of Thoreau's importance to the world, and most also mentioned the value of preserving precious farmland, which was rapidly disappearing from Concord.

Yet, behind the scenes, there was resistance to spending town dollars on such a project. An ACT administrator had stated in his letter to the town that applicants were to show their willingness and ability to provide matching funds equal to 50 percent of the cost of a study. Concord's study was expected to cost $10,000, so the town would have to contribute $5,000 to the work. The application sent from Concord indicated that one-half of the match—$2,500—would be advanced by the Town of Concord and the other half by unidentified "private sources." At least one selectman objected to putting the town on the hook for that amount and for perhaps being called upon to round up the funds promised from "private sources" if they did not fully materialize. There was also a much larger question to consider: if a feasibility study offered clear evidence that the property was indeed historically significant and required immediate stabilization and/or restoration, who was going to fund that work? These quietly expressed hesitations to spend town money on the birthplace would later turn into a more open, contentious debate once the property did come up for sale a few years later. But the early concerns soon became moot. ACT's executive director wrote to the town and the TCAA in February 1992, saying it had received seventeen applications for its current round of feasibility studies and had not chosen the Thoreau birthplace as one of its projects.

The rejection was clearly a big disappointment to Concord Planning Director Al Lima, who had become an avid supporter of protecting the birthplace. Less than a month after receiving ACT's letter of denial, Lima sent a note to the town manager indicating he had been exploring other options for funding a feasibility study on the property. In particular, he suggested asking Congressman Chester Atkins to seek funds from the House Appropriations Committee, an idea that evidently gained a measure of support from town officials and committees.

In April, Lima sent a packet to Atkins's office that included a scope of work for a Historic Structure Report on the Thoreau Birthplace and Homestead. Prepared by Larry Gall at Minute Man National Historical Park, the work would involve an investigation of documents pertaining to the property, an architectural study of the house, an archeological survey, and an assessment of the integrity and significance of the cultural landscape. The study would also include recommendations for rehabilitation of the structure and a determination of the feasibility of moving the house, if it were to be threatened with destruction. The estimated cost of such a study: $70,000.

Given the price tag, it is not surprising that no further word can be found in town records regarding this second try. But these early efforts by Blanding, Brain, and Lima to document the importance of the birthplace would prove to be a great help in the later, more broadly supported fight for recognition.

V

"WE'RE AFRAID THIS COULD BE LOST FOREVER"

In the long run men hit only what they aim at.
Therefore, though they should fail immediately,
they had better aim at something high.

—H.D. Thoreau, *Walden*

When the Breen property became available in the late spring of 1995, the time was right for another try. But it was not until the early days of 1996, once the story had reached a wider public, that the effort to save the property began to surge once again. When that happened, complications set in quickly. As support grew beyond the neighborhood group that had started it all, opinions diverged on the best way to move ahead. The first great divide sprang up between those who believed the Town of Concord should contribute municipal funding to help buy and preserve the Virginia Road property and those who were patently against any town money being put toward the purchase.

At this stage, with James Breen's estate still held up in probate court, the primary focus was on preventing a developer from striking a binding purchase agreement with the Breen family. Little thought had yet been given to what would happen if the property were, in fact, put in the hands of the town. In its current condition, it could not remain standing much longer without stabilization. Who would pay for that? It was a question that troubled even some of the effort's most ardent supporters, and it kept the question of ownership widely open to debate and disagreement.

As the new year approached, Helen Bowdoin, representing the still active, still small, still local Thoreau Country Conservation Alliance, circulated a citizens' petition to have an article placed on the warrant of Concord's 1996 Annual Town Meeting, to be held in late April. She worked with Town Moderator Arthur Stevenson on the wording of the article and secured the ten signatures needed by the Jan. 1 deadline, which assured it a spot on the warrant. Bowdoin's article reflected a cautious approach that would keep the effort moving ahead without committing the town to any concrete action:

Article 28: Protection for Thoreau Birthplace

Located at 341 Virginia Road, the nearly 300-year-old house in which Henry David Thoreau was born in 1817 is threatened. In addition to its literary importance, the property of 18-plus acres, protected on three sides, was home to Captain Jonas Minott, an officer in the local militia during the 1770s. The property is further distinguished as a remnant of vanishing prime farmland, under continuous cultivation since the late 1600s. In recognition of the significance of this property to the community and to the nation, Town Meeting endorses efforts to preserve and protect the Thoreau Birthplace and surrounding land, and requests that the Board of Selectmen work with interested parties to explore all options and take appropriate action toward securing its permanent protection.

At the same time, Concord resident David Stephens, who had alerted his neighbors to the plight of the birthplace shortly after James Breen's death, secured the required signatures for a second birthplace-related warrant article. This one called for a stronger commitment:

Article 29: Funding Support of Purchase of Thoreau Birthplace & Farmland (Virginia Road Breen Property)

To determine whether the Town will vote to raise, appropriate, transfer from available funds, or otherwise authorize, pursuant to the Town of Concord Land Acquisition Program, a sum to be determined, for the sole purpose of assisting the acquisition, with public donations, grants, and other funding sources, the house and other buildings owned by the estate of the late James Breen, containing 18.4 acres, more or less, of arable land upon which stands the house of Thoreau's birth. Located at 341 Virginia Road, for historical preservation, open space, conservation, agriculture, or educational purposes, or take any other action relative thereto.

In the run-up to that Town Meeting vote, during the first few months of 1996, a media campaign and other, quieter efforts to raise awareness beyond Concord succeeded in pointing a spotlight on the town and creating an interest in the decisions its citizens were soon to make. As a small fish in a small—albeit internationally famous— pond, *The Concord Journal* could draw public attention throughout the local area but could not, on its own, rally more distant support. So it was gratifying to see New England's paper of record, *The Boston Globe*, take an active interest in the danger to the birthplace. After *The Concord Journal* broke the story in December, *The Globe* began running stories and opinion pieces by its own reporters and correspondents. It was even more satisfying when on March 4, about a month and a half before the 1996 Annual Town Meeting, an Associated Press article by Robin Estrin was picked up by several newspapers around the country, bringing heightened attention to the effort.

Shortly after seeing that article, Richard O'Mara, a reporter from *The Baltimore Sun*, called me at the *Journal* office to say he had heard of the efforts to save Thoreau's birth house and wanted to write about it for the readers of his paper. He didn't want to depend on other sources but planned to see the house for himself and talk with the people hoping to save it. It was a thrilling moment, because it signaled the start of a broader movement that would likely elicit more widespread support. O'Mara's subsequent visit to Concord deepened his interest in the preservation effort, and his article, "This Could be a Lost Place of Honor," became an important call to action that helped the campaign leap forward.

O'Mara's article, published in the April 14, 1996 edition of *The Sun*, read more like an elegant, expressive creative nonfiction essay than a coolly objective piece of reportage. Clearly, O'Mara seemed to be saying, this was a hard story about which to stay objective.

"The old house rises stark on a small hill over Virginia Road, a thoroughfare with a long life if a short run," he began. "It was the first road into Concord when the town was established in 1635, three miles of curves and plunging hills bordered by alder and birch." Describing what he saw as he approached, O'Mara continued:

> The house stands empty and silent. Conifers embrace its front corners. Rhododendron crawls by the porch. A small American flag decal is fading in a window above the door. A weather-worn Adirondack chair remains outside the back door. It affords a view of the fields and swamps of Concord celebrated by Henry David Thoreau throughout the 44 years of his life in

and around this town. Just a short walk away is the field where James Breen fell down dead last May 26.

A new subdivision could emerge along Virginia Road, already growing dense with contemporary houses and corporate parks farther down and an airfield nearby. A "Thoreau Acres" or "Walden Gardens" might come into being, with split-levels and cute Colonials spreading their placid lawns through all the intimate wild places where gorse now runs and the native Concord grape spills over low stone walls.

O'Mara spent a good deal of his time in Concord talking to local residents and town officials. Author Louise Fadiman told him, "I call it an emergency. It would seem such a travesty to lose not only the house but the lands."

Doris Smith told O'Mara, "We're afraid this could be lost. It could really be lost forever."

O'Mara cited the importance of the property to Concord's long history and the fact that Thoreau is the only literary luminary associated with Concord not to have a house in his name. "Is Concord prepared to allow the birthplace of Thoreau, its son, to be bull-dozed?" asked O'Mara. "Well, yes, but only reluctantly.... Official Concord seems to be waiting for private Concord to take the lead."

Selectman Judy Walpole told O'Mara that the Board of Selectmen was planning to endorse Article 28 at Town Meeting, but that she could not support a suggestion that town funds be committed to help save the property.

O'Mara expressed a degree of sadness at the house's condition, especially after touring it with Gerry Breen, who talked a good deal about her father and grandfather and their close connection to the land. Having stood empty for almost a full year, the house, he wrote, "is a scabrous reminder of life in another time. Its paint is fleeing the clapboards and green shutters, the roof sags, not one of its walls or angles is true."

He ended his article poignantly, quoting activist and Thoreau enthusiast Joe Valentine, at the time head of the Concord Historical Commission and a member of the Save the Thoreau Birthplace Foundation. Valentine told him he felt "a great sense of responsibility to do something to save the place."

"He is outside the lonely house, stepping gingerly over patches of wet snow," wrote O'Mara of Valentine. "The New England sky is gray and turbulent. The thought of losing the house sickens him."

Reading O'Mara's words today evokes the emotional punch that visiting Thoreau's birthplace was having on so many people at the time, even in its decrepitude, including experienced journalists trained to focus on "just the facts, ma'am."

The Associated Press article and O'Mara's plaintive descriptions, combined with continuing local coverage and personal outreach by determined advocates, started to make a difference in both public opinion and town support. Gradually, the previous year's tentativeness was evolving into a more confident, purposeful preservation effort. The publicity and networking brought new supporters to the cause, some of whom would later sign on to help and even contribute to the fundraising effort.

As word spread, advocates held out hope that an "angel" would come forward, just as Don Henley had done in 1990 to protect Walden Woods. Henley himself was fully committed to the Walden Woods project, according to Executive Director Kathi Anderson, but that didn't mean there wasn't another Thoreau disciple with the personal fortune to make an offer the Breens would accept. The amount needed to gain their acceptance appeared to begin at $1 million.

In February, the Save the Thoreau Birthplace Foundation sponsored a talk by Tom Blanding, who presented a comprehensive history of the property and an explanation of its importance to Thoreau's life and work to an audience of more than 100 people. Wayne Rasmussen, an author and former historian for the U.S. Department of Agriculture, introduced Blanding, underscoring the value of the historic farmland to the preservation effort, a consideration that would play a decisive role in all that would follow.

The week before Town Meeting, in the April 25, 1996 edition of *The Concord Journal*, the Save the Thoreau Birthplace Foundation and Thoreau Country Conservation Alliance ran a full-page plea for a yea vote on Article 28, with testimonials from fourteen prominent supporters: authors Bill McKibben, Robert Richardson Jr., John Hanson Mitchell, Jane Langton, Frederick Turner, and Wayne Rasmussen; conservationists Michael Kellett of RESTORE: the North Woods, Claudia Sauermann of the National Trust for Historic

Preservation, T.H. Watkins of The Wilderness Society, and John Andrews of the Sierra Club; professors Lawrence Buell and Richard Forman of Harvard University; Ronald Hoag, president of the Thoreau Society; and State Representative Pamela Resor. Heavy hitters, all.

It is interesting to note that the sponsors of the page did not ask for support for Article 29. Perhaps this reticence was intended to avoid association with the more aggressive article which, if it provoked controversy, ran the risk of sabotaging the more cautious request and shutting down the effort entirely. Or it might have reflected the belief on the part of some advocates that it was too early to ask citizens for the use of tax dollars to help raise funds toward the purchase.

On April 30, 1996, everyone's hard work and outreach efforts were rewarded when Concord's Town Meeting voted overwhelmingly to pass Article 28. The vote was not unanimous, and a couple of dissenters made their opposition heard, but so few voting cards were raised in opposition that no count was necessary. Though this vote was officially nonbinding and limited any action to an *exploration* of the feasibility of purchasing the property, it was a vital first step in making that happen.

It turned out a first step was all Town Meeting was willing to take. Article 29 was moved but failed to pass, with 209 attendees voting nay and 144 voting yea.

Still, it was an important victory, and the editorial in the next issue of *The Concord Journal*, published on May 2, cheered the result, announcing, "Yes on birthplace!" Many who attended that meeting continue to cite the defense of Article 28 by Joe Valentine, which managed to be both reasoned and impassioned, as the decisive factor in the overwhelmingly positive response. I recall his comprehensive presentation, enhanced by visuals displayed with the use of that technological dinosaur, the overhead projector. His argument drew strength from his ability to help the audience envision a number of community-friendly uses for the property, including a small educational center, a working farm, an ecology center, and a site for an environmentally minded nonprofit. Though these ideas were still untested, they served to bring the landscape alive for people and help them imagine how the property might become a community resource while remaining low-key and unobtrusive. True to the magical thinking of the time, Valentine also told Town Meeting he hoped a positive vote on the article would give confidence to potential benefactors, who might be waiting in the wings to gauge community support before committing major funding to help purchase the property.

Though she didn't speak at Town Meeting, Doris Smith was there. Her presence reminded those who knew her role in the success of that evening that it was important to keep in sight the small acts that set the larger ones in motion.

38

Auction set to help save Thoreau's birthplace

A special benefit evening, "Thoroughly Thoreau," will be held on June 15, 8 p.m., at 51 Walden Street, Concord, in an effort to raise money for the purchase and preservation of all 18.4 acres of the Henry David Thoreau birth site on Virginia Road in Concord.

A rare evening has been planned that features an auction and some of the best the area has to offer in art, drama,

music, scholarship and cuisine.

Among the auction items is a full-scale replica of Thoreau's Walden Cabin donated by John Fitzsimmons and his students at the Fenn School. There will also be a number of volumes from the Cameron Collection on Thoreau donated by The Thoreau Society.

Other contributions are still coming in from local artists, authors, innkeepers, merchants,

restaurateurs, and organizations.

Concord tour guide Brad Parker will appear as Thoreau.

Noted Thoreau scholar Tom Blanding will share his extensive research on the birthplace.

Actor Dave Hannegan has been cast as the auctioneer.

Music will be provided by the Squirrel Hill Band, and sweets and savories are being donated by Martha's Catering, Anderson's, the Sudbury Hummus Factory, Concord Teacakes and the Concord Cheese Shop.

Carlisle resident Joan Parker is producing the event.

All proceeds will go to the Birthplace Fund of the National Park Services, earmarked specifically for the purchase of the site.

If you are interested in donating an item to the auction, contact Joan Parker at (508) 369-3973.

For reservations, call (508) 369-7911 or purchase tickets at Snow's Pharmacy on Main Street in Concord center at $12.50/$10 seniors.

STAFF PHOTO BY RICHARD PRI

Fenn School sixth graders are building a 3/4-size replica of Thoreau's Walden cabin. When completed next fall, the finished product will be delivered to the yard of the highest bidder at the upcoming Thoroughly Thoreau Auction. Showing off their carpentry skills are (l-r) Nate Swift, Eli Manna, Ryan Connolly and Zac Toth.

VI

TO COMPROMISE OR STAND FAST?

Compromise makes a good umbrella, but a poor roof.

—James Russell Lowell

Town Meeting voters were not yet ready to commit municipal funds to help save the property; that was clear from the meeting. But the strong vote of confidence in the value of preserving the house and land allowed Concord officials, particularly Selectman Sally Schnitzer, Town Manager Christopher Whelan, Town Planning Director Al Lima, and Natural Resources Director Dan Monahan, to work on soliciting support—and funds—from public entities. It also allowed them to consider what the town might be in a position to contribute based on its established land acquisition guidelines and the funds reserved for capital expenditures.

Meanwhile, working behind the scenes, a tenacious group of citizen activists, including Doris Smith, Helen Bowdoin, Joe Valentine, and Michael Kellett, stayed busy contacting potential private donors and foundations.

One local resident, Joan Parker from the neighboring town of Carlisle, produced a major auction to help raise both funds and awareness. Held on June 15, 1996, "Thoroughly Thoreau" was staged at 51 Walden, a popular performance venue in downtown Concord that is home to the Concord Players community theater troupe. Performers and technical staff from the theater company volunteered their time, and a live band agreed to perform for free. Area restaurants donated food and drink for the occasion. The event raised just under $6,000 for the cause, and by helping build support from neighboring communities, its value as an area booster was greater still.

At some point, however, the efforts of those involved in saving the birthplace diverged. As work to save the house was advancing, so were the Breen family's attempts to sell their property. Though the Breens had not yet acted on any of the several proposals they'd received, Doris Smith and her group of early advocates were concerned the family would be forced to accept an offer that would result in the destruction of the birth house and the eradication of the farmland. They were also troubled by the sluggish response they had received from their Save the Thoreau Birthplace Foundation fundraising efforts. So Smith turned to a developer she and her neighbors knew and respected, Peter Conant, president of CMA Architects of Jamaica Plain, Massachusetts.

Conant responded to the request for help by drawing up a plan to build nine cluster houses on 3.6 acres at the rear of the farmland. Using proceeds from the sale of the new homes, he would restore the house where Thoreau was born as a historic landmark and place the remaining acres in a permanent conservation restriction. Conant said the new homes would be built in a style compatible with that of the restored birthplace and the birth house would be sold to a preservation-minded individual or organization.

Knowing that tension would be aroused whenever the word "development" entered the conversation, Conant hedged his bets from the outset. "I'm only in here to avoid the tragedy that would occur if the house were to be destroyed," Conant said at the time. "I would be happy to bow out if another source of funding comes along. I am a preservationist, first and foremost."

To many people in town, Conant's offer was an appealing proposition. It would not only save the house, it would solve a key problem that naysayers were fond of advancing: no town funds would have to be expended on either the purchase of the house or its stabilization.

On the other hand, there was that pesky detail of the nine cluster houses that would forever alter the rural feel of the landscape. The proposal landed like a grenade into the center of the debate, destroying the yearlong bond that had been forged among local supporters of the preservation effort and splitting them into two intractable camps: those who supported the Conant plan as a worthy compromise and those who opposed any development so near to the house on the last remaining acres of historically and agriculturally significant farmland.

Members of the Save the Thoreau Birthplace Foundation, including Doris Smith, applauded the Conant plan as a creative solution to the problems they were encountering as they tried to raise private funds to save the entire parcel. "What I'd prefer is that all the land be saved," said Smith. "But this is an excellent fall-back position."

Joe Valentine, however, one of the foundation's charter members, could not accept this endorsement of the development plan and resigned from the group. "The proposal that Peter Conant puts forward is probably appealing to many people, but it's development nevertheless," said Valentine in a *Boston Globe* interview published on May 19. "It's no longer going to be a farm; it's going to be another piece of suburbia."

As correspondent Ann Hall pointed out in an op-ed piece published on June 9 in *The Boston Globe*, Smith had the most to lose from Conant's proposal, since she and her husband would be relinquishing their frequent saunters through the fields adjoining their home. "For her, it is a question of 'Yes, in my backyard,'" wrote Hall. "I wanted it all saved," Smith said to Hall. "I will never be able to put into words what I feel when I walk there. It's land that you feel God on."

But others in town wanted to allow time for alternative options to develop—options that would save the entire parcel plus the house—rather than abandon hope at that point. Helen Bowdoin, executive director of the Thoreau Country Conservation Alliance, said she was reluctant to sacrifice the 3.6 acres to preserve the rest. "This is the place where the father of the conservation movement was born," she told Hall. "To have it turn into another slice of suburban development would be a sad mistake."

Conant had not yet signed a purchase-and-sale agreement with the Breen family when he went public with his proposal. It seemed to some observers that he was treating the plan like a canary in a mineshaft, to see whether it lived or died in what had become a heated atmosphere of public opinion. Had he signed such an agreement, the Town of Concord would have had 120 days to decide if it wanted to activate its right of first refusal. Had that right been triggered, it's impossible to know if the crisis would have brought eleventh-hour funders to the fore to supplement whatever the town was willing to contribute—if anything. It would have been difficult, in such a short time, to call a Special Town Meeting or arrange for a town-wide vote to see if citizens would be willing to authorize some level of municipal spending.

The controversy over Conant's proposal delayed his making any agreement with the family and bought more time for everyone involved, including the Breens, to see if another, more comprehensive preservation plan would arise. For the time being, Concord's selectmen, town manager, and staff members continued to work with a variety of entities to piece together financial backing for a purchase.

One of these entities was the Commonwealth of Massachusetts, which offers matching funds to municipalities through the Division of Conservation Services of the Executive Office of Environmental Affairs. The so-called Self-Help grants are intended to aid cities and towns in preserving open land by sharing the cost of land purchases. By providing only part of the cost of such purchases—determined through a complex funding mechanism based on the cost of the property per capita—designers of the program require local citizens to support the acquisitions with their own funds and fundraising efforts. Any land purchased with the help of a state grant, including farmland, must remain open to the public for passive recreation, and the town must provide the state with a plan for such public access and use.

By applying for the Self-Help grant, the town was acknowledging the cultural value and historical significance of the farm on which Thoreau had been born. The grant would not cover any of the costs involved in the purchase and restoration of the house, but there was no doubt that the land was much more valuable as a commercial commodity than the deteriorating structure. Combined with private donations and other organizational funding, town officials believed a state grant toward the value of the land could be decisive in its effort to save the entire property. The state had indicated that Concord would be eligible to receive up to 54 percent of the purchase price. So, with Al Lima and Dan Monahan taking the lead, the application for a Self-Help grant was delivered by the June 1 deadline.

The catch, given the refusal at the Annual Town Meeting to allocate any town funds to the purchase, was that a town applying for a grant had to be willing to commit the total cost of the project before a Self-Help grant would be awarded and some of that funding had to come from the town itself. Another complicating factor was that the grant would not be awarded until the town had voted to acquire the land, though the acquisition could be contingent on receipt of the award. All of this—proof of the ability and willingness to purchase—would have to be demonstrated by the end of the 1996 calendar year to conform to the rules of the program. That was, in the realm of municipal government, a very tight deadline.

"I think everyone is hoping it will be a collaborative effort," Planning Director Al Lima told *The Globe's* Ann Hall. "But that also makes it more difficult because no one agency has the resources to do it."

As did O'Mara at *The Baltimore Sun*, Hall ended her *Globe* piece on a note that revealed her own emotional connection to the preservation effort. "Everyone—including Conant—agrees that the ultimate goal is to preserve the entire property," she wrote. "Concord preservationists and town officials are working hard to save it, but they can't do it alone. What is needed is an outpouring of moral and financial support from everyone who has been moved by Thoreau's ideas and ideals. Concord is his monument, but Thoreau has touched us all."

The rift that developed between the two camps of town activists—those hoping to save the house through a compromise plan that would destroy the farmland and those intent on saving the entire property—became unbridgeable over time, with the second camp ultimately carrying the day. As the late spring and summer of 1996 advanced, discussions between town officials and developer Peter Conant continued. But so did the town's effort to meet the requirements for a state Self-Help grant, which kept alive possible purchase of both house and land.

Since the Save the Thoreau Birthplace Foundation supported the Conant development plan and had adopted a lower profile because of the controversy it had ignited, the Thoreau Country Conservation Alliance, with executive director Helen Bowdoin and members Joe Valentine and Michael Kellett in the forefront, now became the lead citizens' group working with the town to save and preserve the entire property. In a letter to Concord's Board of Selectmen, Bowdoin listed the reasons the property was worthy of preservation and took direct aim at the Conant plan: "A recent proposal to develop four of the property's eighteen acres with a cluster development of nine houses would effectively transform the farmstead into another slice of suburbia," she wrote. "Surprisingly, the land still retains the rural feeling of the nineteenth century. If nine houses were to be built, the birthplace of the father of the conservation movement would be lost forever."

Meanwhile, town officials remained in conversation with the Breen family, through their attorney Nathaniel Brown. Though eager to sell, Ruth and her daughters were generous in their willingness to remain open to the town's overtures. They told Town Manager Christopher Whelan they would consider a funding package that combined an acceptable cash offer with a tax-advantaged gift component. It would take some time, however, for the two parties to agree on the meaning of "acceptable."

Between the requirements of the Self-Help grant and the need to avoid undue delay in either signing on with the Conant plan or securing a separate agreement with the family, the town floated the idea of calling a Special Town Meeting in the fall to open debate and take a vote on acquisition. The tepid support that had characterized the previous year's approach to saving the property had heated up into a fervent effort to make the best decision possible. It would be a shame, many people felt, to let apathy or passivity determine an outcome the town would later regret.

VII

KEEPING OPTIONS ALIVE

Go not so far out of your way for a truer life….
[D]o the things which lie nearest to you but which are difficult to do.

—H.D. Thoreau, Journal

As Ruth Breen and her daughters became more aware of the seriousness of the effort to preserve their house and land, their conversations with Town Manager Christopher Whelan became more serious as well. Perhaps it would be possible for the town to purchase the house with funds from grants and public and private donors, after all. As a sign of good faith, they graciously offered to open the Virginia Road home to interested visitors beginning in the summer of 1996.

Every summer, the Thoreau Society holds its Annual Gathering in Concord, where the organization is based. The four-day event is scheduled to coincide as closely as possible with Henry's July 12th birthday. Scholars, students, and Thoreau enthusiasts arrive in town by the hundreds each year from around the country and the world, joining local participants in lectures, films, readings, saunters, hikes, and paddles that take them from immediate Thoreau Country to Henry haunts as remote as Katahdin in Maine. The Annual Gathering in July 1996 was unprecedented in that it included a visit to the house where Thoreau was born, opened for public touring for the first time in history on Henry's 179th birthday.

In an article in *The Boston Globe* by Andrew Dabilis, published the following day, Gerry Breen is quoted as saying she opened the house to allow Thoreau "followers" to see and experience the setting in the hope they would be inspired to raise funds to save the property. But though several Thoreau Society members who visited the house on Henry's birthday responded with emotion and appreciation, no one expressed the desire to make its preservation a priority for the Society, which had struggled financially for its own preservation since its founding in 1941.

The article stated that many people with the deepest pockets had already pledged support to the Walden Woods Project, which in 1996 was still young. When local activists approached its executive director, Kathi Anderson, about contributing financially to the birthplace effort, she declined on behalf of the organization, saying the project needed to use its funding for its primary purpose: the preservation and protection of Walden Woods.

"We've come up with a lot of possibilities but no hard money," said local historian Joseph Andrews. "A lot of wealthy people were approached and said no."

So halfway through the year, with the Self-Help grant pending, the Conant development proposal still on the table, and the property about to come out of probate, the willingness of the Breen family to hold off on a sale and allow the town more time to consider its options would ultimately make the difference in the final resolution.

In late July and throughout August 1996, the town kept in contact with developer Peter Conant, discussing specific details of his proposal but refusing to commit. At a July 29 meeting, Town Planning Director Lima, Natural Resources Director Monahan, and Health Officer Michael Moore told Conant they had some issues they wanted to bring to his attention. They would, for example, like to have 10 percent of the land area reserved for possible purchase by the town and used for affordable housing. They also hoped that the entire property could be designated as a Wellhead Protection District to ensure purity of the well water, that a drainage swale be created along the western edge of the property as a wetland, and that leaching fields for each of the nine new houses be installed rather than the proposed shared septic system. Perhaps most important of all, they were worried that the Trust for Public Land (TPL) would be averse to purchasing the restored Thoreau birthplace if nine houses were to be built behind it. They thought the TPL would accept three or four, but not the number Conant was proposing.

At some point early in the process of exploring options for saving the property, the Town of Concord had sought counsel from the Trust for Public Land, hoping to strike an agreement by which the TPL would help with the purchase. If the development plan moved forward, Conant would buy the entire property from the Breens and resell the birth house and the acre it stands on, once he had fulfilled his promise of restoring the house to an agreed-upon period style.

Town officials, never wishing to become permanent owners of the house, were interested in partnering with the TPL on its purchase.

The TPL buys property from landowners hoping to preserve their property in perpetuity and then conveys the property or easements on it to public agencies at or below fair market value. If some agreement could be reached with the TPL, the town could purchase the house back at a possibly reduced price and hang onto it temporarily until it could find a nonprofit organization willing to own it and become its permanent stewards. With Conant footing the cost of restoration, a nonprofit would need only commit to maintenance and a public access plan. High on the list of possibilities was The Trustees of Reservations, which owns and operates The Old Manse, one of Concord's most visited historic sites.

Amid all the contingency planning, Conant knew town officials were simultaneously exploring options for purchasing the entire property outright. Clearly hoping to do well by doing good, he demonstrated in his communications with town officials that he harbored a genuine concern for the birthplace. In an Aug. 19 letter to Al Lima, Conant outlined what he understood to be the situation at that moment, an analysis that jibed with others' reports. The state would not inform the town of the status of its Self-Help grant application until late September at the earliest. Once the amount of the grant was known, Town Meeting would have to authorize the remainder, either through town funding or a combination of town and other public/private funding. At the time of Conant's letter, that did not seem a likely prospect.

Conant also said in his letter that Peter Forbes of the TPL had told him his organization would not commit to the purchase of the property on behalf of the town until the required town funding was securely in place, through the Self-Help grant and other sources. He added that the TPL's recent offer of $700,000 was not acceptable to the Breen family and would have to be increased or supplemented to become viable. Finally, Conant noted that his most recent conversations with Concord selectmen led him to believe Town Meeting would not authorize the town funds needed to contribute to the purchase.

"I have been reading lots of articles in *The Concord Journal* and *The Boston Globe* but have not seen any serious money come forward," wrote Conant. There was no arguing with that. As a result, he said, the Breens might be forced to sell to someone who could possibly destroy the house. To prevent that possibility and hold the property in abeyance, he was willing to enter immediately into a purchase-and-sale agreement with the Breens, for a purchase amount "in excess of $1.2 million." Conant added that Gerry Breen had informed him that other developers had approached the family with even higher offers.

"Maybe the prospect of development on the site would galvanize everyone into action," he wrote, noting that "if everyone in Concord contributed $100 per capita, this would produce about $1.8 million, which would be enough to buy the property, restore the house, and establish a maintenance fund. Probably a naïve idea but an indication nonetheless of how little it would take."

Conant acknowledged that "the bad news about my proposal is that it takes some of the land area from the farm and turns it into housing. But the good news is that the [historic] house would be restored, preservation restrictions would be attached to the house and a majority of the remaining land, and an owner-occupant would be maintaining the premises and paying taxes."

One of the most significant messages in the letter was Conant's willingness to convey his purchase rights, as delineated in the purchase-and-sale agreement, to the Town of Concord if, during the duration of the agreement, the town obtained the funds to match his offer.

The list of people Conant cc'd on his letter to Lima offered a glimpse into the extent of the outreach work he had been doing behind the scenes: Doris Smith of Save the Thoreau Birthplace Foundation; Nathaniel Brown, the Breens' attorney; Arthur Fulman chair of the Concord Board of Selectmen; Marcia Rasmussen, town planner; Dan Monahan, Natural Resources director; Michael Moore, Concord health officer; Joe Valentine of the Concord Historical Commission and the Thoreau Country Conservation Alliance; and Peter Forbes of the Trust for Public Land. He was clearly pushing his agenda hard.

But pushing equally hard from the other side were those intent on saving the entire property, and it soon became clear that several town officials were among their number. In a letter to the Massachusetts Historical Commission regarding the town's intention to apply for a Self-Help grant from the state, Al Lima wrote that the

Breen property was being "actively marketed and has received considerable interest from potential developers." Referring to the Conant proposal, Lima wrote, "While this option would save the birthplace house on a large lot, considerable community opposition has been expressed to it because it would result in a compromised setting for this historic building and because the house and its smaller lot may still need to be purchased following the subdivision of the original parcel." He added that "[c]ommunity interest in protecting the historic property has been shown in various ways, including almost weekly newspaper articles in *The Concord Journal* and *The Boston Globe*."

During the month of August, while officials were meeting with Conant, they were also actively soliciting funding help from outside sources. One of these was the Massachusetts Port Authority, or Massport, which oversees Hanscom Field's general aviation operations.

Hanscom Field has been operating as an aviation facility since 1941, when the Commonwealth of Massachusetts acquired 500 acres of land in the towns of Bedford, Concord, Lexington, and Lincoln. During World War II, the Army Air Corps leased the airport and named it the Laurence G. Hanscom Field, in honor of the founding member and commander of the Massachusetts Wing of the Civilian Air Reserve. Military operations dominated Hanscom until it became a joint military and civilian facility in the 1950s. In 1959, the Massachusetts Port Authority assumed control of the state land and in 1974 took responsibility for the general operations and maintenance of the airfield. By this time, military operations had declined to occasional use. Hanscom currently has two runways and is managed as a regional aviation facility, whose major users include corporations, private pilots, flight schools, commuter/commercial air services, and some charters and light cargo planes.

Virginia Road lies directly in the flight path of Hanscom Field's two runways, which are located behind the Thoreau birthplace property. Over the years, as more and more houses were built near the airfield, citizen complaints about noise and pollution had become a major irritant to Hanscom's personnel. Despite the fact that the airfield was there before the residents, who knew of its existence when they purchased their properties, such complaints created a serious image problem for Massport. With this in mind, Al Lima wrote to

Daniel O'Connell, director of business development at Massport. In a letter dated Aug. 29, 1996, Lima informed O'Connell of the town's wish to acquire the historic birthplace property. He said that though Concord was eligible for a state grant that could cover up to 54 percent of the acquisition costs, he had been told that limited funds and a high level of competition meant the town was unlikely to receive that full share. "Since Massport owns property on the northern and western boundaries of the Thoreau site—and given the inherent conflicts in having residential uses developed at a site situated at the end of a runway—I wish to explore with you Massport's possible interest in becoming a partner with the Town, the Commonwealth, and private interests in preserving this significant site," wrote Lima.

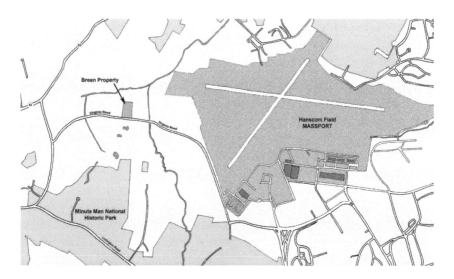

Meanwhile, Peter Conant was beginning to get the message that the town was not as enthusiastic about his development proposal as he had hoped it would be. A second letter from him to Al Lima, dated Aug. 23, indicates that the town was putting up too many obstacles to his plan. The letter refers to a site visit to the Breen property on Aug. 20 by representatives from the state's Executive Office of Environmental Affairs, as part of their evaluation of the town's application for a Self-Help grant. Though he didn't state it explicitly, Conant seemed to be suggesting that the timing of the visit might indicate the state's willingness to inform the town of its decision on the grant earlier than anticipated.

In addition, Conant wrote that he had just learned of the town's intention to propose a new conservation bylaw that would affect the wetlands setback requirements for the site. Even though the new bylaw would require a Town Meeting vote, which could not occur before spring of the following year, the requirement would take effect retroactively to the very first public hearing on the matter, which would fall into his construction period.

This letter was shorter and less energetic than his earlier missive. Conant wrote that "it has been suggested that I should wait until the potential for state funding is determined before proceeding with any purchase offer," a suggestion he appeared willing to take. This suggestion was likely made to delay triggering the town's right of first refusal, which would need to be exerted within four months of the signing of a bona fide purchase-and-sale agreement.

Conant added in this letter that he would need time to determine the impact of the proposed new bylaw on his development plan and ended by saying he would be "studying the situation before making a decision." It turned out to be the last scene of a classy production.

Virginia Road and surrounding farmland as it looked in 1890 to
local photographer Florence Richardson.

VIII

TAKING A STAND

Things do not change; we change.

—H.D. Thoreau, *Walden*

As autumn came on, interest in the Conant development proposal waned. There was no discernable moment of epiphany, but at some point early that fall Concord's collective consciousness rose high enough to turn saving the birthplace and its farmland into a town imperative. It felt as though people suddenly realized: Hey, this is Henry David Thoreau's birthplace, and no other town in the world can lay claim to it. If the house were to be destroyed and the land on which Thoreau's mother had grown up and Henry had first seen the light of day were sliced into pricey suburban house lots, how could Concordians hold up their heads? So, while everyone waited for an answer about the state's Self-Help grant, efforts to enlist financial support to save the entire property ramped up on all fronts.

In September, members of the Board of Selectmen enlisted the services of George McCully, a development consultant they hoped would help draw up an effective fundraising plan. On Oct. 3, he laid out his suggestions in a memo sent to Selectman Sally Schnitzer and former Selectman Judy Walpole, who had become part of an Ad Hoc Committee to Save the Thoreau Birthplace comprised of town officials and citizen activists. "There should be no doubt that sufficient funds can be raised for this project," he wrote encouragingly, advancing an opinion that was not yet shared by many in town. In proposing detailed suggestions for how to proceed with a successful capital campaign, he offered one piece of particularly important advice: the town would have to come up with at least a portion of the acquisition cost if it hoped to attract other donors. "The larger the Town's financial commitment, the easier and quicker it will be to secure the remaining funds," he wrote, "not just because fewer dollars will remain, but because donors will be more willing to give if the Town is strongly behind the project."

At the same time, McCully advised the town against becoming the permanent manager of the entire property. "I expect the Town ...

will see the wisdom of minimizing its potential problems and exposure by limiting its role to that of friendly sponsor, catalyst, and broker of this project rather than that of permanent and sole administrator of the entire site and its diverse activities...." He suggested dividing the property into three administrative entities: 1) conservation land, which could be managed easily by the town; 2) agricultural land, which could be leased to an appropriate farming entity; and 3) the historic house, which could be leased or sold to an educational institution or museum.

McCully was clear that raising the funds to buy the property would have to be conducted as a public-private collaboration because "neither the public nor the private sector has the funds by itself to protect and preserve Thoreau's Birthplace." He also urged the town to be cautious about asserting its vision for how the house and land would be used. There should be some attempt at defining future use, he said, in order to demonstrate the potential value of the property. But that vision shouldn't be so restrictive as to discourage any appropriate funders. "This definition of ultimate usage should be done advisedly, with technical assistance," he wrote, "because every restriction will affect fundraising for better or worse."

McCully continued to advise the committee throughout the next several months. His observations about the philanthropic climate were astute, and committee members ended up adopting many of his suggestions, in large part, because most of them affirmed their own thinking. They had already launched a public-private partnership, enlisting the help of the state, the Trust for Public Land, Massport, the Thoreau Country Conservation Alliance, and the Save the Thoreau Birthplace Foundation. They now turned to a new potential partner: EDCO, the Education Collaborative for Greater Boston, to help them imagine how the property could be used.

IX

THE SEEFURTH CONNECTION

We can't always do all we would like to do,
but we always have an attentive ear when Thoreau is mentioned.

—Nathaniel Seefurth

When Courtland Booth, then director of the Concord-Carlisle Adult and Community Education programming, was spearheading a new town-wide curricular initiative called the Concord Program, he turned to the Education Collaborative for Greater Boston (EDCO) to help fund the project. Founded in 1969 by a small group of area school superintendents, EDCO began as a private, nonprofit consortium with the goal of providing opportunities for staff and students in urban and suburban districts to work together on joint initiatives. Over time, participation grew, and by 1996 EDCO had become a public entity comprising twenty-one school districts, including Concord. Its services also grew to include professional development for teachers, special education and alternative education programs, and curriculum development across disciplines.

The Concord Program turned out to be a perfect fit for EDCO. It was a collaborative curriculum designed to coordinate visits to Concord's historical, cultural, and environmental landmarks. As stated in a published brochure, the program's purpose was to explore the significance of Concord's heritage as a center for revolutionary ideas, literary genius, and conservation advocacy in order to "strengthen the connections in Concord between people and nature and to share the lessons learned with a local and national audience."

Booth, who had become an active member of the Ad Hoc Committee to Save Thoreau's Birthplace, recognized in EDCO a potential partner in the effort to preserve and use the property. When he discussed the Concord Program with Jack Green, EDCO's longtime executive director, Booth mentioned that a major unit in the curriculum was entitled "Thoreau and Friends." Green then told him of EDCO's great benefactor, the late Nathaniel Seefurth. After serving in World War I and earning a law degree, Seefurth had made his fortune practicing estate and tax law. In 1952, at the age of 56, he had established the Seefurth Foundation in his native Chicago, intending the philanthropic fund to serve as "a means to care for, educate, and encourage boys and girls of limited financial means who show promise of having unusual qualities of character and leadership and who indicate a desire to devote these talents to the service of their fellow men rather than for their own personal advancement." Green told Booth that Seefurth had greatly admired Thoreau and the town of Concord and would have supported the curriculum EDCO was about to fund.

Nathaniel Seefurth

In fact, Seefurth had an admiration for Henry Thoreau that bordered on the evangelical. In an essay entitled "Nathaniel Seefurth—Friend of Thoreau," published in the Fall 1976 issue of *American Transcendental Quarterly,* his friend Kenneth W. Cameron wrote that Seefurth "at some point … arrived at the opinion that if he might only encourage young people to read Thoreau's [*Walden*], its self-reliant message would leave its mark on their lives as it had on his."

Seefurth even wrote a small book, entitled *Thoreau: A View from Emeritus,* which the Seefurth Foundation distributed at no cost to a number of college libraries in the late 1960s. The copyright page of the volume declares its intention to acquaint students "with the man who proclaimed to youth, 'If you have built castles in the air, your work need not be lost; that is where they should be. Now put the foundations under them.'"

In 1969 Cameron, a professor at Trinity College in Hartford, Connecticut, and a respected scholar of Transcendentalism, came across the book and began a sustained correspondence and friendship with Seefurth that lasted until Seefurth's death in 1976, at the age of 79. In the course of their written exchanges, Cameron put Seefurth, then living with his family in Walnut Creek, California, in contact with an inspiring educator he greatly admired: Jane Dorgan, a fifth-grade teacher at the Louise Duffy School in West Hartford, Connecticut. Dorgan, who later became principal of the nearby Bridlepath School, was an early proponent of experiential, hands-on education. She was also a believer in the positive effects Thoreau's writings could have on children. Each year, she would take her fifth-graders on an exchange program with an elementary school in Concord and would return to Hartford with some Concord pupils in tow.

Seefurth was intrigued. That fall he and his wife traveled to Connecticut to meet Dorgan, who arranged for a group of her former students to re-create a typical class "in which Thoreau was taught, discussed, illustrated, and written about in themes, notebooks, and term papers." That visit cemented Seefurth's belief in the value of teaching Thoreau to the young, and he agreed to fund a primer written by Dorgan for 10-to-14-year-olds, *Henry David Thoreau: An Exploration Into His Life, Thoughts, and Friends*, which the Seefurth Foundation published in April 1970 and distributed, again free of charge, to interested schools.

The visit with Dorgan also became the seed for a dream that occupied the remaining years of Seefurth's life: the establishment of a Seefurth Center in Concord that could be used by schools as an overnight facility for students of American literature, history, and ecology during a visit to the many historical and natural sites the town has on offer. Seefurth envisioned the center as a place for students and teachers from around the country to gather and enhance their field trip through an immersive experience that would keep them centered in the place they were studying.

The idea for the center was planted in Seefurth's mind by Dorgan herself. She reported that response to the primer she had written had been "overwhelming." By the spring of the first year the book was in print, more than 600 schoolchildren were using it in their classrooms. "I have been contacted by schools from all over the United States requesting copies of this book to use with young people," she wrote. "The one problem that everyone encounters is the distance to the Concord area with no overnight facility for the youngsters and teachers or educational facility for seminars, lectures, and so forth."

Not a man to ignore a need or sit on a good idea, Seefurth began immediately exploring possible sites for such an educational center and, when in 1970 he found one he thought would be ideal, he bought it. The five-acre lot on Barrett's Mill Road in Concord was owned by the McGraths, a local farm family. Anne McGrath, curator of the Thoreau Lyceum, a now-defunct but once cherished gathering place for Thoreau enthusiasts in the heart of downtown Concord, was only too happy to sell a piece of her family's land for the purposes Seefurth had in mind.

But things did not go smoothly. When Seefurth presented the town with plans for a Seefurth Education Center, neighbors of the property rose up in protest. They worried that a residential center meant to house potentially large groups of students transported by school buses would have a negative impact on the neighborhood. The building inspector denied Seefurth a building permit on the grounds that the intended use—educational—was not permitted in the historic district. In a long, detailed presentation to the Board of Appeals on March 3, 1971, Seefurth and his supporters sought to dispel these worries and assure all concerned that the "Literary and Historic Journey to Concord, Massachusetts" being facilitated by the Seefurth Center would not be disruptive to residents. The appeal was again denied, and ultimately Seefurth had to sell the land and abandon the hope of fulfilling his dream during his lifetime.

It is impossible to know today if Seefurth would have prolonged his efforts to build a center in Concord had he not suffered a major heart attack in July 1971 that put him in a prolonged coma and from which he never fully recovered. The property he had purchased in Concord was sold to the town as permanent conservation land, and the proceeds invested in a Seefurth Fund. To keep his dream alive, less than a year before Seefurth's death his family transferred all the assets of the Seefurth Fund to the Education Collaborative for Greater Boston in the hope that a center would someday be built in his name and realize his vision. In the meantime, while efforts to locate a site for the center continued, proceeds from the Seefurth Fund would be used to support educational programming in line with his philosophy, such as the Concord Program.

Twenty years after Seefurth's death, EDCO's Jack Green—with the encouragement of Court Booth—saw a way to resurrect his dream. Green had always admired Seefurth's devotion to education and regretted that he had not been able to carry out Seefurth's goal of establishing an educational center in Concord. He told *The Concord Journal* he had always considered it a "personal and moral commitment" to find a home for the center. When he heard about the availability of the Breen property, Green saw his opportunity at last. If the Town of Concord were able to raise the funds to purchase the house and land, perhaps EDCO could work with town officials to construct a barn on the site that would fit neatly into the agricultural landscape and become the long-hoped-for Seefurth Center. Green could imagine Seefurth's delight at opening his center on the very farm where Thoreau was born. In fact, Mrs. Seefurth told Green she was "tickled pink" at the possibility of a Seefurth Center located "in Henry Thoreau's backyard."

Residents gear up for big decisions in 1997

By Richard Fahlander
STAFF WRITER

It was crystal ball gazing time on Saturday morning, as town officials presented their best laid plans for next spring's Town Meeting. If the prognosticators are right, those who attend the annual legislative session will vote on several measures of lasting import to the town. A new visitors center, the saving of the Thoreau birthplace and farmland and the allocation of Hapgood Wright's $330,000 legacy are among the issues likely to attract interest.

And while not every warrant article will be a magnet for debate, taken together, they all make a difference in the fabric of the town. Here is the lowdown on what was presented at last Saturday's coordination meet-

See DECISIONS, PAGE 14

Town moving on Thoreau birth house

A seed that was planted by preservationists last spring is taking root, as the town moves closer to purchasing the Thoreau birthplace.

On Saturday Arthur Fulman, chairman of the Board of Selectmen, announced that by the end of this month he expects to have in hand a purchase and sale agreement for less than $1 million with the Breen family, the house's current owners.

Fulman said he is "cautiously optimistic" that the pieces of the purchase puzzle will fall into place in time for spring Town Meeting.

Last month the town was awarded a $160,000 self-help grant from the state to be used toward the purchase of the property. Fulman said he expects the town to contribute about $150,000 from the capital fund. The birthplace also is one of a number of projects mentioned for funding from the Hapgood Wright Centennial Fund.

In addition, Fulman said several private organizations have expressed interest in contributing to the purchase. Massport, which operates nearby Hanscom Field, has indicated its willingness to purchase conservation restriction rights.

Fulman said the plan presented to Town Meeting will include provisions for ongoing programing and financial support. One option could be leasing the farmland to a local farmer and building a small educational center on the property. The house itself would be restored.

— Richard Fahlander

X

THE STARS BEGIN TO ALIGN

Success in preservation requires perseverance,
tenacity, mastery of the facts, and collaboration.

—Stanley Smith, *Historic Preservation for Professionals*

In early October 1996, more than a year after the Breen property came up for sale, the fate of the Thoreau birthplace remained uncertain. The town's efforts to gain support and funding to purchase the house and land simmered steadily, but quietly, on a back burner. Before the heat could be turned up again, the town needed to hear from the state about a decision on the Self-Help grant. The answer finally came on Oct. 31, and it was disappointing. Funds had been low and competition fierce. Though Concord had been eligible for up to 54 percent of the purchase price of the property, which could have amounted to as much as half a million dollars, the grant from the Executive Office of Environmental Affairs was for only $160,000.

Surprisingly, rather than having a dampening effect on the effort, the modest grant became the catalyst for action. A Nov. 7 article in *The Concord Journal* reported that the grant announcement "immediately set off phone calls and meetings among town officials and local preservation activists who are laying the plans for the next step."

That step, which demanded citizen approval, was a decision on whether or not to accept the grant. The date for acceptance had been set by the state at Dec. 31. But given the impossibility of convening a Special Town Meeting in time to vote on the grant and meet that deadline, Planning Director Al Lima requested and received an extension until the end of January.

Complicating the process were two key requirements: the town would have to vote to appropriate the entire purchase price—still estimated at around $1 million—before it could accept the grant, and the grant funds would have to be spent by the end of the fiscal year, that is by June 30, 1997. The fact that Town Manager Christopher Whelan, a steady, cautious administrator, went on record to say meeting these requirements was "do-able" hinted at just how much lobbying of potential funders had already been conducted privately, well behind the scenes.

"We did not receive the amount we had hoped for from the state," said Selectman Arthur Fulman at the Nov. 4 Board of Selectmen's meeting. "So others need to step up to the plate on this issue." Fulman revealed that night that Massport had been receptive to the town's requests for financial help. "For Massport, if the land isn't developed with homes, that's one less person complaining about Hanscom [Field]," he said. Fulman acknowledged, however, that the airfield's unpopularity among town residents, especially those who lived closest to it, might lead to objections about accepting Massport funding. But Fulman believed those objections would be misplaced. "Massport's here and we're here, and sometimes you have to work together," he said.

Names of other potential donors were being withheld until they had signed on officially and agreed to go public, so from an observer's perspective, the situation still appeared tenuous and the goal beyond reach. But Selectman Sally Schnitzer sounded an optimistic note when she told *The Concord Journal*: "We expect to have to ask the town for some funding. But our intention is to have all other commitments in place by Town Meeting." Suddenly, after so many months of discussions and talks and waiting, time was short.

Leading up to the state's announcement, Christopher Whelan had continued negotiating the purchase price with the Breen family attorney, Nathaniel Brown. At the time the state grant was announced, no agreement had yet been reached. But all parties knew that a firm figure had to be in place in order for funders to come out from behind the curtain and commit. By the end of the calendar year, after several offers and counter-offers and solid assurances by the town that all the money could indeed be raised, the Breen family agreed to sell the house and land to the town for the below-market price of $960,000. Part of the difference between that price and what the family could have received from a developer was offset by the tax advantages of designating a portion of the property as a gift. It was a generous offer, and Whelan expressed confidence the terms could be met. When the negotiation was finally completed, the Breens also agreed to close on the property by the end of June 1997, which would meet the state's requirement that the Self-Help grant be spent by the end of the fiscal year.

By the end of the final quarter of 1996, all private offers to purchase the property—even the creative, though ultimately unsatisfactory, solution presented by developer Peter Conant—were taken off the table, and the town set about rallying potential funders to make their support official.

"The clock is ticking," warned Al Lima when the state grant had been announced on Oct. 31. In fact, despite the confidence and optimism spurred by the awarding of the grant, the timing was simply too tight for the town to gather all the necessary funding for a Special Town Meeting vote in January. Many of the potential funders had to secure a final commitment from boards of directors or other decision makers and could not turn things around that quickly. Once again, town officials reached out to the Executive Office of Environmental Affairs to request a further delay in the established deadline for accepting the state grant. In a letter dated Nov. 21, 1996, Board of Selectmen Chair Arthur Fulman told Conservation Services Director Joel Lerner that "a consortium of town officials, nonprofit organizations, individuals, and educational/historic groups have been working diligently to identify sources of funding. We remain guardedly optimistic that all the funds can be raised, but not in the January-February timeframe. Bringing the appropriation issue to a vote in January would be premature, we believe, because it would cause the town to commit to the full purchase price (which it cannot afford to do) without being assured of funding from other sources…. This is a risk the Selectmen cannot responsibly undertake and could result in the failure of efforts to date."

As a consequence, Fulman asked Lerner to extend the state's deadline for accepting the grant until Concord's 1997 Annual Town Meeting the following spring. Fulman assured Lerner that if Town Meeting voted to approve the appropriation of funds in the spring, the money would be spent by the end of the fiscal year, as required. He added that if it appeared at any point that the full price for the property would not be forthcoming, town officials would let Lerner know in time for the grant to be reallocated.

Significantly, Fulman included in his letter a detailed account of the town's conversations with the Education Collaborative for Greater Boston. He revealed that EDCO would be willing to contribute to the purchase of the Breen property if an arrangement could be worked out for the collaborative to build a "barnlike structure" on the property and operate it in conjunction with the restored birth house as an educational facility for visiting students. Fulman said EDCO had already submitted a preliminary site plan and would be meeting with permitting boards before the spring Town Meeting. Though the Self-Help grant was intended to protect the land only and not any structures on the property, Fulman wanted Lerner to know that the multiple uses planned for the birthplace would enhance its appeal to funders and raise the chances of acquisition and preservation.

Lerner, who from the start had enthusiastically supported the town's wish to preserve the property, responded quickly to Fulman's request. In a letter dated Nov. 26, he said that delaying a vote until the April Town Meeting "appears to be a good strategy" for putting all the funding sources together. He was especially delighted to hear that Massport was interested in contributing to the cause in exchange for an easement on the property that would prevent new houses from being built there. "Keeping houses out of Hanscom Field's flight path is an objective which benefits both the town and Massport," Lerner wrote. "If some should say, 'Isn't this tainted money?' I would say 'Tain't enough!'"

Meanwhile, two new citizen initiatives were launched in the fall of 1996 to build awareness and advocacy for the birthplace effort. Thoreau Society member Peggy Brace, a supporter of the Thoreau Country Conservation Alliance, printed self-addressed, stamped envelopes and set them on the counter of the Shop at Walden Pond, with a hand-written note urging shoppers to write statements of support for saving Thoreau's birthplace that would be sent to Gov. William Weld. Signing her note "an alarmed Concord citizen," Brace wrote, "This is not a local issue. This is a national and international issue."

Brace had already tried out her idea at the Thoreau Society's Annual Gathering that July, and the response had been "overwhelming," according to Helen Bowdoin. The postcards received the same enthusiastic welcome at Walden Pond. The shop's manager, Stephanie Kornfeld, told *The Concord Journal* at the time that her customers were enthusiastic about sending the postcards and that hundreds had already been filled out. Some people were offering to pay for the cards and others insisted on donating a few dollars to support the effort. "Even children dig into their pockets for change," she said. "It's obviously a hot issue. We're happy to be part of this community action."

Several of the postcards' messages were reproduced as an accompaniment to the *Journal* article. "Please don't destroy what has taught so many of us," read one. In a note more personally directed at Governor Weld, one sender wrote, "It is a poor nation that does not honor its heroes or value its treasures. As one whose family has been so deeply intertwined with the Commonwealth since its founding, surely you can see the necessity of saving the Thoreau birthplace in the home of American liberty."

Whether or not the hundreds of postcards sent through Brace's effort exerted any effect at the state level, her bright idea definitely inspired local citizens by demonstrating the powerful feelings evoked by Henry David Thoreau and the value people placed on the house where he was born.

Another, very different effort was put forward by Concord resident Christine Rinaldo, who founded a nonprofit corporation in September 1996. Historic Concord, Inc., which continues to exist today, was originally incorporated to advocate for threatened historic resources in Concord, raise funds to enable the town to accomplish its goals for saving historic properties, and provide education on historic preservation. While its stated goals were broad, the announcement of its founding listed the saving of Thoreau's birthplace as one of its primary objectives. The organization would succeed in raising $10,000 toward the birthplace purchase, and its public support would add one more influential voice to the cause.

As such efforts proceeded on all fronts to gather in the necessary funds, the town stepped up as well. The Board of Selectmen, which prepares in December the warrant for the following spring's Annual Town Meeting, drafted articles requesting approval to purchase the Breen property and contribute $160,000 of town money toward the cost of the property. That amount, which matched the funding offered by the state grant, would be drawn from land acquisition funds the town held in reserve. It was an important moment and something of a risk. On the one hand, town officials knew, from their fundraising consultant's advice and their own instincts, that funders needed solid proof of town support before committing themselves. On the other hand, the voters at the 1996 Town Meeting had not been willing to provide that support, and selectmen had no idea if public opinion had evolved enough to change that outcome. They also understood these articles would have no chance at all of passing unless the rest of the purchase price—over and above the $320,000 from the state and town—was securely in hand.

In the Dec. 12 issue of *The Concord Journal*, reporter Richard Fahlander wrote, "If the prognosticators are right, those who attend [the 1997 Town Meeting] will vote on several measures of lasting import." Among these, he noted, was the decision on whether or not to save the Thoreau birthplace by purchasing the Breen land. Selectmen Chair Arthur Fulman expressed his optimism that the vote would be positive, yet offered no detailed evidence of the town's ability to raise the purchase price. For undecided citizens, it was still a waiting game.

With the December holidays approaching, Frederic Winthrop Jr., director of The Trustees of Reservations (TTOR), sent a letter of encouragement to the Board of Selectmen. As the owner and operator of The Old Manse in Concord, TTOR had been working for years with local groups to develop a series of integrated thematic tours of the town's historic sites. "The Thoreau Birthplace would add greatly to the experience of these visitors and to their understanding of key elements of Concord," wrote Winthrop. "As the oldest working farm in Concord, this ... site should not be developed. We believe a far better use would involve utilizing this property as an orientation center for school groups and others who wish to understand not only the historical and literary associations of the town, but also the evolution of the Concord landscape."

As the busy year wound down, all eyes were on April 1997, and attendance for the pivotal vote on the Breen property was expected to be huge.

XI

"I'M BEGINNING TO BELIEVE
WE MIGHT ACTUALLY DO THIS!"

*Maintaining the identity of tangible historic places
is one of the hallmarks of civilization…. [It is a way] to bequeath
the best of our present and past to succeeding generations.*

—Stanley Smith, *Historic Preservation for Professionals*

Exclamation points punctuated the first four months of 1997. Group after group, person after person stepped forward at last to offer their public support—in the form of real dollars—for saving Thoreau's birthplace. "There are a lot of fishing lines out," said Selectman Sally Schnitzer to *The Concord Journal* in mid-February. Gradually, they were all being reeled in.

There was now a preliminary plan in place for the future use of the property, prepared by the Ad Hoc Committee to Save Thoreau's Birthplace, which included representatives from the Board of Selectmen, the town staff, the Thoreau Country Conservation Alliance, and other citizens' groups. The plan allowed people to envision what they were supporting, and that helped a great deal. The birth house would be restored and used as a way to honor Thoreau's life and legacy; the farmland would be kept in agricultural use, most likely through a lease with a local farmer; portions of the land would be managed by the town's Natural Resources Commission and used for walking trails; and a modest barnlike structure would be constructed by EDCO as a small education center. This plan was just specific enough for several different advocacy groups to embrace. Some donors were most interested in preserving the house where Thoreau was born, while others felt more of an emotional connection to the historic farmland. EDCO's plan drew in educators who felt that the Seefurth Center could fill a void and serve to enliven the Concord experience for a new generation of young people. In order to assure neighbors that any future use would not be disruptive, the plan contained a provision against opening a gift shop, bookstore, or snack bar on the property.

By the end of February, the town had signed a formal purchase-and-sale agreement with the Breen family for the agreed-upon price of $960,000 and set a tentative closing date for May 27, a few days before the state's prescribed deadline for spending its Self-Help grant. The town estimated that an additional $20,000 or so would be needed to cover legal and other transaction costs.

On March 10, Peter Blute of Massport informed the town that the agency would be donating $200,000 to the project in exchange for a deed restriction on the property "to ensure no conflicts arise between the use of the property and impacts from airport operations." Massport's Jeremy Crockford told *The Concord Journal*, "It's a good idea to preserve the land where Thoreau was born. So I think this conservation restriction benefits both the town and Hanscom." It was a huge moment. This was the largest donation made by any single entity. It came after months of negotiation and buoyed spirits as Town Meeting loomed. "I'm beginning to believe we might actually do this!" said Selectman Sally Schnitzer. "It's very exciting."

Also that month, EDCO's board of directors voted to donate $300,000 to the property acquisition, $160,000 of which would be a direct contribution and the other $140,000 a loan to be reimbursed when the amount was raised by other sources. This strong commitment made a significant difference to the bottom line and cemented EDCO's relationship with the town, which in exchange for the donation and loan agreed to grant EDCO a thirty-year lease, at a cost of $1 per year, of a small portion of land adjacent to the birth house for the construction of an education center. It was becoming ever clearer that a Seefurth Center would figure prominently in any future planning and fundraising for the property. A site plan called for parking spaces for two school buses at the rear of the property along with limited parking for staff. The only difference between this plan and Seefurth's original dream was the absence of overnight facilities. That plan had already been rebuffed during Seefurth's earlier attempt to build in Concord, and the dormitory component was deemed too risky to attempt again.

The Ad Hoc Committee to Save Thoreau's Birthplace had been hard at work on the fundraising effort. At its March 21 session, dubbed "Countdown to Town Meeting!", the agenda filled two pages with details that needed to be nailed down during the coming weeks. These included how best to handle the fact that the Self-Help grant was only for the land and not for the house, how to reach out to town residents for donations, how to structure the Town Meeting presentation, how to ensure that all promised funding was squarely in place, and how to assure Town Meeting voters that they would not be asked to fund the restoration of the house or the future use of the property. It was a head-spinning list of tasks, to be accomplished by a handful of already busy people. And a follow-up meeting was scheduled in ten days time, in case anyone had thought of dragging his or her heels.

In early April, a Boston-area foundation made an anonymous donation of $180,000 to the cause. That major gift erased the $140,000 debt the town owed EDCO for its loan and brought success within reach. Helen Bowdoin, of the Thoreau Country Conservation Alliance, pronounced herself "on pins and needles" as the finish line was drawing near. As if to offer a wake-up call to others in town, she said there was no time left to sit back and wait. At this point, there was less than $100,000 left to raise. "We are facing the prospect that the entire effort could go down the drain for lack of less than 10 percent of the purchase price," said Bowdoin to *The Concord Journal*.

In an attempt to close the funding gap, the ad hoc committee sent out a town-wide mailing in mid-April. The letter told residents that "the effort to save Thoreau's birthplace is led by private citizens who believe our town will suffer irreparable loss if we fail in this endeavor.… Now we turn to you. … Most of the funds pledged to us so far were done so with the understanding that private citizens would also come to the rescue.… One of the reasons we live in such a wonderful town is because neighbors band together to preserve its unique heritage and unique standing in the American landscape."

The letter also promised that "all contributors of $1,000 or more will be permanently recognized on a bronze plaque to be prominently displayed on the first floor of the Thoreau House." In a *Concord Journal* article announcing the impending appeal, reporter Richard Fahlander noted, "Without individual contributions, the complex Thoreau Birthplace house of cards could come tumbling down."

On Thursday, April 17, just short of two weeks before the highly anticipated vote was set to take place, the editorial in *The Concord Journal* summed up the collaborative work of the previous two years and ended by calling for citizens to respond generously to the appeal letter:

A town-wide mailing will be sent out this week in the hope that, in the remaining days before Town Meeting, enough citizen donors will come through to close the gap. Selectmen have said they do not support asking the town for one dollar more than the $160,000 they had planned, so it is essential that that goal be reached before a vote is taken.

Any contributions that go beyond the goal will be put toward restoring the birth house, the next step in this important initiative. ...

Please open the mailing when you receive it and consider making a donation, however small, to lend your hand to the citizen efforts that have taken this grassroots initiative to the point of near victory. And please plan to attend Town Meeting and vote "Yes" on Article 35.

In the end, more than 269 contributions, ranging from $5 to $5,000, were received from local individuals and families. A group of young environmentalists, who called themselves the Green Beans, proudly offered a donation of $27.05—all the profits from their lemonade stand.

A week later, the Thoreau Country Conservation Alliance (TCCA) published a full-page exhortation, largely consisting of brief testimonials, in *The Concord Journal*, similar to the one it had co-authored before the previous year's Town Meeting. Quoting Thoreau's words about being born "into the most estimable place in all the world, and in the nick of time, too," the brief text read: "The time to save Thoreau's birthplace from development is fast running out. The time for Concordians to act is now. The nick of time is all that's left."

Many of the printed testimonials were submitted by members of a Thoreau Birthplace Advisory Board that the TCCA had set in place earlier that month to help the tiny group advance a giant of a cause. The six-member TCCA (J. Walter Brain, Vidar Jorgensen, Michael Kellett, Joe Valentine, Jeffrey White, and Executive Director Helen Bowdoin) had been shouldering a great deal of the work on behalf of the birthplace and decided to call on the advice and support of a larger group of advocates to buttress their own efforts. I agreed to join the new Advisory Board that spring and contribute advice on media relations. The twenty-five other advisors came from a wide range of backgrounds, and I list them here to offer an idea of the number of people from all walks of life who had been rallied to the cause over the previous year: Kathi Anderson (Walden Woods Project); John Andrews (Sierra Club); Court Booth (Concord-Carlisle Adult and Community Education); Peggy Brace (Thoreau Society); David Brower (Earth Island Institute); Lawrence Buell (Harvard University); John Clarke (Massachusetts Audubon); Theresa Cohen (environmental engineer); Barbara Forman (The Concord Program); Richard Forman (Harvard University); Ronald Hoag (Thoreau Society); Michael Kellett (RESTORE: the North Woods); Anne LaBastille (author); Bill McKibben (author/environmentalist); John Hanson Mitchell (author); Theodore Osgood (Concord Historical Commission); Grace Perez (Concord Natural Resources Commission); Wayne Rasmussen (historian); Pamela Resor (state representative); Ian Thompson (businessman); Frederick Turner (author); Judy Walpole (Board of Selectmen); Joe Wheeler (consultant in sustainable development); Beth Witherell (Thoreau Society); and Claudia Sauermann Wu (National Trust for Historic Preservation).

The testimonial page also included comments from Superintendent Nancy Nelson of the National Park Service, Thoreau biographer Robert Richardson, and Congressman Marty Meehan. It stands as one of the strongest public displays of support that had yet been advanced by any group, and I'm convinced it had a positive effect on the outcome.

That same week, Town Manager Christopher Whelan wrote a thank-you letter to another anonymous donor, a local resident who had just contributed $75,000, the gift that at last put the town over its $960,000 fundraising goal. "Just a few weeks ago, it seemed the goal was insurmountable," Whelan acknowledged. "However, ... pledges have been arriving these past few weeks from a wide variety of corporate, individual, and foundation donors, and the excitement is mounting."

Thoreau birthplace deserves your vote

In late December 1995 The Journal ran a front-page story about the Thoreau birth house on Virginia Road. Its owners, the Breens, had put it on the market after the death of the family patriarch, and a small group of concerned citizens, headed by Doris Smith, was making a quiet but determined effort to safe the property, which included 18.4 acres of historic farmland.

So much development had already occurred on Virginia Road, and now here was the house where Thoreau was born — moved from down the street but still sitting on the same original farm — likely to yield to yet another clump of cluster homes.

Gradually, with some important research help from Thoreau scholar Tom Blanding, these citizens began to get the attention of other citizens.

In a particularly discouraging moment, when it looked like a sale might be imminent, one enlightened developer stepped forward to offer to restore the house and design a compromise development plan. But even he stressed that his first preference would be to save the entire property, and he later withdrew his proposal.

Through the efforts of a citizen-run auction, which was as important for the attention it drew as for the funds it raised, and the persistent, behind-the-scenes work of the Thoreau Country Conservation Alliance, support for saving the property grew.

No one really knew just how much support had grown — certainly not town officials — until an exhilarating moment at the 1996 Town Meeting, when people voted overwhelmingly to ask the town to take a leadership role in helping preserve the house and land.

From then on, with the leadership of Selectman Sally Schnitzer, the energy and know-how of Town Manager Chris Whelan and Director of Planning and Land Management Al Lima, and the continued support of a corps group of concerned citizens and other town officials, a state grant was secured, a purchase price of just under $1 million was negotiated and donations were gathered from private sources.

The Education Collaborative stepped forward with one of the missing pieces: How would the property be used? They hope to build a small center from which to do their work of promoting the teaching of Thoreau to school children, and they made a substantial donation in the bargain.

Now another Town Meeting is here, and citizens will have the chance to close the loop they opened in 1996. Article 35, which will likely be taken up Wednesday, April

Excerpt from *Concord Journal* in advance of the 1997 Town Meeting vote.

XII

CONCORD COMMITS

What a country chooses to save
is what a country chooses to say about itself.

—Molly Beattie, U.S. Fish and Wildlife Service

At last, on Wednesday, April 30, the day arrived when the fate of the Thoreau birthplace would be determined. It was the third night of the 1997 Town Meeting, which would conclude the following evening, and attendees overflowed from the high school auditorium into the adjoining cafeteria, where the proceedings were broadcast on a closed-circuit TV.

The Board of Selectmen, Finance Committee, Planning Board, Natural Resources Commission, Concord Land Conservation Trust, and Concord-Carlisle League of Women Voters all formally recommended passage of the acquisition article (see Appendix A for the full text of historic Article 35), and several residents rose in support as well. Saying that "Concord can't afford not to purchase this land," resident Reinier Beeuwkes demonstrated through a series of slides the fiscal impact on the town of a new housing development on the site, which would cost far more in local services, including school services, than the town would spend to purchase the property. It was an argument that had not yet been made, and it clearly caught people's attention.

Making the case for the Board of Selectmen was Sally Schnitzer, an advocate for the property's preservation from the beginning and a member of the Ad Hoc Committee to Save Thoreau's Birthplace, which had spearheaded the town's fundraising efforts. Schnitzer recalled the previous year's Town Meeting vote, which directed selectmen to "work with interested parties to explore all options and take appropriate action toward securing the permanent protection of the birthplace of Henry David Thoreau." She noted that despite the enthusiasm generated by that article, it was clear to both town officials and concerned citizens that the town could not afford to purchase the property on its own. In outlining the array of funders that had joined the town's effort, she reported that in the end, only 17 percent of the

$960,000 purchase price would need to come from town coffers.

As she outlined the detailed plans for the property, including leasing portions of it to be used as a farm and an education center, Schnitzer said the town would likely lease the birth house and an area of surrounding land to a "qualified nonprofit" interested in becoming its steward. Before closing and moving Article 35, she gave voters three assurances: the town would not use the property in a way that would prove disruptive to residents; any donations that exceeded the purchase price and closing costs would be used to stabilize the birth house; and, no additional tax dollars would be spent to fund restoration of the house. To that last point, she added, "Concerned citizens and organizations have already begun to step forward to work on this task."

It was evident from the start of the discussion that momentum was moving toward approval and those in attendance were ready to commit. That week's *Concord Journal* had already gone to print, so the paper's reporting on the results of the vote would have to wait until the following week's May 8 edition. That issue's front page highlighted the success story, written by reporter Bryan Davis. It began: "A victorious orange wave capped a year of fundraising and support building last Wednesday night as Town Meeting voters thrust their colored ballots into the air, overwhelmingly supporting the purchase of the Thoreau birth house and surrounding farmland on Virginia Road." Only two "no" votes were cast, a result that brought tears to the eyes of many that night, including mine. "We thought that maybe Thoreau would have liked the two dissenting votes," Helen Bowdoin told *The Boston Globe*.

Those who had worked so hard to make the moment possible were both thrilled and a little stunned by the huge outpouring of support. "The success of the funding effort really blew me away this week," said Schnitzer after the meeting. "Just two or three weeks ago, we were asking ourselves what we would do if we fell short. Now, here we are, and it feels great!"

Donations from individuals and families responding to the town-wide appeal continued to come in throughout the month of May. In the end, defying all early predictions, the town received approximately $87,000 beyond the purchase price.

The major donors lined up as follows:

Town of Concord: $160,000

State Self-Help grant: $160,000

EDCO: $160,000

Massport: $200,000

Anonymous foundation: $180,000

Welch's Foods, Inc.: $20,000

The Sudbury Foundation: $10,000

Concord Land Conservation Trust: $10,000

Historic Concord, Inc.: $10,000

Anonymous donation from an individual: $75,000

Smaller donors included the Colonial Inn, Cambridge Trust Co., Federal Savings Bank, Concord Historical Collaborative, the Thoreau Tennis Club, Middlesex Bank, the Thoroughly Thoreau Auction, and the Cheese Shop of Concord, all groups with local roots.

As Schnitzer noted during her Town Meeting presentation, the range of donations—both in size and source—demonstrated the breadth and variety of community support that had built up over the preceding year. It was a testament as well to all the public officials and private citizens who had worked together, sometimes in unlikely allegiance, to transform a longshot into a sure thing.

Though Doris Smith says today that she was only "a small cog in the events that took place" to save the property, it was around her table that a precarious, low-tech preservation effort gained the necessary strength and momentum to become a *cause célèbre* in town and beyond. A journal she kept of those early days is astonishing in its detailed depiction of the time, patience, resourcefulness, and energy it takes to launch a citizen initiative. The journal contains comprehensive notes from the regular meetings she hosted with engaged activists and invited guests and cites scores of contacts, all of whom she called for advice or help even though most of the leads led to dead ends. It must have been a tedious process, day after day, and Smith was not always applauded for her efforts, especially after she supported developer Peter Conant's compromise plan for the property. As time went on, other entities took over the lead and, never one to claim the limelight, Smith was more than willing to pass the torch. But there was no doubt that her hard work, outreach, and persistence in the early stages helped make it possible for others to succeed later on. Smith will always be remembered as a pioneer in the saving of the birthplace, and she remains an inspiring example of what can be accomplished when a concerned citizen works to make change happen, one person at a time.

"I was the last person anyone would think of to start a historic preservation effort," Smith wrote on the last page of her journal. "Well, it has been an experience."

The Thoreau birth house at the time of its 1997 purchase by the Town of Concord.

XIII

"WE'RE TAKING A LITTLE BIT
OF A BREATHER"

What do we do now, now that we are happy?

—Samuel Beckett

In the lead-up to the 1997 Town Meeting, the spotlight remained squarely on raising the money to purchase the Thoreau birthplace property. No one was ready to discuss publicly how the rehabilitation of the historic house might be handled except to assure Concord taxpayers that no additional town funds would be used for its restoration. Shortly before the Town Meeting, when asked by *The Concord Journal* how the house would be restored, Helen Bowdoin replied, "Right now, that is a problem I would love to have."

Well, Concordians awoke on May 1 to that very problem. Soon, when the town closed on the purchase of the Breen property on May 23, the birth house and land would become theirs. Almost exactly two years after James Breen Jr.'s death, the house had been uninhabited for so long that it was in serious need of help. Since town officials had never wavered in their refusal to take on the restoration task, it would be up to private organizations to raise the money and get the job done.

In an April 10 letter to the Board of Selectmen, members of the Ad Hoc Committee to save Thoreau's Birthplace had written, "It is recognized by those who have worked for the acquisition of this property that the Town of Concord is not expected to absorb the costs of stabilizing, restoring, and administering the homestead itself. Rather, the [acquisition] will give an opportunity for private parties to propose restoration and preservation plans for the birthplace home." Any plans for the house, according to the committee's letter, would have to limit activity to "an appropriate level" for the neighborhood; be compatible with the planned agricultural use of the land and the activity at the educational center; and comply with the deed restriction against new housing negotiated with Massport.

At the end of the letter, the committee offered a qualification that never made it into the public presentation at Town Meeting or the newspaper articles at the time. If efforts to restore the birthplace did not prove successful "within a reasonable amount of time," the town might be forced to "remove the house." It is not clear from the letter how much time would be considered "reasonable" and what it would mean to "remove" the house from the preserved open land. But it *was* clear that even these ardent supporters of saving both the house and the land felt the need to address the concern that the deteriorating structure would become a permanent burden to the town. The vague reference to "a reasonable amount of time" meant that once the town acquired the property, the clock would start ticking once again.

Behind the scenes leading up to the acquisition of the property, the ad hoc committee had quietly been studying potential options for the future of the birth house. At a committee meeting held on March 21, former Selectman Judy Walpole had presented eight possible scenarios, including pros and cons for each.

In the first, the town would sell the house for $1 to a developer, who would restore it and resell it to a private family to cover restoration costs. This option would remove the need to raise additional funds for restoration and have no undue impact on the neighborhood. But it would prevent the public from visiting the historic site and perhaps conflict with the planned farm and educational center.

In a second imagined scenario, the house would be restored and leased as affordable housing, which has always been in short supply in Concord. This option would add no new traffic on the neighborhood road, but would have the same negative effects as the first option and require the town to raise funds to restore the house.

Scenario three entailed leasing the house in exchange for the "sweat equity" needed to restore it. This strategy had been used in the 1970s to restore the so-called Harrington House in town, which drew a number of local volunteers to the task. Besides presenting the "cons" associated with the first two options—no public access and the need to raise more funds—this option raised the question of whether a tenant could be found to take on the difficult work of restoration.

A fourth possibility would be to restore the outside of the house and only the birth room on the inside. The rest of the house would be used as storage space for EDCO and the birth room opened to the public on weekends, perhaps on a seasonal basis. This option had the advantage of allowing public access to Thoreau's birthplace, with minimal traffic expected to disrupt the neighborhood. Though additional funding would be required, it would involve much less of an expenditure than a full restoration. But who would manage the visitor activity? How would the town comply with the Americans with Disabilities Act, since the birth room was on the second floor? And would EDCO need office and storage space in addition to what it would have in its own building? "Probably not," wrote the committee.

Scenario five was the one that most people had put forth when the subject was raised at all in public. A nonprofit organization would be found to restore and then manage the house for modest public access. In this case, the town would either lease or sell the house to the nonprofit entity, which would raise the restoration funds through grants and private donations. If this were to happen, the town would not have to take responsibility for either the fundraising or the management of the house. But concerns were cited about a possible conflict with EDCO's use, and the need for additional parking for visitors, guides, and possible management staff. The committee also wondered if charging for visits would cover operational costs moving forward.

The sixth option appeared to be the least likely, but it seemed worth including. What if the town could convince the state, which managed Walden Pond, or the federal government, which managed the Minute Man National Historical Park, to restore and manage the house for public visitation? This option would allow public access to the historic birthplace at no cost to the town. It would, however, change the character of the neighborhood and remove the property from town control. In fact, conversations had been held with the superintendents at both the pond and the park, and both had said it would be difficult to secure funds for management of a new property at that time. Still, both the town and the committee did not want to give up on this option entirely until all efforts had been exhausted.

Option number seven was perhaps the most creative—and complicated—and would remain on the table for serious consideration moving forward. The town would seek grants to restore the exterior of the house and the birth room and lease the rest of the interior space to artists, craftspeople, a nonprofit group whose mission was compatible with the spirit of the property, or a Thoreau scholar in residence. The birth room would be open on weekends, perhaps from April through Thanksgiving. Again, someone would have to manage the visitor activity to the birth room. And could the town find grants to make the interior usable and possibly habitable? Would rental fees sustain the cost of maintaining and operating it?

In the eighth and final scenario, the committee envisioned a future for the house that would essentially place it in an induced coma. The town would retain ownership but would only work to stabilize the structure to keep it standing and then maintain it in a "mothball" condition, with no public access and no activity whatsoever. Though uninspiring, this solution would likely have to be implemented for the short term, since no immediate plans for stewarding the house had been put in place. Once it became clear that funds had been raised beyond what was needed for the purchase of the property, the town could afford to make a few improvements, perhaps enough to enhance the curb appeal of the house, which was an eyesore at the time. The committee acknowledged that this scenario would need an "eventual resolution," since the town would not have the means to continually maintain the building over a long period of time, and some degree of public access to Thoreau's birth house was necessary if the town hoped to honor the wishes of many who had contributed to its purchase.

Town Planning Director Al Lima had estimated it would cost about $200,000 to protect the house from further deterioration and perhaps as much as $800,000 for a full restoration. In the meantime, the town began immediately after Town Meeting to work on quick fixes. The Department of Public Works began mowing the lawn to improve its appearance from the road and contracted with a local handyman to repair leaking windows and patch up the foundation. A crew also sprayed the poison ivy around the house, which was rampant and would require continued vigilance as people began working on the property.

Meanwhile, when asked by *The Boston Globe* what next steps were planned by the Ad Hoc Committee to Save Thoreau's Birthplace, Helen Bowdoin said in a May 18 article, "We're taking a little bit of a breather. But not much. We're looking at a second major round of fundraising to restore the house. First, it needs to be stabilized so it doesn't just fall down."

XIV

"THIS PROJECT HAS BEEN ABOUT PARTNERING"

I sometimes awake in the night
and think of friendship and its possibilities.

—H.D. Thoreau, Journal

A few weeks after the Town Meeting vote, on May 19, 1997, the Town of Concord held a large reception in the Town House on Monument Square to recognize all those involved in the successful, two-year effort to save the Thoreau birthplace. Being there was not only a privilege, it was a visual reminder of the number of people who had made it all happen.

A hallmark of the effort to save the birthplace was the public-private collaboration that had proved both fruitful and inspiring. Small-town politics can often distance those officially in charge from those who vote to put them there. Concord remains a beautiful place, often cited as a quintessential New England town, in large part because of its five regulated historic districts and the strict oversight of its permitting boards. The price of this beauty has frequently thrown Concord into discord. The experience of working together to save the birthplace allowed public officials and private citizens to get to know each other in the best way possible—by sharing both the goal and the work.

The words expressed by a visibly moved Sally Schnitzer, who hosted the celebration on behalf of the Board of Selectmen, are reproduced, verbatim, in Appendix B. Her remarks deserve to be retold as she said them, not only because they cannot be improved upon, but because they reflect an intimate knowledge of the breadth of support that had been mustered—support that had seemed unimaginable two years earlier. "This project has been about partnering," she said, as she began her generous recognition of the people and organizations that had contributed to the effort. But her litany of thanks omitted one important name: her own. Gracefully closing the gap between "official" Concord and its private citizens, Schnitzer had brought the best of both worlds to the work. To me, she has always embodied the successful partnership being celebrated that day.

Once Concord closed on the birthplace property on May 23, 1997, townspeople set about claiming the place as their own. Town officials had received scores of support letters during the year leading up to the vote, and it was time for pride. It was also time for much-needed TLC, which many residents and staff members would provide as the house continued to lie dormant.

On June 5, a group of volunteers from a local environmental group called the Concord Greenpeople gathered at the house for a work party. Under the direction of Natural Resources staff, they removed broken trees and shrubs damaged by winter storms, dug up invasive plantings, pruned the sprawling red oak at the front of the house, and cleared the path to the door. As an added touch, they installed two bluebird houses, which were immediately visited by two pairs of tree swallows in a buoyant moment of serendipity.

The Ad Hoc Committee to Save Thoreau's Birthplace met on June 13 to discuss the future use of the property and the pressing question of restoring the house. As yet, no single organization had come forward to take responsibility for the house and no *deus ex machina* appeared poised to descend from the clouds and assure its restoration. Since the goal of the committee—to save the property from development—had been met, members felt a new group should be formed to help the town find a best way forward. Selectmen said they wanted the new group to work in the same manner as the ad hoc group had done, by welcoming members from municipal agencies, nonprofit organizations, and the private citizenry.

With that directive in mind, the committee chose to reorganize as the Thoreau Birthplace Task Force. They didn't know it at the time, but this group would end up shepherding the birthplace property through the next ten years. Several members of the original ad hoc committee stayed on to anchor the new task force. One of these, Community Education Director Court Booth, recalls a number of committee members vowing to each other that if the purchase of the property were approved by Town Meeting, they would stay active in the future planning, and they made good on that vow. Along with Booth, Selectman Sally Schnitzer continued to be a key member of the new group, as did former Selectman Judy Walpole, Planning

Director Al Lima, Natural Resources Director Dan Monahan, and Town Manager Christopher Whelan. Michael Kellett and Helen Bowdoin remained on board representing the Thoreau Country Conservation Alliance, as did Joe Valentine from the Historical Commission, Christine Rinaldo of Historic Concord, and Jack Green from EDCO. Joining the new task force were Désirée Caldwell, director of the Concord Museum, and Joseph Wheeler, a town resident.

Wheeler had joined the earlier committee partway through its work. He had an avid—and very personal—interest in preserving the Breen property, having been born at 215 Virginia Road in the house that had been built on the original site of Thoreau's birthplace. Wheeler's mother, Ruth, a journalist and local historian, wrote a well-received book, *Concord: Climate for Freedom*, which continues to be a valuable resource for scholars and historians and lends the Wheeler home a special significance of its own. After a distinguished career as a manager of overseas economic development programs, primarily with USAID (Agency for International Development), Wheeler and his wife, Verona, had retired to Concord and become active members in community life. Joe had been involved in many town initiatives, but saving and preserving the birthplace would become the one closest to his heart.

Joe Wheeler

Missing from the new group was Doris Smith, who had begun to move out of the frame as other players had moved in. That summer, she dissolved the nonprofit she had co-founded, the Save the Thoreau Birthplace Foundation. Once the property had been saved, Smith did not feel compelled to continue her fundraising efforts, though she and her husband, George, remained generous supporters of the cause from behind the scenes.

The ad hoc group that met on June 13 listed a number of tasks that needed to be done over the next several months. These included having a survey done of the property, tending to the overgrown landscape, establishing a process and timetable for putting the farmland back into active agricultural use, and working with EDCO on plans for the educational center. Subsequent meetings throughout that summer highlighted the daunting responsibility the town had assumed by purchasing the property, with its deteriorating historic house and large swath of arable land, and by making a bargain with an educational entity eager to collect on the promise of a building site.

As a first step in its stewardship of the property, the town contracted with Ganteaume & McMullen, a Boston architectural and engineering firm, which conducted a preliminary structural investigation of the house on July 11. Though the engineers didn't find anything they would characterize as dangerous, they noted several areas of serious deterioration. Not surprisingly, the firm recommended that the town arrange for a more comprehensive investigation "to insure the structural integrity" of the house. But even their one-day visit convinced them that the house needed a new foundation that could be kept dry for future upkeep of the building. A survey of the entire property that summer also revealed that it was slightly larger than originally thought: 20.3 acres, rather than the 18.4 that had been cited in earlier documents.

To give structure and direction to its work, the new task force needed an overall vision for the property, and its members would have to divide up responsibilities if they hoped to make that vision a reality. Their regular meetings through November of that year, supplemented by many hours of outside work, culminated in a detailed proposal to the Board of Selectmen, which the task force presented on Dec. 1.

The proposal comprised a vision statement, an outline of urgent and long-term issues that would need attention, and six recommendations. The vision statement contained no surprises, since it was compatible with all that had been said before about the property. It should be devoted to educational programming related to Thoreau and his contemporaries and used for agriculture appropriate for the setting. Its historic house should be restored and interpreted for the public. An education center "in a simple style" compatible with the restored house and the surrounding landscape should be built, and a portion of the land kept as open space and conserved accordingly. This early vision imagined that the house might be restored to its appearance in 1817, the year of Thoreau's birth, and some of its interior spaces restored to that same period. The heating, plumbing, and insulation would be updated for current use, so the house could support educational programming and be opened to the public on a limited basis.

The proposal noted that plans for the educational center were already in progress and that construction was expected to begin within the following six to eight months. As a result, "it is now time to focus energies on the house."

Among the things that needed immediate attention, according to the task force, was a detailed plan for the stabilization and security of the house. At a minimum, the group felt that the foundation needed further work beyond the little that had already been done, the house must be made weather tight, and the façade could use cosmetic work to make it more "presentable."

In the longer term, the task force urged the town to decide a use for the house that would remain faithful to the spirit of the farm landscape and be guided by what was "uniquely possible there." In a significant admonition, they advised selectmen against duplicating or trying to supplant "resources or services available at other venues in the area." This last was an important point. The task force was hoping to help the town discover a niche for this property that had not already been filled. It would be important to respect the work of other historic entities in a town that boasted many. These organizations had supported the acquisition of the property, and the task force was determined to retain them as partners, not turn them into rivals. Another reason for including this piece of advice was to advance the cause of the planned education center. There was nothing like it in Concord at the time, and the task force believed the property offered a unique chance to provide something both necessary and meaningful.

At that point, approximately $63,000 of the donations received for the property acquisition remained in the Thoreau Birthplace account held by the town. The task force recommended that selectmen use these funds to take several steps:

1) Recognize through appropriate plaques or signs the generosity of donors.

2) Fund a professional study of what it would take to stabilize and weatherproof the house, restore it to its 1817 appearance, and modernize its utilities.

3) Encourage the Natural Resources Commission to sign an agricultural lease for the farmland within the next six months, in time for the 1998 summer growing season.

4) Send out a Request for Proposals inviting concerned groups and individuals to form an organization devoted to the restoration and operation of the Thoreau House.

5) Continue to take steps to stabilize the house until a professional assessment could be completed.

6) Encourage the Concord Historical Commission to complete the necessary work for placing the house on the National Register of Historic Places.

The Board of Selectmen unanimously accepted the vision and the recommendations that night, and the decision effectively changed the course of events as the new year approached. In the past, efforts had focused on finding an established nonprofit to take over responsibility for the house. By accepting the task force's recommendations—notably, number four—town officials were signaling their willingness to consider a newly formed group, at least partly composed of private individuals, to shepherd the house toward its as-yet undetermined future.

And in that gleam of an eye, the Thoreau Farm Trust was conceived.

XV

THOREAU FARM IS BORN

If one hesitates in his path, let him not proceed.
Let him respect his doubts, for doubts, too, may have some divinity in them.

—H.D. Thoreau, letter to H.G.O. Blake

When the Thoreau Birthplace Task Force made its recommendations to Concord's Board of Selectmen, its members had already laid the groundwork for a new, citizen-based organization that would guide the historic house through its early days—perhaps years—as a town property. Town officials had made it clear that municipal involvement would be minimal, and no established organization or agency had come forward. So, shortly after selectmen approved the committee's recommendations on Dec. 1, the group moved ahead with plans to establish a nonprofit group composed of local citizens willing to take on the difficult challenge of raising funds to restore the house and then manage the restoration process.

Leading that effort were Michael Kellett, Helen Bowdoin, and Joe Valentine, three of the people who had played major roles in helping save the birthplace property. On Jan. 9, 1998, Kellett sent a letter inviting several other advocates to a meeting at Helen Bowdoin's house on Jan. 21. "With the encouragement of the Thoreau Birthplace Task Force," wrote Kellett, "I am convening a meeting of people who might be interested in the creation of a new nonprofit organization, called the Thoreau Farm Trust."

It was an interesting choice of name. Though the new citizens' group was meant to focus its work on the restoration and re-use of the birth house, its founders sought to honor the entire landscape on which the house stood and its significance as part of the history of agriculture in Concord. It was important to know and appreciate the Henry who first saw light on a simple farm that his mother had called home for fourteen years and that she and her husband had struggled to manage.

The property did indeed have a lot to say about the history of farming. Thoreau's birth in 1817 coincided with a shift in farming practices within Concord and throughout New England. Large commercial enterprises began to supplant subsistence farms and those producing food for local markets, exploiting the burgeoning rail system to transport their goods farther afield. Thoreau is often mischaracterized as having little respect for farming and farmers. But though he hated the idea of being mindlessly yoked to work of any sort, especially work done primarily for profit, he admired farmers who labored for love of the land. He enjoyed talking regularly to George Minot (spelled "Minott" by Thoreau, using an accepted alternative spelling of the time), whose farm was located close to Ralph Waldo Emerson's house and who was a descendant of the Minot family that owned the house where Thoreau was born. He wrote often of this friend in journals, including this entry from Oct. 4, 1851:

> Minott is perhaps the most poetical farmer—who most realizes to me the poetry of the farmer's life—that I know. He does nothing with haste or drudgery, but as if he loved it. He makes the most of his labor, and takes infinite satisfaction in every part of it. He is not looking forward to the sale of his crops or any pecuniary profit, but he is paid by the constant satisfaction which his labor yields him. ... He cares not so much to raise a large crop as to do his work well.

So, the name Thoreau Farm felt just right. It reflected Thoreau's origins more faithfully than a mere "birthplace" moniker and would reflect the new organization's mission of bringing Henry out of the woods and back into the heart of his hometown.

Two Concord officials attended the Thoreau Farm Trust launch session, Selectman Sally Schnitzer, chair of the task force, and Planning Director Al Lima. Also in attendance were Court Booth, Jack Green from EDCO, Joe Wheeler from the task force, and Theresa Cohen, an environmental engineer who had been a public supporter of saving the property. During the next month, members of this core group met twice, on Feb. 3 and 24, to review drafts of goals and bylaws prepared by Kellett, Valentine, and Wheeler, who had been asked to serve as interim chair. They also drew up a list of people they would solicit to become charter board members of the newly formed Thoreau Farm Trust.

By the end of March, the bylaws had been approved and board members elected. The purpose of the organization, as stated in its bylaws, was to support the restoration, maintenance, and use of the Thoreau birth house under the "policy direction" of Concord's Board of Selectmen. Since the Town of Concord intended to issue a Request for Proposals for the future stewardship of the house, as recommended by the task force, the Trust could not categorically state that it would fulfill its goals. But "pursuant to agreements which may be entered into with the Town of Concord," the Trust planned to prepare stabilization, restoration, and preservation plans for the house; raise funds for that purpose; manage the restoration; maintain the restored house, which would be used to advance education about Thoreau, nature, farming, and conservation; and recommend and implement integrated management plans for the entire property.

I was one of those invited to become a charter member of the group based on my support as editor of *The Concord Journal.* My presence on the Advisory Board of the Thoreau Country Conservation Alliance had allowed me to get to know many of the others intent on saving the birthplace in the best way possible: by working together. I grew to admire the passion and dedication of the early adopters and loved being part of a cause I believed in. So in March 1998, I agreed to sign on as one of the fifteen founding members of the Thoreau Farm Trust Board of Directors and became its first clerk/secretary. The other fourteen charter members were Joe Wheeler (president); EDCO's Jack Green (vice president); Court Booth (treasurer); Helen Bowdoin; James Callahan of Welch's Foods; Désirée Caldwell from the Concord Museum; Theresa Cohen, Brian Donahue; professor of Environmental Studies at Brandeis University; educator Jayne Gordon from the Concord Museum; Michael Kellett; preservation professional Barbara Lambert; Planning Director Al Lima; Christine Rinaldo of Historic Concord,;Inc., and Joe Valentine from the Concord Historical Commission.

We all signed on with the understanding that the Trust might not be chosen by the town to complete the goals it had set forth. The Request for Proposals, yet to be drawn up, might be answered by other, more experienced organizations better equipped to raise funds and guide the work. "If The Trustees of Reservations or the Society for the Preservation of New England Antiquities came forward and offered to take on responsibility for preservation, restoration, and use of the house, it might well be in the Town's interest to accept their offer over one from a new and untried organization like the Trust," wrote Joe Wheeler in a note to board members. "If this happened, we might want to turn ourselves into a support group for their effort. ... Admitting the possibility of such a scenario is another way of reminding everybody that the Trust has no inside track and ought not to have one. ... If it turns out that we are the only ones in the field, we all know we will be taking on a very serious job."

The recent example of what had occurred with the Walden Woods preservation effort, when the local citizens' group had been superseded by a more polished operation, stood as both a caveat and a challenge. The founders of the Trust knew we would have to work hard—and show results—to earn the confidence of town officials. But we also knew that the effort to save the birthplace had turned into a source of local pride. A citizen-driven effort to restore Thoreau's house seemed a fitting continuation of what had become a community cause. Perhaps a more established organization might eventually take over permanent stewardship of the house, but in the spring of 1998, the Thoreau Farm Trust was peopled by known individuals who were on the spot and ready to tackle the goals they had helped to shape. Michael Kellett and Joe Wheeler assured town officials they would visit the house regularly to check on its welfare. The Trust may not have claimed an inside track, but it did immediately assume a proprietary attitude toward the house, which it was intent on protecting.

The most challenging task facing the Thoreau Farm Trust at the time was the prospect of raising the money necessary to restore the house, estimated at $800,000. Common wisdom held that donors are more willing to give to programming than to buildings, so EDCO's partnership was considered essential to the Trust's future success. For that reason, the Trust treated EDCO as a partner in its work from the outset. By taking on the role of board vice president, after serving on both the ad hoc committee for the acquisition and the task force following the purchase, EDCO's executive director, Jack Green, continued to be a key player in all that was happening in regard to the property.

XVI

FROM HARE TO TORTOISE

Adopt the pace of nature: her secret is patience.

—Ralph Waldo Emerson

Unlike the effort to purchase Thoreau's birthplace, which was propelled by the urgency of deadlines and the fear of imminent destruction, the next steps in the story progressed with the slow deliberation more common to the life of a municipal government. It is tempting to say they slowed to the serene pace of a Thoreauvian saunter, but that would be exaggerating their speed. The excitement of the chase had been replaced by the less exhilarating work of tending to the prize.

Since Concord now owned the entire birthplace property, decisions about its future had to take their place among the many other issues on the busy town's docket. Complicating the process was the three-pronged shape of the vision that the Thoreau Birthplace Task Force had advanced and the town had endorsed. Instead of focusing on one entity, as it had done when working to acquire the property, the town now had to arrange for the management of three separate components: the farmland, the house, and the education center. Each demanded careful attention to detail and required approvals and permits from a number of boards and committees. In addition, there were now two groups serving in an advisory capacity on all proposals, decisions, and actions: the task force and the Thoreau Farm Trust. At times, all three of the property's initiatives remained in a state of suspended animation while the people closest to those efforts took deep breaths—and waited for their cue to start moving again.

Before they turned the historic house over to another entity, town officials needed more information on its current state and historical features. That would be a first step in determining the extent and cost of restoration. The second step would be the development of a more concrete plan for how the house would be used. With the help of the task force, Town Planner Marcia Rasmussen crafted a Request for Proposals (RFP 65), which she sent out in

November 1997. The RFP invited architectural firms specializing in historic preservation to apply for a contract to conduct an in-depth structural study and evaluation of the birth house.

The study outlined in the RFP was meant to be comprehensive, and the scope of work was broad, comprising ten tasks: 1) to research and prepare an analysis of the historical and architectural significance of the structure; 2) to analyze the structural integrity of the building; 3) to identify and prioritize steps to stabilize the house and prevent further deterioration until it was ready for future use; 4) to analyze the issues involved in moving the house, either temporarily or permanently; 5) to assist the town in deciding to which period the building should be restored and to what level of detail; 6) to assist the town in complying with all applicable codes and requirements while preserving the historical and architectural integrity of the structure; 7) to develop a plan for implementing the restoration in three stages: stabilization; limited first phase; and final completion; 8) to draft a site plan for the landscape around the house; 9) to develop cost estimates for all phases of the work; and, 10) to develop an action plan for the sequencing of tasks, ending with completion. It was a tall order.

By the Dec. 15, 1997 deadline, the town had received nine responses. A selection committee chose five firms to invite for interviews on Jan. 20 and, a week later, made its choice: the New Hampshire-based Preservation Partnership, a small, well-respected firm headed by architect Maximilian Ferro.

Ferro and his partners undertook their study at about the same time the Thoreau Farm Trust was establishing itself. Several of the Trust's board members were historians, by profession or avocation, and would keep a close eye on Ferro's work and subsequent findings.

XVII

GAINING GROUND SIGNS ON
TO FARM THE LAND

*[Thoreau] especially loved to raise melons. I once went to a melon-party
at his mother's ... and he, the gardener, came in to help entertain the guests.*

—E. Emerson, *Henry Thoreau as Remembered by a Young Friend*

By all measures, the easiest piece of the Thoreau birthplace puzzle to set in place was the agricultural component. Concord boasts a long history of agricultural use of the land and, though most of the Colonial-era farmland has been reforested, and development has largely transformed the 26-square-mile town into a mown suburban landscape, there remain today several prominent farm families who continue to cultivate their land and sell their produce and plants at local farm stands. Virginia Road, once a thriving farm neighborhood, had yielded its acreage to homebuyers. But the Breens had maintained a 300-year tradition by farming their twenty acres from the time James Sr. purchased the property in 1909 until James Jr.'s death in 1995. Since that time, though most of the fields had lain fallow, the prolific rhubarb kept sprouting up to remind visitors that the land was still alive and waiting to be sown.

As town officials and task force members gauged interest among local farmers, they hoped to avoid leasing the land to people who would use it as nothing more than a peripheral field devoted to pumpkins or other crops they could not fit on their primary land. When Concord resident Jamie Bemis came calling, they realized they had found the right tenant. In fact, it was a match so perfect they could never have imagined it.

In 1990 Bemis, whose husband's family had long owned the popular Hutchins Farm on Monument Street, founded a nonprofit farming entity at her family's Liberty Street home that she called Gaining Ground. The mission of the small organic farm was to grow fresh, healthful food for hunger relief. With the help of volunteers of all ages, including school groups and teens assigned court-mandated community service, Bemis donated all the produce—often on the very day it was harvested—to food pantries and shelters in the Greater Boston area.

In 1997, Bemis had gained permission from The Trustees of Reservations to cultivate a Gaining Ground garden at The Old Manse. It was a particularly apt choice, since Thoreau had planted a garden there in 1842 as a wedding present for the Manse's tenants, Nathaniel and Sophia Hawthorne. Thoreau was a welcome visitor to the Manse, and Hawthorne wrote in his journal that Henry would come by to check on the garden and admire the melons that especially thrived there.

By 1998, Bemis had begun looking for another site for Gaining Ground, one that could accommodate more crops and replace the small plot she was cultivating at her home. The availability of the Thoreau birthplace land came at just the right time for her—and for the town. She began negotiations with town officials early in the year, but there were enough details to work out, including the length of the lease and the need for water and electricity at the site, that a deal was not made until the fall of 1998, too late for that year's growing season. When all the details finally fell into place, Gaining Ground signed a three-year lease for nine acres of farmland, with the first growing season set for 1999.

From the time it had purchased the property, the town had stipulated that all activities related to its use must complement each other and co-exist comfortably. As things developed, the Thoreau Farm Trust became the meeting ground for all the entities taking part in birthplace activities. EDCO's Jack Green had been a founding board member and now Jamie Bemis would be invited to join the board as well, as a liaison with Gaining Ground. Bemis hoped Gaining Ground could use part of the birth house, once it had been restored, as office space for the farm operation, and there was also the question of shared driveway access and parking spaces. All three organizations—EDCO, Gaining Ground, and the Thoreau Farm Trust—would benefit from close collaboration. Although the Trust was the only one of the three not to have a commitment from the town nor the funds to fulfill its ultimate goals, most of its members had helped save the property from destruction, and the presence of the other two organizations on its board granted the new nonprofit a certain standing, however unofficial.

XVIII

"WE SHOULD NOT PRETEND THAT OUR JOB WILL BE EASY"

The mere vision is little compared with the steady, corresponding endeavor thitherward.

—H.D. Thoreau, Journal

For the fledgling Thoreau Farm Trust, the year 1998 was filled with promise. Most of that promise, however, was verbal. A great many people were exchanging ideas with a great many other people. They were good ideas, and those less experienced in civic activism or nonprofit management were learning from those with more. Still, at the time, the work took on the stolid gait of treadmill tedium. But in retrospect, I now see that the exercise—though accomplished mostly in place—was making us fit for the long-term effort, which was emerging as a marathon, not a sprint. Racing to the finish line was out; pacing ourselves for the long run was in.

"We should not pretend that our job will be easy," wrote chairman Joe Wheeler to Thoreau Farm Trust board members in April. "We are constituted to represent many interests and points of view, and it will be necessary to take the time to resolve these into a consensus among ourselves, with the Town, and with other interests not directly represented on the board."

That spring, meetings of the Trust were held at the Ripley Building, which housed the administrative offices of the Concord School Department, an arrangement brokered by board member Court Booth. But in May, they were moved to the home of Joe and Verona Wheeler, a decision that brought the work back to the locus of the whole enterprise—a concerned citizen's kitchen table. For the next several years, the official address of the Trust would become the Wheeler home, at 129 Westford Road in Concord.

During the rest of that spring, summer, and fall, the Trust's members worked together on several fronts: setting up nonprofit operations; helping clean up and stabilize the house; aiding in the interpretation and implementation of the study being conducted by

Max Ferro's firm; developing a fundraising strategy; and working with EDCO, Gaining Ground, the Concord School Department, and the town's Historical Collaborative on programming possibilities.

The Trust had exactly $50.06 in its new Middlesex Savings Bank account in the spring of 1998 and no executive director to guide the work, so board members carried out all the early tasks ourselves. Court Booth contacted a Concord resident who was a partner at the Boston legal firm of Hale and Dorr, which agreed to provide pro bono services to shepherd the Trust through the process of incorporation and help secure its status as a 501(c)(3) nonprofit, a necessary step that would allow us to carry out our philanthropic and fundraising objectives.

Barbara Lambert led a group of board members and their spouses on visits to the state registry of deeds in order to research the ownership history of the land and the house. Joe Valentine and I worked on the first drafts of a fundraising brochure. Brian Donahue explored possibilities for using the agricultural history of the land as part of the programming for the house. Other members were charged with reaching out to organizations that might be interested in partnering with the Trust in the restoration and operation of the house, including the Society for the Preservation of New England Antiquities (SPNEA), The Trustees of Reservations, the National Trust, and the National Park Service. Everyone had a job to do, and each of us dug in.

Along the way, the Trust benefited from the help of a number of generous volunteers. John Walker, a talented news photographer from Community Newspaper Company, which at the time published *The Concord Journal*, offered to take photographs of the house that we could use to document current conditions and illustrate our brochure and other publicity materials. Fred Stott, an experienced development professional (who also happened to be my father-in-law), graciously offered his time to help us with our fundraising strategy. Members' spouses and friends also donated hours of their time to help with everything from financial analysis to lawn mowing. We were all learning, some more literally than others, what "grassroots" activism really meant.

In one note to the board late that summer, Joe Wheeler mentioned his dismay that attendance at meetings had been low and his worry about the difficulty of "getting enough of you busy people together." Fred Stott had mentioned to him during one of his visits that what the Trust was experiencing was normal. "The good news is that you have very busy people on your board who are in high demand. The bad news is that you have very busy people on your board who are in high demand." At one point that spring, Wheeler noted, "For the last board meeting, two members used the excuse that they had just had or were about to have a baby. All right—and congratulations! But just don't try to use that excuse too often!"

Virginia Road neighbor Tim Rodgers and supporter Verona
Wheeler (wife of Joe) discussing the condition
of the birth house in 1998.

XIX

"THE HENRY DAVID THOREAU BIRTHPLACE IS A DISAPPOINTMENT"

Passion, though a bad regulator, is a powerful spring.

—Ralph Waldo Emerson

When in mid-July 1998, noted historic architect Maximilian Ferro submitted a draft report to the town following a structural study of the birth house, it managed to raise temperatures during what was already an unusually steamy summer. Aware of Ferro's deep experience and outstanding reputation, members of the task force and the Thoreau Farm Trust were eager to know what he thought about the condition of the house and the prospects for its restoration. When they came, however, his assessment and recommendations set us back on our heels. "As it now presents itself, the Henry David Thoreau Birthplace is a disappointment," he wrote. "As we shall see in this report, that need not remain so."

As everyone knew, the house had been moved in 1878 to a more easterly location on the original farm, about 300 yards along Virginia Road. When that happened, it was lifted off its foundation, and its large central chimney and rear lean-to shed were left behind. When the task force submitted its recommendations to the town, they included the hope that the restoration would bring the house back to its appearance in 1817, the year Thoreau was born in it. For that to happen, the chimney and lean-to would have to be reconstructed.

The question of what date should be used as the target restoration year was of primary importance, of course. Nothing could be done structurally to the house until that question was resolved. Ferro had a definite opinion on the subject: "As I investigated the [birthplace], it became absolutely clear to me that it should be returned to its former splendor," he wrote in his report. By this he meant that a central chimney and rear lean-to shed should be reconstructed and the exterior and interior returned to their 1817 appearance, as closely as that could be determined. Ferro wrote that he was "absolutely convinced that the house should once again look its rightful age and re-embody its lost dignity."

Ferro had expressed some of his opinions orally while his firm was conducting its investigations, and they had already begun to affect events. One of the frustrations that kept emerging at each Trust board meeting was the failure of the Concord Historical Commission to complete and submit the necessary paperwork for the house to be listed on the National Register of Historic Places. The commission had been apprised of the earlier effort to earn a listing for the house, when Doris Smith had persuaded the commission to inquire about an application. That overture had received an encouraging response from the Massachusetts Historical Commission. What had held the town back from completing the application was the long process of deliberation at the state level, which would not have been resolved in time to save the house from potential destruction. But in 1998, time was not a factor, and Trust members did not at first understand the delay in applying. The answer came in the form of a warning from Max Ferro, who had told a commission member what he would later put in his report: if the house were to be listed on the National Register of Historic Places, the town would have to abide by the state's restrictions prohibiting the full restoration of a property back to its original state by replacing lost elements. Ferro stated that the restoration should be done with private support alone, which would allow complete freedom of choice in how to proceed. Once the restoration had been done, with neither help nor interference from state or federal agencies, the house could be submitted for listing on the National Register.

Ferro pressed his case for complete restoration hard. He interpreted the earlier response from the Massachusetts Historical Commission, which acknowledged the house's associations with the 19th- and 20th-century agricultural history of Concord, as another way of saying it was "eligible as a squalid, degraded reminder of the demise of farming as a lucrative pursuit in the Town of Concord. In this context, graduate students can wax eloquent on how the stripping off of all decorative carving evokes the dust bowl mentality, or on how the upside-down old door to the cellar splendidly underlines the transition between the educated, gentlemanly builders of the house and the poor, ignorant people who became its later tenants."

Earlier in his report, Ferro had used words like "shoddy," "ghastly," and "monstrosity" to describe some of the more modern features of the house that he felt should be removed. Though some of us were taken aback by the strong language, no one could deny Ferro's passion for restoring the house to its more stately appearance during Thoreau's time—and several local advocates agreed with him completely.

"The Massachusetts Historical Commission wants us to understand that the Thoreau birthplace has no historic validity as such, but only as an example of decrepit farm architecture of the present century. Don't you believe it! To me and to thousands, perhaps millions of others, the real significance of the house is as the birthplace of one of America's greatest literary figures, and steeped in the beauty and elegance of his parents' and grandparents' time, not on the squalor of the near-present. We know what we have lost—or shall I say temporarily mislaid. Let's act to get it back." [All emphasis his.]

In fact, Ferro was not being entirely accurate about the response the town had received from the Massachusetts Historical Commission back in 1996. After acknowledging the agricultural history of the house, the commission included an entire paragraph about its significance as Thoreau's birthplace. Far from dismissing this factor, the commission explicitly stated that its association with Thoreau, however short, would definitely bolster the house's chances of being listed on the National Register. Ferro's interpretation of the commission's response underscored his determination to convince the town that a full restoration was the only path to take.

Reactions to his plan from members of the task force and Thoreau Farm Trust board were mixed. Some, including Joe Wheeler, shared Ferro's desire to see the house restored to its 1817 appearance and so were ready to accept his argument. Others believed the house should reflect the story of its entire existence, revealing the changes it had undergone and honoring its entire habitation history.

The Trust's Désirée Caldwell, director of the Concord Museum, reported at a July 29 board meeting on a conversation she and Joe Wheeler had had with Brian Pfeiffer of the Society for the Preservation of New England Antiquities. Pfeiffer told them that the public and many contemporary preservationists were now interested in both the original fabric of a historic house and its evolution over time. Pfeiffer himself favored this "holistic" approach, which seeks to maintain both the original and the new elements of a house. He said he believed it was important to show visitors the process of preservation.

Caldwell noted that the two approaches, Ferro's and Pfeiffer's, represented two ends of a spectrum. Both were acceptable practices depending on the wishes of the property owner, she said. "But if we choose, we can come out somewhere in between."

The Trust's Brian Donahue, who managed the community-based Land's Sake Farm in his Weston hometown, believed that it made sense philosophically to feature the process. He hoped, he said, that the Trust would show in its interpretation of the property how the farmhouse had evolved over time as the agricultural landscape—and farmers' lives—had changed.

Helen Bowdoin advised that the Trust "not risk locking ourselves into a rigid decision on restoration right now. If we remain flexible, we will be able to do what we feel is right with each room." She added that we must keep in mind the "large picture" of the house and property. "People who lived there deserve our respect."

By the end of that July 29 board meeting, we had reached a consensus to remain flexible. But we agreed that whatever we decided about the big picture, we would keep Thoreau "at the heart of what happens." Michael Kellett summed up the mood of the room when he said the Trust should treat Max Ferro's report as a foundation to build on. "But it is our own vision that should drive the work."

While we wrestled with a decision on the restoration's parameters, discussions of the pros and cons of a listing on the National Register of Historic Places also roiled the waters. Kellett and Valentine believed that even if Ferro's concerns were justified, as they would later prove to be, a listing on the Register was essential to our fundraising effort. "We're not going to get the money to do this if we're not recognized on the Register," said Kellett. "We need all the validity we can get." So the Trust decided to encourage the Concord Historical Commission to work on the documentation necessary to nominate the house so the paperwork would be ready to submit when the time was right.

Viewed in retrospect, Ferro's strong opinions were exactly what we needed at the time. They jostled us into thinking more deeply about the birth house's long history and set us on the path to making some of our most important decisions about its future.

XX

THE TRUST EARNS ITS INC.

The voyage of the best ship is a zigzag line of a hundred tacks.

—Ralph Waldo Emerson

As the fall of 1998 approached, the Thoreau Farm Trust had yet to submit its articles of incorporation to the Secretary of State's office. With concerns about protecting the house increasing as winter loomed, and fundraising an urgent necessity, that step suddenly became a top priority. Finally, with the generous pro bono help of Hale and Dorr, the paperwork was completed and, on Oct. 7, the Trust received its official stamp of approval as a 501(c)(3) nonprofit corporation, legally sanctioned to carry on "charitable and educational" activity in support of "the restoration, maintenance, and use" of the historic farmhouse.

It was an important turning point, because the official designation allowed the Trust to begin soliciting donations from public and private sources. Jack Green had been communicating with the editors of the *Massachusetts Catalogue for Philanthropy* in the hope that the Trust could be included in that fall's edition. With its nonprofit status now in place, our newly minted charitable organization was now eligible for inclusion in the influential publication, which offers thumbnail descriptions and contact information about more than 100 philanthropic organizations and is sent to thousands of households throughout the state. It was exciting to see the Thoreau Farm Trust among that year's chosen organizations, especially when we were told we were among the youngest nonprofits to be included. In describing the restoration of the Thoreau birthplace as a "truly once-in-history giving opportunity," the catalogue ended with an explicit plea for donations: "This is your opportunity to help create a national, and world, memorial to one of America's greatest writers and philosophers."

When the catalogue was published in early November, Joe Wheeler told *The Concord Journal*, "This is the embarkation of our fundraising boat." With an estimated $800,000 to raise for the restoration, that boat would sail the waters for quite a while.

Successful incorporation also meant the Trust would be able to respond to the town's Request for Proposals when it was released, which was expected to happen in December. This RFP would ask for proposals from nonprofits willing and able to raise the funds to restore the house, manage its restoration process, and operate it for educational and cultural purposes. The chosen organization would receive a long-term lease to the house and two acres of the land on which it stood. As a new organization, the Trust had no track record. So if we hoped to be chosen, we had to demonstrate that our members had proven expertise in fundraising, historic preservation, and education and that, collectively, we were up to the job. Originally, we were told that proposals would be due by Jan. 22 and a nonprofit chosen by the end of February. If all went as planned, a lease would be signed on April 19—Patriots Day.

Until that process was completed, the Thoreau Farm Trust found itself in an awkward position. In order to strengthen our case to the town, we needed to prove we could raise a substantial amount of money. But we couldn't raise much real money until we were recognized as the official stewards of the house. Though we would always assure donors that any funds raised by the Trust would be put toward the restoration and maintenance of the house, no matter what role the Trust continued to play over time, it would be the rare donor who would commit to a brand-new nonprofit without proof of that organization's standing. To capitalize on the tradition of end-of-year

In the year following its purchase, the house continued to deteriorate.

giving, we sent out notices to those who had helped with the birthplace effort and knew of our past work, introducing the new nonprofit and inviting interested people to sign up on our mailing list and consider making a donation. As expected, that early solicitation produced only a small response—about $2,000. But it was a start.

In late December, Max Ferro submitted his formal report, which included a list of the tasks that needed to be done to stabilize the house and in what order. It was decided that the town would use some of the remaining funds in the acquisition account to re-roof the house (as inexpensively as possible, since the roof would likely need to be replaced again during the historic restoration) and complete structural repairs to stabilize the foundation, patch holes, and fix broken windows. Once these repairs had been completed, the town would pay to have the house painted. The peeling white clapboards were looking decidedly depressed and would benefit enormously from a fresh coat of color. Joe Wheeler and Barbara Lambert were entrusted by the town to choose the color and, after consulting with Max Ferro and the Society for the Preservation of New England Antiquities, would ultimately decide on brick red.

In 1998, the Town demolished the 20th-century porch at the front entrance.

For all involved in the Trust's early days, this was a challenging period. The needs were pressing and the process slow. It was difficult to maintain momentum in the face of continuing uncertainty. At the end of 1998, no one had yet signed a contract with the town to use any part of the site. Gaining Ground was on board to bring the farm alive again, but it would take another several months before a formal agreement would be reached. EDCO's negotiations with the town were dragging on and preventing the collaborative and the Trust from settling in as long-range planning partners. And though the Trust had its bona fides in place, we had no guarantee of future stewardship.

During my time at *The Concord Journal*, I had been taking a hiatus from my teaching career at Concord Academy. I had turned to journalism and freelance writing in part to experience the immediate gratification of having my labor transformed into a tangible product. Being part of the Thoreau Farm Trust was my first foray into citizen activism, and I was finding it rather similar to being in the classroom again. From time to time, I would find myself thinking, "Maybe one day I'll see that what I'm doing here has made a difference. But it won't be today."

Thinking back on that time, Town Planner Marcia Rasmussen said she remains impressed by the willingness of both town officials and citizens, in what she acknowledges to have been a frustrating time, "to hammer away and keep things going."

After being reshingled, the house was painted brick red in the fall of 1999.

XXI
A DREAM DEFERRED

Our whole purpose in what we are attempting is to encourage as many young people as we can reach to become acquainted with Thoreau, to absorb into their own lives some of the values he stands for, one in particular—the value of an independent life.

—Nathaniel H. Seefurth

S truggle became the watchword of 1999. Everything concerning the Thoreau birthplace property was delayed. Gaining Ground would emerge from the year as the only winner, having signed a lease in March and planted its first crop during that growing season. It was a thrilling development, celebrated by all as a meaningful way for the historic farmland to serve the community. But EDCO's plans would falter, and the Thoreau Farm Trust would suffer peripheral damage. Over the course of the year, communication between EDCO and the town gradually broke down, to the regret of all concerned. And because the programming partnership with EDCO was so integral to the Trust's hopes for what the house would become, its vision also shattered.

Back in 1996, the plan for opening a modest Seefurth Center in a new barn adjacent to the birth house had become a centerpiece of the advocacy and fundraising efforts that allowed the town to purchase the property the following year. Not only had EDCO contributed $160,000 to the purchase, but the inspiring story of Nathaniel Seefurth and his devotion to Henry David Thoreau had helped supporters imagine generations of young people spending time in the room where Henry was born and gathering in the barn to share all they had absorbed from their visit to Concord.

On Oct. 23, 1997, exactly five months after the town had closed on the birthplace property, Concord's Board of Selectmen hosted a reception and celebration of the planned Seefurth Center. The program, held on the Virginia Road property, included a welcome by Town Manager Christopher Whelan, an overview of the plans for the birthplace property by Selectman Sally Schnitzer, and an introduction to the day's special guests: Marian Seefurth, widow of Nathaniel, and

Thoreau ed center fêted

BY BRYAN DAVIS
STAFF WRITER

Last Thursday, as a gesture symbolic of new growth, silvery slivers of rye seed were cast across a patch of land at the Thoreau birthplace on Virginia Road.

The ceremonial planting was in recognition of a new educational center that, once final approvals are in place, will rise behind Thoreau's birth home.

The purchase of the birthplace by the town this spring set the stage to fulfill a dream that has been decades in the making. Nathaniel Seefurth, Chicago businessman, philanthropist and Thoreau scholar, tried for years to get build such a center in Concord, and after his death bequeathed funds to the Educational Collaborative of Greater Boston.

Seefurth's widow, Marian, was on hand and beamed as speakers

Marian Seefurth

recounted her husband's commitment to building a center where others could come and learn about Concord's native son.

"I can't believe the center is finally becoming a reality after all of these years," she said, a wide smile on her face. "I feel as though my husband is here with us. He would have been so overwhelmed, excited . . . just thrilled."

But until the birthplace was saved, EDCO could not find a home for the Seefurth Education Center, said former director Jack Green.

The center is being developed in cooperation with the EDCO, the Thoreau Birthplace Task Force, Concord-Carlisle Regional School District, the Concord Program, and historic sites in Concord and Lincoln.

Concord Selectman Sally Schnitzer, credited with leading the board's efforts to save the birthplace, said it was symbolic that the second-grade students were at the

SEE **NEW CENTER**, PAGE 16

Dr. Jane Dorgan, the pioneering educator who had ignited the Seefurths' interest in building a student center in Concord more than twenty years earlier.

It was an emotional moment, rivaling in goose-bump factor the event held to celebrate the property acquisition itself. After a series of readings, Natural Resources Director Dan Monahan and Concord teacher Dorothy Prendergast led Mrs. Seefurth, Dr. Dorgan, and other guests in a dispersal of seeds on the land as a symbol of the hope and possibility this place would cultivate. After the reception, EDCO hosted a luncheon in the Daniel Chester French Room of the Concord Museum. Among those attending were members of the Thoreau Birthplace Task Force and the Thoreau Farm Trust, and representatives from the Concord Schools and several organizations developing curricular materials for the future Seefurth Center under the auspices of the EDCO-funded Concord Program. Though Nathaniel Seefurth was not there in person, he was everywhere in spirit.

The celebratory gathering—treated as a groundbreaking ceremony—was a testament to how intricately the Seefurth Center had been woven into the vision for the property's future. A site plan, drawn up by Maugel Architects, Inc., called for the construction of a

40-by-60-foot post-and-beam barn structure with a wood-shingled roof, barn-board siding, and sliding barn doors. The barn conformed to the size limits of the zoning district, and EDCO was seeking no variances. The architects' submission to the Planning Board noted that the barn had been designed "to coordinate and work in conjunction with the Thoreau Birthplace House." There would be parking spaces for two buses and nineteen cars, which would be located behind the barn to obscure their view from the road. The Planning Board had approved the site plan in the fall of 1997, and construction was set to begin in 1998.

But things began to unravel early that year. Jack Green, EDCO's longtime executive director and the devoted torch-bearer of Seefurth's dream, retired from his position at the end of 1997, not long after the groundbreaking ceremony. Green remained on the Birthplace Task Force and became a key member of the founding board of the Thoreau Farm Trust, but he yielded his role at EDCO to a new executive director, Thomas Scott. Scott had been superintendent of schools in Concord before assuming his new role. His association with both the town and EDCO, of which he had been a board member, meant that he was well aware of the property's acquisition and EDCO's role in it.

As Scott worked with EDCO's board on plans for funding the construction and maintenance of the Seefurth Center, his board members raised concerns about the small return the organization would receive for a sizable financial outlay. EDCO held approximately $1.5 million in the Seefurth Fund, some of which had been used to contribute to the purchase and plan the education center. At least another $500,000 was expected to be needed for construction. The board felt it should retain a substantial amount of remaining funds as a quasi endowment to ensure there would be enough to maintain the Seefurth Center in perpetuity, putting no financial burden on EDCO's programming. To address those concerns, the board asked Scott to revisit the site plan and increase EDCO's presence at the site. They wished to locate their School Services staff at the barn to defray some of the costs, which would mean constructing office space there, and they wanted a larger structure to accommodate teacher workshops and curricular programming across all disciplines. In their view, the center should serve EDCO's wider purposes at the same time it was fulfilling Nathaniel Seefurth's vision of becoming a gathering place for students learning about Thoreau and his legacy.

Accepting the board's directives, Scott returned to EDCO's architects, who worked throughout the year on revised drafts for a new barn with a larger footprint and a higher profile. EDCO intended to put offices on a newly added second floor to house its School Services team, and the education plan also called for teacher workshops in all subjects, not just those related to Thoreau.

The revised site and use plans took months to complete and delayed construction and lease negotiations throughout 1998, the year the center was meant to be built. It was clear from the time town officials saw the site plan revision, which didn't happen until May 1999, that they did not support the proposed changes because they significantly altered the way the barn would look and feel. To complicate things further, the town was beginning to hear concerns about increased traffic on Virginia Road, as Gaining Ground began to bring farm vehicles and volunteers to the site, and the town initiated plans to build Elm Brook, an affordable housing complex directly across from the birthplace. A larger educational center with increased use would surely add to neighbors' anxieties.

In June 1999, after more than a year of discussion, Concord Selectman Ruth Lauer sent a letter to EDCO's Tom Scott confirming the board's strong commitment to the creation of the Seefurth Center, but only as "originally envisioned." They had, she said, always embraced the plan for a "simple, rustic barn-like structure, the purpose of which would be to educate students about Henry David Thoreau and his contemporaries." But they could not accept the proposed expansion in use, which included administrative functions and non-Thoreau-related curriculum development. Lauer wrote that selectmen believed "the inclusion of these other functions would change the focus of the Seefurth Center, might result in higher levels of traffic and other neighborhood impacts, and is inconsistent with the commitments made to the Town and the neighborhood during many months of discussions leading up to the Town Meeting in 1997."

The letter appeared to leave no room for negotiation or compromise concerning the revised proposal. But it did hold out hope for ultimate resolution. "EDCO was an early and critical partner in the campaign to purchase the farm...," wrote Lauer. "We look forward to the opportunity to work further with you on plans for this site, which accomplish the mutual vision for Thoreauvian education as articulated by Nathaniel Seefurth and as agreed to by the Town and EDCO."

Members of the Thoreau Farm Trust board were understandably dismayed by the turn of events. Tom Scott had begun attending board meetings as the liaison to EDCO. He kept us informed about EDCO's struggle to devise an acceptable plan that would meet the collaborative's needs and satisfy the town. But communication faltered at every stage, and by the middle of 1999, resolution appeared unlikely. "To be honest," he told us at that point, "I don't feel EDCO is welcome any longer in the town."

The impasse led to some tension among the Thoreau Farm Trust's board members. A majority supported EDCO in its effort to meet its institutional needs at the Seefurth Center. These members felt we and EDCO had always considered ourselves partners, and we should remain loyal to that partnership. They also believed EDCO's demands were reasonable. Having more people regularly use the center could help with oversight of the birth house and improve security.

I found myself in the minority on this issue. My head understood the need of EDCO's board to exercise its fiduciary responsibility, always the primary task of any board of directors. But my heart had been won by the original plan, which would maintain the quiet simplicity of a rustic setting and feature a serene retreat for learning and reflection rather than a bustle of professional offices. I and a few other members believed we should attempt to persuade EDCO's board to honor the purposes for which the Seefurth Fund had been set up. To us, the Thoreau Farm Trust's unconditional support of EDCO's revised plans felt like a betrayal of Nathaniel Seefurth, whose vision had so inspired us.

After repeated, often heated discussions, the majority prevailed, and the Thoreau Farm Trust linked its fate to EDCO's. "We will go down this path together," concluded Joe Wheeler.

While EDCO was revising its plans for the Seefurth barn, the Trust kept busy solidifying its internal functions, launching a modest fundraising initiative, sharing its goals with the public, responding to the town's Request for Proposals, and working with town staff on stabilizing the house. We had $1,642.88 in our account in January

1999, after spending $569 on such things as government fees related to our incorporation and application for nonprofit status. Concerns about the need for an audit were put to rest by Michael Kellett, who informed us, rather wryly, that we were well below the financial threshold for such a requirement.

With plans for the affordable housing development under way, and Gaining Ground launching its farm operation, we felt it was incumbent upon the Trust to engage the neighbors in our work in order to ease any concerns that Virginia Road would become a noisy, traffic-snarled thoroughfare. As a first step, we invited Virginia Road resident Tim Rodgers to join the board. Rodgers had rolled up his sleeves with Trust members and friends at a cleanup day on the property the preceding fall, and he and his son had been volunteering their time to mow the lawn. Besides being a mean guy with yard tools, Rodgers was adept at computer use and set up the Trust's first website. He also developed a group email list that he used to keep neighbors informed of our actions and solicit ideas and concerns from them. At that point, not everyone on the Trust board even had email, and Tim would be instrumental in making us all more Internet savvy and, consequently, more communicative.

On March 3, 1999, the town finally issued its Request for Proposals soliciting responses from nonprofits interested in funding and restoring the birth house. Applications were due by April 2. We submitted our comprehensive response to the RFP on March 31, and it turned out we were the only nonprofit to respond by the deadline. We mused about this for some time and ultimately concluded that the absence of other bidders was likely due to the active involvement of our members since before the property's acquisition. The public was aware of our hope to continue as stewards of the house, at least through the restoration phase, and perhaps other organizations had held back as a result. Yet it was possible the town would still reject us as unqualified to carry out its desired goals for the property and choose instead to extend the deadline, so we were taking nothing for granted.

Into our response to the RFP we poured all our hopes for the birthplace property. We envisioned the house as an enhancement to the neighborhood and as a place to be used in the public interest. The restoration would be done in an environmentally sensitive way, using cost-effective, energy-efficient strategies that reflected Thoreau's status as the father of American environmentalism. The educational activities we would plan for the house would complement those of the Seefurth Center and, to a lesser extent, Gaining Ground, and would coordinate as well with programming at other institutions in Concord, including the library, the museum, other historical houses, and the National Park Service.

Our application acknowledged that fundraising for the restoration would likely take up to three years, so we proposed shepherding the house through a "mothball" stage during that period, at a cost of no more than $5,000 per year. We estimated restoration costs of at least $500,000 and a long-term endowment goal of $2 million to ensure the house's future health.

By that point, the Trust had raised approximately $5,000, enough to cover the first year of the "mothball" stage. For the three years devoted largely to fundraising, we proposed to operate largely through the work of volunteers, mainly our board members.

In late May, we were thrilled to hear that our response to the RFP had been accepted. The selection committee had chosen us to become tenants of the house and one acre of surrounding land. It was, without a doubt, a leap of faith on the part of town officials—and we were leaping along with them. But it had taken a great deal of work to reach that point, and it felt like the perfect way to celebrate the end of our first fiscal year that June. Based on the experiences of Gaining Ground and EDCO, we knew lease negotiations could drag on for several months and involve multiple drafts, but the responsibility conferred on us by the town strengthened the confidence we had in ourselves and catalyzed us into action on the strategic planning and fundraising fronts.

By April, the house had been reshingled and, late that fall, it was finally repainted the brick red recommended by the Trust. The result was transformative, a welcome improvement that lifted its appearance and everyone's spirits.

The house's facelift also had a pleasing effect on the neighbors. "What a difference a coat of paint makes," enthused one of our regular correspondents. But the positive spirit was dimmed when, on Dec. 20, Tom Scott and other EDCO administrators made a presentation to the Board of Selectmen, which several Virginia Road neighbors attended or watched on TV. Scott presented the revised plan that continued to show a larger structure and included the planned increased use by staff conducting multidisciplinary curriculum development and teacher workshops. In an executive session held immediately following that board meeting, selectmen voted to reject the proposal.

In a letter to Scott confirming that vote, Selectman Ruth Lauer again expressed support for the original design and use. "The Town remains committed to this vision and is anxious to see the fulfillment of the Seefurth Center…," wrote Lauer. "We continue to believe that the student-centered barn would be beneficial to furthering the programs of many of the cultural institutions in our area and is consistent with the 'Thoreauvian purposes' for which the property was acquired."

Selectmen realized, said Lauer, that since that time, EDCO's board had likely undergone turnover. They understood, she said, that the needs of EDCO might have changed during the two years since the original proposal had been advanced by Jack Green. "It may be the case that a rustic building as originally discussed does not fulfill EDCO's needs at this time," wrote Lauer. "This is a decision that only the EDCO board can make."

Though continuing to leave open the option of returning to the earlier plan and reiterating the Board of Selectmen's "strong desire to work with you at the Thoreau Farm," this letter was less conciliatory than the one she had written the previous June. There were only two choices, and EDCO had to decide between them. "Because the future of the Seefurth Center has a profound effect on the efforts to preserve the Thoreau Birthplace, it is important for the Town to know whether EDCO wishes to proceed with the original plans or wishes to withdraw its proposal to build the Center," wrote Lauer. "Therefore, I ask that you advise the Town Manager at your earliest convenience as to what EDCO's plans are in the matter."

Although Lauer didn't send that pointed letter until Feb. 10, 2000, perhaps hoping that EDCO would reconsider in the interim, Town Manager Christopher Whelan had phoned Scott after the board's executive session in December to inform him of the refusal of the new plan. So at the end of 1999, it appeared certain that Nathaniel Seefurth's dream would remain unrealized.

XXII

TRYING TO PICK UP THE PIECES

*Painful as it may be, a significant emotional event can be
the catalyst for choosing a direction that serves us
—and those around us—more effectively. Look for the learning.*

—Louisa May Alcott

During the next year and a half, from January 2000 through June 2001, the Thoreau Farm Trust board was thrust into the role of mediator between EDCO and the Town of Concord. It was in everyone's interest to make this partnership work. The town had accepted a substantial donation from EDCO toward the purchase of the birthplace property and had always promoted the Seefurth Center as integral to its future. The Trust's proposal to restore and re-use the house was founded on the assumption that EDCO would become its educational arm. We were counting on the professional expertise of its staff to shape learning activities related to Thoreau, with the birth house serving as a perfect enhancement to the Seefurth vision.

Town officials, eager to be released from responsibility for the house, were hoping to conclude a lease agreement with the Thoreau Farm Trust. Now that Gaining Ground was up and running and a true point of pride for the town, it was important to restore the birth house and begin using it in appropriate ways for the public good. In May 1999, the house had been struck by lightning, destroying some of the newly laid roof shingles. Though the town's insurance covered the cost of the repair, town officials had become ever more eager to shift responsibility for the safety and security of the structure to a non-municipal steward. But the Trust's board did not wish to sign a lease without the Seefurth Center as a partner. So throughout those eighteen months, the Trust advanced several proposals as potential compromises while trying, with limited success, to keep discussions alive between EDCO and the town.

Holding up those discussions was EDCO's urgent need to relocate its headquarters in neighboring Lincoln. The collaborative was about to lose its office space as well as the classroom space it had used in the Lincoln schools, which were expanding and needed to reclaim the rented space. As early as January 2000, Tom Scott and his staff were exploring other locations in Lincoln from which to run their entire operation. While a search for new quarters was going on, Scott decided not to press the town on a decision about its revised plans for the Seefurth Center, which had become a less pressing concern. So communication between the two entities essentially shut down for several months.

A number of possibilities remained open: EDCO could wait to see if turnover in the Board of Selectmen would change the town's stance; it could locate all its staff in its new facilities and build a rustic barn in Concord to use solely as a classroom space; it could build the center and turn its operation over to the Thoreau Farm Trust; or, the Trust could choose to raise additional funds to build its own education center and use EDCO as a consulting agent. But nothing could be done until EDCO and town officials resumed their conversations, which had come to a complete halt. Until EDCO's board came to a decision, the Trust chose to leave its own lease unsigned. If no Seefurth Center were in the offing, the Trust would have to evaluate the wisdom of moving forward on its own.

In late April, Joe Wheeler mentioned for the first time that the Trust might have to "to fold its tents." But Trust member Al Lima, who had recently left his position as Concord's planning director while remaining on our board, reminded us that we were in this for the long haul. "We must not get discouraged when we take a half-step forward and two steps backwards; that is the way these efforts usually proceed," said Lima. Encouraging us to "stick with the process and remain steadfast," he mentioned an effort he had worked on that took eight years to succeed. "Determination will win in the end, and we will see a good result," he assured us. We very much wanted to believe him.

During the 1999-2000 fiscal year, which ran from July 1 to June 30, our board underwent a few changes. Christine Rinaldo of Historic Concord, Inc. and Joe Valentine left the board, though both remained connected to the ongoing efforts at the birthplace. Virginia Road resident Tim Rodgers and Gaining Ground's Jamie Bemis had joined, as had Concord resident and Thoreau Society member John Mack. I left *The Concord Journal* to return to "civilian" life in July 1999 and resumed my earlier career in education at Concord Academy, where my husband, Sandy, taught a popular course called "Thoreau and

Kindreds." Through his work and my own relationships with students, I was again seeing firsthand evidence of the magic that happens when young people discover in Thoreau's writings a mind to contend with. The author Joyce Carol Oates once wrote, "To read Thoreau in adolescence is to read him at a time when such statements carry the weight, the promise, of prophecy." I was learning that all over again.

As we continued to try to broker an agreeable arrangement between EDCO and the town, the Thoreau Farm Trust stayed busy on the tasks it had laid out for itself. Brian Donahue secured a grant from Brandeis University, where he was a tenured professor of Environmental Studies. During that summer, he and Barbara Lambert used the funding to conduct research on the use of the birthplace property over time. Donahue also mapped the property and surrounding area using Geographic Information System equipment borrowed from Brandeis as a way to visualize the habitation and use history of Virginia Road. Lambert continued to search through deeds and probate records with help from other members of the Trust board, and Tim Rodgers was developing a more informative, interactive website. Though fundraising had remained very low-key pending lease negotiations, we had received a $5,000 grant from a family foundation that boosted our assets to $11,548.54 by May 2000. Each time we reviewed these figures, we reminded ourselves that our assets would amount to a much larger figure if we were to factor in all the person-hours donated by board members and other volunteers and the pro bono help from Hale and Dorr. It was important to stay positive.

In September 2000, EDCO and town officials resumed their dialogue. The process, though cordial, remained fraught. Selectmen had taken charge of the negotiations and begun to set up strict limits on what EDCO could and could not do at the site, including how many classes could be held per week and how many students could be there at any one time. EDCO's administrators chafed at these new restrictions, and came to believe the town was simply trying to force them to stop trying for resolution. It was clear the restrictions were formulated in response to the revised plans for an enlarged and more heavily used Seefurth Center and would likely not have applied to the original site and use plan, which had already been approved.

As the first year of the new millennium waned, there appeared to be no compromise in sight. Rick Wheeler (cousin to Joe), the new chair of the Board of Selectmen, sent a letter to Tom Scott just after Thanksgiving asking for "closure." While reasserting yet again the town's support for the original conception of a Seefurth Center at the birthplace, Wheeler said, "It was becoming increasingly clear to our Board that we were constraining what you and your associates might have considered to be normative activities." EDCO had decided by that time to house its School Services staff at its new headquarters in Lincoln, and Rick Wheeler seemed to be saying the town was willing to continue discussion, but only on its terms.

That letter and EDCO's growing reluctance to engage any further with the town prompted Joe Wheeler to ask the Thoreau Farm Trust's board if we should let the town know that "we are close to pulling out." But selectmen encouraged us to sign a lease that would allow us to proceed with raising the funds and restoring the house. They suggested we limit the lease to that purpose and postpone the plans for an education center and ongoing operational stewardship until that first purpose was safely under way. Unwilling to accept this "restoration only" approach, our board voted unanimously to reject the idea. We did not believe we could raise the money to restore the house unless we had compelling programming to offer once it was opened to the public. Before asking donors to commit their resources, we would have to tell them exactly how the restored house—and their contributions—would be used for the benefit of the community.

To address these issues and attempt to revive the discussions with EDCO, the Trust appointed Court Booth, Jayne Gordon, and me to serve as a negotiating team with the town. On Jan. 3, 2001, Booth wrote a letter to Town Planner Marcia Rasmussen outlining where we believed things stood. Gaining Ground was actively cultivating nine acres and conducting educational visits to the land. The Thoreau Farm Trust had already engaged with the farm, through our liaison Jamie Bemis, to devise ways to be mutually supportive. Booth added that EDCO had recently come up with a new strategy, which would allow the Thoreau Farm Trust to assume day-to-day, site-based management of the Seefurth Center barn. This idea was still largely undeveloped, but the two organizations were discussing possible ways to make it work for the benefit of both. Booth also informed Rasmussen that the Trust and EDCO would coordinate scheduling at the center to ensure sufficient parking behind the buildings, and no parking would be permitted on the road. He outlined a minimal use plan that would not encourage large numbers of visitors, either to the house or to the education center.

We hoped the letter would reassure the town that EDCO was willing to make some serious concessions to guarantee the creation of a Seefurth Center at the birthplace.

But while accepting the details that Booth had outlined for the Thoreau Farm Trust's plans for the house, selectmen continued to question EDCO's intended use of the proposed barn. It was clear they were having great difficulty overcoming their unhappiness with the way the original plans had been changed. They asked that teacher workshops be limited to a maximum of ten per month and that, on an annual basis, at least 30 percent of programming at the site be Thoreau-related. This second requirement represented a significant compromise, since the town had originally understood that the Seefurth Center would be completely devoted to Thoreau-related material. Even so, Scott and other EDCO administrators raised concerns about the difficulty of measuring curricular initiatives in percentages, especially given the evolving needs of the many school systems they served.

By late winter, EDCO had grudgingly agreed to the two stipulations, but relations remained strained, and the lease situation was still tenuous. Our negotiating team told selectmen that, with the uses and conditions in place, we hoped the board would permit Town Manager Christopher Whelan to pursue lease negotiations. "The challenging work of fundraising and restoration still lies before us, and we are eager to get started," we said in a March 17 letter. But the Board of Selectmen was laboring under a burdensome workload and could give only limited time to the birthplace issue, so a resolution remained distant.

As the Thoreau Farm Trust's Annual Meeting, scheduled for May 23, approached and we still had not received a nod from the Board of Selectmen, we decided at the request of Joe Wheeler to treat that meeting as our watershed moment. We would ask selectmen through our negotiators to let us know by that date whether or not they were ready to resume lease negotiations with both EDCO and the Trust, understanding that the two organizations were partners in the project. If they agreed to authorize the town manager to negotiate, we would use that meeting to plan our fundraising strategy. If not, we would use it to plan our exit.

Ultimately, the decision was taken out of the hands of both the town and the Trust. On May 21, Tom Scott and his top administrator, Eileen McSwiney, met with our negotiating team and let us know that EDCO could not continue discussing the construction of a Seefurth Center with the town. Though disappointing, this announcement was not surprising. Scott said he and his staff believed the town had erected so many roadblocks to their work that effective programming would be compromised as a result. Despite that conclusion, EDCO stood behind its $160,000 investment in the birthplace acquisition as a way to honor Nathaniel Seefurth's memory, an extremely generous decision. Scott also left open the possibility of building a modest barn and forging a partnership with the Thoreau Farm Trust at some future date, or perhaps using additional Seefurth funds to support Thoreau-related programming at the house. But given the mood of the moment, that all seemed unlikely.

So on May 24, 2001, Booth, Gordon, and I met with Sally Schnitzer and Ruth Lauer, the lead negotiators for the Board of Selectmen, and Town Manager Christopher Whelan. We handed each of them a copy of a letter we had hoped never to have to deliver: our notice that we were suspending negotiations on a lease that would have allowed us to fund and manage the restoration of the Thoreau birth house. Signed by our president, Joe Wheeler, the letter said in part, "We judge that without the educational component—a component central to our interests—we would not be able to raise the funds for the restoration and operation of the house. Therefore, we suggest you seek a new partner."

We added that we wished to be as helpful to the town as possible moving forward and would share all the research and other foundational work we had done during the past year and a half. This work included summaries of more than 700 property deeds, historical maps of the area, structural studies of the house, and records dating from the earliest efforts to save the property. We also said we would maintain our organizational framework as a corporate nonprofit in case that would be useful for another group choosing to pick up where we had left off. And, of course, all donations we had received would be devoted to preserving and restoring Thoreau's birth house in whatever way that could happen.

It was an emotional moment, to be sure, and those of us from the Trust could see that others in that room shared our sadness. We all knew there were no villains in the picture and understood the realities of running an organization with many masters, as EDCO and the town were both doing. But we also knew that the five of us shared an allegiance to the original vision for the Seefurth Center. I'm sure I was not alone in thinking that if the plan we had all embraced in 1997 had remained in effect, the doors to a new Seefurth Center would have already opened, and the Thoreau Farm Trust would be well on its way to raising funds to restore the house.

On June 5, the three organizations—the Thoreau Farm Trust, EDCO, and the Town of Concord—issued a joint press release announcing a halt to our plans for the birth house and education center. Along with everyone else on our board— most of us founding members—I was struggling with a deep sense of loss. It was a blessing for me that I was no longer editor of *The Concord Journal.*

XXIII
THE TRUST IN MOTHBALLS

Not till we are lost, in other words, not till we have lost the world,
do we begin to find ourselves, and realize where we are
and the infinite extent of our relations.

—H.D. Thoreau, *Walden*

In the wake of our profound disappointment at losing our educational partner, the Thoreau Farm Trust, Inc. remained alive, barely. We had told the town we would maintain our nonprofit corporation and share our resources with whatever organization might come forward to adopt the house, and we kept that promise. After devoting so much of our time and emotional energy into saving, protecting, and planning to preserve the house, board members would have found it difficult to walk away from the birthplace—and each other. The decision to keep our organization intact throughout all the events that would transpire over the next two years—from mid-2001 to mid-2003—would prove to be the determining factor in the future of the birthplace. But no one could have predicted that at the time.

Concord's staff and selectmen, who had expected the historic house to be someone else's responsibility by that time, did their best over those years to keep it from crumbling. Meanwhile, throughout the town and beyond, quiet conversations began to percolate, sustaining hope that a perfect candidate would bubble up and take over restoration planning from the Trust. Joe Wheeler was elected chair of the Concord Historical Commission in 2001. So, though the Thoreau Farm Trust did not meet officially as a board during the second half of that year, effectively joining the birth house in its "mothball" state, Wheeler was perfectly positioned to keep us informed of the activity surrounding the property.

Gaining Ground, which continued to enjoy success on the land and benefited from being the only tenant on the birthplace property, expressed interest in using the house when they negotiated a new five-year lease with the town in 2001. But it was unclear to what extent the organization would rehabilitate the structure, since the farm's primary function was philanthropic. Though pleased with Gaining Ground's presence and purpose, town officials preferred to lease the house to an organization dedicated to restoring it and using it to celebrate and advance Thoreau's life and work.

The most significant conversations took place between the town and the Thoreau Society and continued for almost a year. Shortly after our own negotiations with the town broke down, Trust members Joe Wheeler and John Mack, who were also on the board of the Thoreau Society, began corresponding with the Society's other board members and its executive director, Tom Harris, about the possibility of the Society taking over the house.

At the time, the Thoreau Society was headquartered at the Thoreau Institute in Lincoln, the scholarly center founded and operated by the Walden Woods Project. Founded in 1941, the Thoreau Society is the oldest and largest organization devoted to an American author. Today, its 1,200 members hail from all fifty states and twenty countries. The Society once had a footprint in downtown Concord, when its worldwide headquarters was located in a small building on Belknap Street called the Thoreau Lyceum, which shut down in 1995 when the Thoreau Institute opened. The Society's board was tempted by the opportunity to relocate in Concord and understandably interested in inhabiting the actual birth house. The problem was money. They had very little of it and slim prospects for raising enough to cover the cost of renovation and continued maintenance. The Society's board estimated it would take $400,000 to complete the first phase of a restoration project and close to $1 million for a full restoration. In addition, board members were loath to commit without an endowment whose income would fund maintenance of the house in perpetuity. That was a steep hill to climb for an organization that was about to announce a $50,000 budget deficit for FY02 and present an FY03 budget with a projected deficit of $30,000.

During the fall of 2001, Executive Director Tom Harris had several meetings with Concord's town manager and Selectmen Sally Schnitzer and Ruth Lauer, who had been serving as liaisons to the birthplace negotiations. With the town's cautious encouragement, Harris prepared a formal proposal developed by the Society's board, many of whose members were scattered at colleges and universities around the country. Locally, Joe Wheeler and John Mack remained involved, which meant the Thoreau Farm Trust was kept apprised of the Society's collective thinking. To show our support for the proposal, we offered to cover the cost of keeping the house in "mothballs" for four years—the time the Society's board believed it would need to raise funds for the first phase of renovations. The proposal stipulated that if it could not raise that much in the designated time, the Society would return the house to the town.

Despite all the positive feeling, the Thoreau Society's foray into potential ownership felt precarious from the start. Tom Harris submitted a comprehensive proposal to the town on Dec. 15, 2001, which included an overview of the funds to be raised, a plan for modest educational programming, and a desire to restore the house to its 1817 appearance. The proposal also called for office space for an executive director and two staff members and reflected the town's wish that parking be limited to four or five cars. The Thoreau Society's board members added, however, that they would not have the formal authority to move ahead until after their board meeting in late January, at the earliest.

Meanwhile, selectmen were in the process of preparing the 2002 Town Meeting Warrant, which had to be completed by early January. In order for the town to convey the house to an appropriate nonprofit, Town Meeting would have to approve a sale, so selectmen decided to write an article requesting such approval and include it on the warrant as a "placeholder," to be moved if the Society chose to advance its proposal.

Late in December, Selectman Sally Schnitzer wrote to Tom Scott at EDCO informing him of the Thoreau Society's interest in purchasing the birth house and adding that she believed it was worthy of selectmen's consideration. "The Town would be greatly relieved to find a party willing to undertake the expensive restoration project and long-term maintenance and upkeep of this historic house," she wrote. "The house would be open to the public on a limited basis, but use of the site would be kept at a very modest level." Schnitzer told Scott that the sale or lease of the house and the land around it "would have the effect of forever precluding a future presence by EDCO." Noting that EDCO appeared to have no further interest in building a Seefurth Center on the site, she asked Scott for his thoughts on the recent developments and offered to meet with him and Town Manager Christopher Whelan to discuss his response in person.

Though it was clear that Schnitzer's letter was sent as a good-faith effort to keep EDCO informed and confirm the collaborative's decision to look elsewhere for a site, both the Society's board and some Trust members were alarmed by the communication. The limits on parking and use felt restrictive to the Society, whose plans were largely unformed at that point. And the Trust had never believed that selling or leasing the house to the Thoreau Society would preclude the eventual construction of a Seefurth Center, if that opportunity should arise in the future.

But we needn't have worried. Just before the 2002 Town Meeting in April, the Thoreau Society informed the town that it would not seek to acquire the birthplace "at this time." While not closing the door on a future proposal, the Society's board indicated that the organization did not feel capable of raising the necessary funds on its own and would take a more "cautious approach" by seeking other partners. Considering the cost of restoration, operations, and long-term maintenance on the circa 1730 birth house, the board estimated that it would actually need to raise upwards of $2 million. In retrospect, it seems likely that when the Society's board polled its membership, it did so in the hope that a major donor from within its ranks would step forward. But that didn't happen. With the Society's own operational finances on such precarious footing, most members must have felt it would be foolhardy to proceed with a major acquisition. Though the town would agree to sell the house for only $1, the prospect of failing to raise the restoration funds and having to return the house to municipal ownership was unsavory. It would not reflect well on the Society, nor would it be in the best interests of the house.

Although the Thoreau Society was out of the picture by the time Town Meeting convened in the spring of 2002, selectmen decided to move Article 62. If passed by a two-thirds majority, the article would "urge the Board of Selectmen to continue its efforts to identify a suitable organization, institution, or agency willing and able to undertake the historic restoration of the nationally significant Thoreau Birth House located at 341 Virginia Road, and ... authorize the Board ... to sell for nominal consideration, or lease, the birth house, together with up to 2 acres of the surrounding land, ... to such an organization ...."

After polling Thoreau Farm Trust board members and receiving our approbation, Joe Wheeler spoke in support of the article on the Town Meeting floor on April 29, as did John Mack. Both the town and the Trust were concerned about the condition and safety of the house and believed the authorization to sell would allow selectmen to act quickly should a good opportunity present itself in coming months. The article passed with only a few dissenting votes, giving selectmen the green light to seek a savior.

As Town Meeting approached, the Thoreau Farm Trust had begun to meet regularly again, after about nine months of relative dormancy. The original catalyst for our re-emergence was our support for the Thoreau Society's desire to take over the birth house. Though many of us recognized the idea as a pie-in-the-sky proposition, we had to acknowledge the town's favorable attitude and the fact that there was no better option in play.

To prepare ourselves for the Town Meeting vote and determine how we might aid the Thoreau Society in its effort to acquire the house, we invited the Society's president, Ron Bosco, to a Trust meeting on March 6. At that point, Bosco was still hoping to make a formal proposal to the town in time for the Town Meeting vote. In an attempt to define our role in that proposal, we discussed whether to dissolve our organization and give the $12,612 in our account to the Thoreau Society; donate part of the money but remain active ourselves; or reorganize ourselves in a more minor role as Friends of the Thoreau Birthplace. It seems surprising now, considering our recent removal from the fray, that we decided unanimously that night to remain active in our original iteration as the Thoreau Farm Trust. We also voted unanimously, in the event that the Thoreau Society purchased the house from the town, to donate $20,000 over the next four years—some of which we had on hand and some we believed we could raise from board members over the four-year period—to cover house expenses during the Society's fundraising stage.

By the time of our fourth Annual Meeting on May 14, 2002, the Society had withdrawn from consideration, and Town Meeting had voted to approve the sale of the house to an acceptable nonprofit. Everything, in other words, was still in flux. Everything, that is, except our Thoreau Farm Trust board, which remained intact for another fiscal year. It was a loyal group, indeed, if a bit tired. We agreed to keep lines of communication open with town officials as they continued their search for a buyer, but we imagined putting ourselves back in mothballs for another fiscal year, that is, until June 30, 2003.

As it turned out, we would shake off the mothballs long before our next Annual Meeting during what would become a very eventful year for the Trust and for the town.

The west-side parlor downstairs showing the extent to which repairs were needed.

XXIV

"STARS IN THEIR EYES, NOT A NICKEL IN THEIR POCKET"

Tomorrow is a new day; begin it well and serenely
and with too high a spirit to be cumbered with your old nonsense….
It is too dear, with its hopes and invitations, to waste a moment on yesterdays.

—Ralph Waldo Emerson

In the summer of 2002, the birth house was vandalized. No one was caught, but police suspected a group of young people had managed to enter the abandoned house and spray paint the walls. The event was not catastrophic, but it served to highlight the structure's vulnerability and refocus attention on finding an organization to protect it. "It reawakened us to the fact that it could be lost," said Selectmen Chairman Gary Clayton at the time.

By the fall of that year, though the exterior of the house sported a new roof and a recent paint job, the interior was in deplorable condition. Some of the walls had started to crumble, ceilings were flaking, floorboards had warped, linoleum was yellowing and curling, and wallpaper was slinking off the walls. Stairs leading up to the second floor were dangerously unstable, and there was unpleasant evidence that critters had been making the place their home despite efforts to repair cracks and holes in the foundation, clapboards, and windows. After the enormous effort to save the property that had begun seven years earlier, it would be tragic to see the house fall down for lack of a rescuer.

The Thoreau Far Trust's board, urged on by RESTORE director Michael Kellett, encouraged town officials to request help from the National Park Service (NPS), stewards of the Minute Man National Historical Park. In 1965, the NPS had acquired the Wayside, once home to the Alcotts, the Hawthornes, and Margaret Sidney. Located on Lexington Road in Concord, the 18th-century house was the first literary site the Park Service had ever owned. That acquisition had set an important precedent, and the Trust hoped the Thoreau birthplace would be considered another worthy addition. In fact, the birth house seemed an ideal complement to the Park Service's holdings because one of its early inhabitants, Captain Jonas Minot, figured prominently in the American Revolution after joining his fellow Minute Men at the Old North Bridge on the morning of April 19, 1775.

In early conversations, Park Superintendent Nancy Nelson expressed strong interest in both the Revolutionary and literary significance of the farmhouse. The Thoreau Farm Trust was among several Concord organizations that made formal presentations to the Board of Selectmen in support of enlisting the Park's help in establishing a public-private partnership at the birthplace. If the Park would take ownership, the Trust and the Thoreau Society promised to sign on as fundraisers, educational consultants, and stewards.

But the idea never took root. Superintendent Nelson informed the town in early 2003 that the time was not right for the Park Service to take responsibility for another historic house in Concord. Funds were much tighter than they had been in 1965, and Nelson's tentative overtures at the federal level had not met with encouragement. A spokesperson for the Park Service told *The Concord Journal* that Secretary of the Interior Gale Norton had decided that budget constraints would suspend the addition of new Park Service acquisitions for the foreseeable future.

With the Park Service initiative looking grim and the situation dire, the town turned to a new Concord resident, "This Old House," for help. The production company for the popular Emmy-winning PBS home-improvement series had moved in May 2002 to a renovated barn on Virginia Road and so had become a near neighbor to the Thoreau birth house. Passing by the house each day, the cast and crew noticed its deterioration and decided to reach out. Though they were not interested in taking on the project themselves, they offered to raise awareness by featuring the house in their magazine, which devoted its final page each month to a property in need of saving. Town Manager Christopher Whelan gave his approval for what was essentially a real estate ad for the house, and the illustrated feature appeared in the issue of the magazine dated November 2002 (which appeared in print during the month of October). The piece ended with the news that "[t]he Town is offering the two-acre property for sale to someone who will agree to faithfully restore the house for the benefit of Thoreauvians everywhere and open the home for public tours on a regular basis."

The operative word in that message, to those of us who had been involved in the effort to find an interested nonprofit, was the word "someone." It was becoming clear that the selectmen, who had placed disposition of the house on their priority list for the year's work, were now willing to consider selling the house to a private individual, given the right circumstances.

In an email responding to questions from Trust board member Helen Bowdoin, Christopher Whelan wrote that town officials were "gauging what level of interest there is in a private restoration (or any other ideas we might hear). This could take the form of a private citizen acquiring the property, with historic preservation covenants and possibly a first-right-of-refusal clause regarding resale."

Whelan also told Bowdoin that the town was considering allowing a tenant or caretaker to move into the house as it had done with another town property, the historic Harrington House. In the 1970s, the house and farmland were saved and preserved through a municipal purchase and then leased to a tenant for $300 per month in exchange for continuing maintenance. In the arrangement, the house is opened to the public once each year. That situation was quite different, however, since the house was habitable from the start and did not carry the significance of the Thoreau connection. Whelan estimated it would cost at least $150,000 to make the Thoreau house minimally habitable, a sum the town could not put to that purpose. "No public or nonprofit groups have stepped forward, even with modest resources for the care of the property," wrote Whelan. "So we're asking the public if they will help."

Within a month of the article's appearance, the town had received more than 400 calls from interested parties. It had also received alarmed responses from Thoreau Farm Trust board members, who continued to hope that the house would be put in the care of a preservation-minded nonprofit. In the rash of emails and phone calls that immediately followed the magazine's publication, board members advanced a number of ideas, including encouraging the town to reach out again to The Trustees of Reservations and the National Park Service. Joe Wheeler contacted the Thoreau Society's Ron Bosco to suggest that the Society make the relatively modest investment of the $150,000 the town believed it would take to secure an occupancy permit for the house. If the Society could afford that sum, it could transfer its headquarters to the birth house, saving the annual rent it was now paying the Thoreau Institute, and rent a couple of rooms to fellow nonprofits to help pay expenses while it worked to raise money for a complete restoration.

None of these ideas would bear fruit. But it was also true that the town did not have the authority to sell or lease the house to a private individual. That authority would have to come from Town Meeting, which would not meet again until spring of the following year. So though there was obviously a great deal of interest in the property, we knew the town could not act precipitously in the direction of a private owner.

That constraint turned out to be a blessing when, in mid-December 2002, multimillionaire Donald Saunders, co-owner of the Boston Park Plaza Hotel and Towers and former husband of actress Liv Ullman, offered $1 million to save the birth house. As reported by Thomas Grillo in a Dec. 14 article in *The Boston Globe*, Saunders expressed interest in establishing a nonprofit trust whose proceeds would be used to repair the house and install new systems. Part of the proceeds from the trust would then be used to staff the house as a museum. Saunders told *The Globe* that he had already helped restore several properties, including a large Victorian in Gloucester, Massachusetts, which he purchased for $364,000 in 1998. He had the house gutted and restored and had recently placed it on the market for $3.3 million. "But I'm not seeking to profit from the Thoreau home," he said. "In exchange for turning the house into a museum, I would occasionally like to have dinner at the house with my family."

To those of us at the Trust, Saunders's proposal felt completely wrong for the house, which was never intended to become a relic of the past. But Selectman Gary Clayton said the idea intrigued him. "A lot of people have called with stars in their eyes and not much more than a nickel in their pocket," he told *The Globe*. "This is not a handyman special that can be fixed up on weekends."

The idea of selling the house to a private individual, Saunders or another interested party, prompted mixed reactions. Ron Hoag, a board member of the Thoreau Society who had been involved in the Society's abortive proposal to the town, said he believed private ownership of the birth house could work, as long as it came with deed restrictions regarding renovation standards and public access. But Trust member Michael Kellett was adamantly against the notion. "This is public land and a public home, and it's too important to trust that a private individual will do the right thing," he said. "It would be like renting out Independence Hall to a computer company. This historically significant piece of property attracts people worldwide and deserves better."

On Dec. 16, the Concord Board of Selectmen decided to place an article on the 2003 Town Meeting Warrant that, if moved and passed, would authorize the town to sell the birth house to a private individual for $1 in exchange for assurances that the owner had the means to fund a historic restoration and would open the house for occasional public viewing. But selectmen continued to express their hope that a nonprofit or government agency would take over the house, so they also agreed to ask the Planning Department to send out a letter later that month to two dozen organizations in the hope of finding an interested buyer among them. The letter announced that a Request for Proposals would be issued during the early months of the new year seeking a nonprofit or government agency to restore the house according the Secretary of the Interior's Standards for the Treatment of Historic Properties and "consistent with preserving the character-defining features of the house." The letter also stated that "[i]n the event that a suitable group, agency, or institution is not identified, the Board of Selectmen may decide to also seek Town Meeting authorization to lease or sell the house to an individual. If the Town Meeting authorizes such action, the Town is required to follow another Request for Proposal process."

To keep all options open as they approached a new Town Meeting season, the Planning Department agreed to convene a roundtable meeting in January for any groups or individuals interested in acquiring the house. The information session would allow the town to explain the current state of the structure and the financial implications of taking it over and to outline its requirements for restoration and use of the house. Interested parties would then have the information they needed to ask questions, present their own ideas for all to hear, and make a decision on whether or not to move ahead with a response to the Request for Proposals when it was issued. It was hoped that one or more participants in that meeting would submit a serious proposal that could be addressed in a timely way and implemented as soon as possible after the April Town Meeting.

By the time the letter was sent and the roundtable scheduled for Jan. 21, the calendar was about to turn once more, with the birth house—having remained vacant for seven and a half years—in serious disrepair and facing another punishing winter. The town ended the year by putting out feelers in all directions in a flailing attempt to find a rightful owner. And the Thoreau Farm Trust, hoping to keep the original vision for the house alive, found itself on the verge of making a New Year's resolution to retrieve our hat and throw it back in the ring.

The front stairwell in the birth house, early 2000s.

XXV

A POTENTIAL NEW PARTNER COMES A-COURTIN'

Every path but your own is the path of fate.
Keep on your own track, then.

—H.D. Thoreau, *Walden*

As promised, on Jan. 21, 2003, the Board of Selectmen and the Planning Department convened a roundtable discussion on the Thoreau Birth House for "agencies, institutions, groups, or individuals interested in acquiring the property." The afternoon meeting drew representatives from a number of organizations, including the Thoreau Farm Trust, the Concord Museum, the Thoreau Society, the Walden Woods Project, the National Park Service, The Trustees of Reservations, the Wellesley Management Group, the Sons of the American Revolution, and the New England Watercolor Society. Neither Donald Saunders nor a representative from his corporation attended. Though he never issued a public withdrawal of his $1 million offer, Saunders failed to respond to the town's December letter or the invitation to the January gathering. A notoriously private man, Saunders may have chosen to shy away from the town politics and publicity that would accompany any major activity concerning the Thoreau birthplace.

Selectman Gary Clayton and Planning Director Marcia Rasmussen facilitated the roundtable, presenting a comprehensive overview of the town's intentions for the property and outlining the possible terms and conditions of a purchase-and-sale agreement. Though Concord's Board of Selectmen and its leadership had evolved over the nearly eight years since the property was put on the market, the town's plans for the birthplace had never wavered. Historic preservation, agricultural use, land conservation, and public access had always been part of the vision, as had educational programming related to Thoreau.

The list of possible terms and conditions that would be applied to a future sale was lengthy, including presence on the property to ensure security; shared access and parking with Gaining Ground; interpretative materials at the site; documentation of the restoration process for the town's archives; the employment of a qualified historic preservation architect and contractor; assurance of sufficient funding for restoration, maintenance, and operation of the house; and an acceptable proposal for educational programming and visitation practices. In case the nonprofit or agency dissolved or needed to sell the house, the town would seek a right of first refusal for 180 days.

Discussion at the meeting was lively. Not all those present were actually interested in acquiring the house. Several, including representatives from the National Park Service, the Concord Museum, and the Walden Woods Project, were there to gather information and consider a possible supportive role but had no intention of stepping up. Many of us were there to see who else would appear and what ideas they would bring with them. Though no concrete plan was advanced that day, one point of consensus did emerge: we all agreed that a nonprofit organization would be the best choice to own and manage the property. Before ending the meeting, Clayton told the participants that he hoped we would talk among ourselves and try to "craft a proposal that will work."

The roundtable and attendant publicity prompted four letters of interest. One came from Michael W. Bowie, representing the Massachusetts Society of the Sons of the American Revolution (MASSAR). Bowie proposed restoring the house to its appearance before its 1878 move, returning the birth room "to the exact configuration of its condition in 1817," creating a library and resource center for MASSAR's holdings and genealogical research, creating a conference room for use by MASSAR and "associated groups," and using the outdoors for special events on Patriots Day and Thoreau's birthday. His plan also included a new barn addition that would be turned into single-room occupancy units for ten disabled veterans or other "eligible individuals."

Another response came from Ilex Construction, a Maryland-based landscape architecture company that sought to restore the house but did not have the capacity to operate it.

The Thoreau Society wrote to express interest in managing the property in partnership with another organization, preferably the National Park Service.

The fourth letter came from the Thoreau Farm Trust. Four of us on the board had attended the roundtable, Joe Wheeler, Michael Kellett, Jayne Gordon, and I. There we had met developer Joseph Mullin, president of the Wellesley Management Group, and one of his partners, building contractor Christopher Marano. Mullin's company had recently purchased and renovated a former mill complex in Maynard, Massachusetts, known as Clock Tower Place, and he had moved his office to that location. One of Mullin's corporate objectives was to give back to the community by creating a nonprofit wing of his development corporation, which he named Bay Trust, Inc. When he learned of the opportunity to restore an at-risk historic site in Concord, Mullin saw an opportunity for Bay Trust to make its philanthropic mark at a high-profile property.

During the week following the roundtable, a group from the Trust's board met with Mullin to discuss his interest in the project. At that session, Mullin placed a generous offer on the table: Bay Trust would advance the necessary funds for the immediate restoration of the house—a figure now estimated at approximately $800,000. A portion of that advance, an amount he did not specify, would be a donation. Over time, the Thoreau Farm Trust would repay the remainder through a fundraising drive, which Mullin would help us conduct, adding his local and national contacts to our own.

Amid years of reticence on the part of other deep-pocketed groups and individuals, Mullin's offer appeared out of nowhere as our dream come true. It would mean the house could be saved from further deterioration without our having to plan and execute a multi-year fundraising campaign before work would begin.

The town was asking for expressions of interest to appear quickly, so the Trust had little time to decide whether or not to accept Bay Trust as a partner in a renewed effort to acquire and restore the house. It was a difficult offer to ignore. We did indeed have "stars in our eyes and not much more than a nickel in our pocket," and here was a potential partner telling us he was willing to front the money. Should we agree to collaborate?

There were many factors to make us wary. At a meeting to decide possible next steps, our board members raised a number of concerns: Bay Trust was an unknown quantity; fundraising might be difficult once the house was fully restored and the risk of its collapse averted; we would be taking on the enormous workload and responsibility of restoration planning and management; and, perhaps most important of all, we were still a bit bruised from the earlier negotiations with the town that had lasted much too long and yielded nothing. Yet, there was no doubt that Mullin's sudden appearance was the serendipity we had always been waiting for. It felt impossible to walk away from the prospect of a major funding partner and the promise of immediate restoration. So, despite our misgivings in the face of vague promises and missing details, the Trust's board voted to sign on.

At the end of January, we sent a letter to Marcia Rasmussen expressing our interest in working with Mullin and Bay Trust to restore the house. The Thoreau Farm Trust's role would include guiding the restoration plans, developing programming for the site in conjunction with the Thoreau Society and other educational partners, and raising enough money to repay Bay Trust and maintain the house for the long term. We would engage a historic architect to help us determine the date to which the house should be restored and craft plans for the restoration. Our letter added that we would consider installing a permanent tenant in the house or in an adjacent barn to help with oversight and to provide income. We also suggested using some space in the house for an office so the Trust would have a regular presence there. Finally, we said we would pursue an eventual partnership with the National Park Service, which we still hoped might assume oversight of the house from us while we continued to support the property and raise funds for its well-being. Despite the messages we had received about the Park Service's reluctance to commit to the house, we continued to hold out hope that Congress might authorize the Secretary of the Interior to conduct a site assessment and historical survey and allow a process of federal acquisition to begin. Though we were willing to work toward the restoration, members of the Trust's board understood that a small nonprofit like ours might not have the wherewithal to maintain such a culturally significant historic property forever.

During February and March, as we awaited the town's Request for Proposals, the Trust board met several times with Joe Mullin and exchanged numerous emails about how we should respond once the RFP was issued. During that period, we were still thinking of restoring the house to its 1817 appearance, with a newly installed central chimney and lean-to. We also hoped to replace the three existing outbuildings, which were falling down and would soon be removed, with a small barn designed to match the one originally presented by EDCO and approved by Concord's Planning Board back in 1997.

The RFP finally appeared on April 2, several weeks later than expected and too late to ensure a choice of respondent by the time Town Meeting convened later that month. But the document was worth the wait and demonstrated the town's abiding commitment to the birthplace property. To help determine the conditions an applicant would need to fulfill and assess the historic properties of the house, the town had hired McGinley Hart & Associates, a consulting firm of historic architects and preservation planners. The firm conducted a comprehensive historical evaluation of the site and prepared a valuable set of illustrations and design guidelines for the future restoration.

By this time, the house—officially known at the state level as the Wheeler/Minot Farmhouse/Thoreau Birth House—was in the final stages of being approved for listing on the National Register of Historic Places, a process that had been going on for at least two years. To write the text of the application, the Concord Historical Commission had wisely enlisted the services of architectural historian Anne McCarthy Forbes, a local resident, a respected authority, and an early ally of the birthplace effort. Though some consultants had advised against requesting a listing until the restoration had been completed, most of those involved with the property—including McGinley Hart—believed a register listing would serve to establish the site's historical standing once and for all.

The firm determined that the house had been built circa 1730, somewhat earlier than originally thought. Rather than advocating for a single restoration option, as consultant Maximilian Ferro had done in his 1998 study, McGinley Hart highlighted the complicated evolution the house experienced during its long life. "Several architecturally and historically significant features of the house as it existed at its former site, and some that were present at its new location after the move, have since disappeared, making the question of preservation/restoration philosophy a complex one," they wrote in their evaluation. To the prospective new owner, they offered three alternative periods for the dating of a future restoration plan: the period just before and after Thoreau's birth (1814-1818), before the house was moved to its current location; the late-nineteenth-century "tenant farmer period" (ca. 1878), after the house was moved; and the mid-20th-century Colonial Revival period (ca. 1950) during the Breen family's ownership.

Meanwhile, the Thoreau Farm Trust had been working with Joe Mullin since late January on a proposal that would reflect a future partnership arrangement. The plan we put forth in our response to the RFP was based on the funding Mullin had promised to advance and the construction expertise of his for-profit enterprise, the Wellesley Homes Corporation. We also agreed, on Mullin's recommendation, to name Richard Wills, president of the architectural firm of Royal Barry Wills Associates, as our design architect. Mullin's firm had evaluated the house and estimated the cost of a first phase of construction, which would include stabilization and complete restoration of the house, at $1 million. A second phase, the building of the barn, would add an estimated $600,000. The numbers were daunting, and Mullin told us Bay Trust did not have the $1 million in hand but was intending to raise it through a loan and tax credits in advance of a fundraising campaign. The second phase would depend on the success of that campaign. These details differed somewhat from Mullin's initial overture, which was effusive in its offer to advance dollars that seemed to be at the ready. The Trust's board was hesitant to commit under these new circumstances, but extended conversations with Mullin and his associates reassured us that they were acting in good faith and would offer substantial help in raising the necessary funds.

Our other hesitation involved our inability, as a volunteer board, to deliver the educational programming expected to take place at the birth house, which we had initially delegated to EDCO. But the close relationship we had developed in the past year with the Thoreau Society led to a memorandum of understanding designating the Society as a "cooperating organization" that would help design and implement Thoreau-related programming. So though we continued to harbor concerns about the enterprise we were about to launch, the Trust decided to proceed with our response to the RFP, which we delivered by hand on May 2, the deadline day.

The Trust's plans for the house, as expressed in our cover letter, continued to feature the construction of a modest barn. Since our last vision statement, we had sharpened our focus somewhat, and the re-use concept we presented in our RFP response would form the bedrock of our permanent vision. The house, we believed, was ideally suited to become a lasting tribute to Henry David Thoreau, especially in the context of his relationship to his family and community. We also wished to honor the three centuries of farming the house's occupants had perpetuated by working cooperatively with Gaining Ground and offering educational programming on the evolution of farming practices over time. The barn would reflect the vision of Nathaniel Seefurth, though without his imprimatur, by becoming a place where teachers and students could gather to synthesize their educational visit to Concord and include a lecture space for guest speakers. Finally, we sought to honor the community that had rallied to save the historic site by designating an interior space for local groups to meet. We emphasized in our proposal that our plans were devised to treat the house not as a separate entity but as an inextricable part of the land on which it stood.

Looking back now on those early months of 2003, I am struck by the burst of enthusiasm that infused our RFP response. Though we had expected to remain in a dormant state throughout the fiscal year, our response revealed that we had never lost sight of our dream and had built up a great store of potential energy. Court Booth and Jayne Gordon drafted the educational programming component of our proposal; Brian Donahue provided the agricultural overview; Barbara Lambert helped with the restoration planning; and the rest of us offered fundraising, writing, and editing help. We were once again functioning as a cohesive group, led by the indefatigable Joe Wheeler. It felt awfully good to be back.

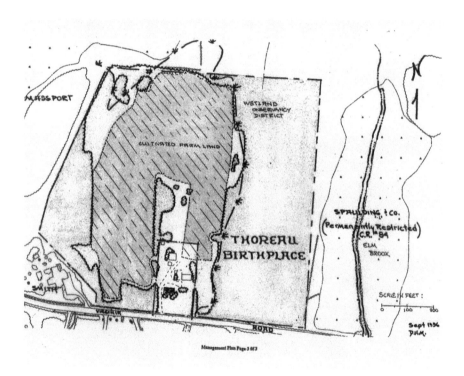

An early, undated rendering of the birthplace property
by Concord's Natural Resources Director Dan Monahan.

XXVI
CHOSEN

Make the most of yourself,
for that is all there is of you.

—Ralph Waldo Emerson

While we and Bay Trust awaited a decision by the town on the responses it had received to the Request for Proposals, selectmen moved to request Town Meeting approval for conveyance of the property to a private individual. Though the current RFP stipulated that submissions must come from corporations, nonprofits or charitable institutions, business associations, or joint ventures, selectmen did not want to take the chance that no appropriate respondent would apply and so sought broad authority to act. Article 48 was moved on April 29 and read as follows:

> To determine whether the Town will vote to authorize the Board of Selectmen to sell for nominal consideration, the property at 341 Virginia Road …, commonly referred to as the "Thoreau Birth House," including 2.5 acres, more or less, together with the structures existing thereon, to any interested individual, group, organization, or public agency, under terms and conditions approved by the Board of Selectmen, provided such buyer agrees to restore the structure to a standard acceptable to the Board and agrees further to preservation covenants to be imposed by the Selectmen, or take any other action relative thereto.

The article passed easily, by a declared majority vote, a development that lent even greater import to the town's deliberations concerning responses to the current RFP.

Only three proposals were received, and two of these were immediately deemed unacceptable because they did not come from entities stipulated in the RFP. So our joint proposal became the only response under consideration by the review committee, which included former Selectmen Sally Schnitzer and Judy Walpole, current selectman Peggy Briggs, Historical Commission member Deborah Bier, and the Concord Library's Curator of Special Collections Leslie

Perrin Wilson. We knew the committee would have concerns about the potential impact of our proposed uses, our partnership with Bay Trust, and our ability to raise the necessary funds, since we could show only the meager $13,000 we currently held in our coffers. So we girded ourselves for a long process of negotiation, which we expected to last at least through the fall.

Meanwhile, the Thoreau Farm Trust board was undergoing a few changes. Our fifth Annual Meeting, on May 13, 2003, included the election of new officers. Court Booth became vice president and John Mack, treasurer. Joe Wheeler had asked to step down from the presidency but agreed to serve as clerk/secretary, and I was elected the new president. Earlier that year, I had changed my last name from Daniel, which I had been using professionally for many years, to my more recent, married name, Stott. I had been reluctant to make the change for a long time but it felt right and proved to be a smooth transition for everyone concerned, though it does make for some confusion on the research front. Most of the other members remained on board, including Helen Bowdoin, Jayne Gordon, Brian Donahue, Désirée Caldwell, Barbara Lambert, Michael Kellett, and Tim Rodgers. Tendering their resignations were former Concord Planning Director Al Lima, who had been a key advocate for saving the birthplace, former EDCO director Jack Green, who had kept working with the Trust long after the EDCO-town negotiations had fallen through, and Concord resident Theresa Cohen, who would remain a loyal supporter and advocate. Now that EDCO's formal involvement at the birthplace had ended, current Executive Director Tom Scott also left the board that year, as expected.

With optimism as our co-pilot, our eleven board members voted to engage development consultant Kristin DeBoer, a staff member at RESTORE, to develop a preliminary fundraising strategy for use in the event we were chosen by the town. Recommended by Michael Kellett, DeBoer was an experienced grant writer and fundraising consultant with a strong interest in Thoreau and the environment, and we were pleased to welcome her to our team.

Meanwhile, the town's hope—and our own—that the birth house would be listed on the National Register of Historic Places continued to be stymied at the state level. Holding up the nomination was the plan, stated in the nomination documents, to reinstall a central chimney and rear lean-to, both features of the house as it existed on its original site when Thoreau was born. Michael Steinitz, who was overseeing our application for the Massachusetts Historical Commission, objected to the addition of any element that was not part of the house after it was moved in 1878. As Max Ferro and others had predicted, the commission demanded a say in how the house would be restored as a condition of its inclusion on the register. While we progressed with our planning, we and the town had to decide which was more important, securing a listing or restoring the house to its 1817 appearance. For the time being, we decided to continue to press our case for a central chimney and lean-to.

Negotiations with the town proceeded deliberately, as we had expected. But by the end of July, we were told that the town had "designated" the Thoreau Farm Trust and Bay Trust to complete the restoration project. Town officials had always hoped to avoid turning the house over to an individual since, among other considerations, private ownership might conflict with the active and sometimes noisy work being conducted on the site by Gaining Ground, which was now welcoming hundreds of volunteers of all ages to the farm. Though Bay Trust was an unknown factor, we were not, so they chose to put their faith in the nonprofit sector.

In order to help us launch a fundraising drive as soon as possible, selectmen offered to write a letter informing us of their decision, even before formal negotiations had begun. The letter stated that the two nonprofits were "actively negotiating" for the purchase of the house and that the town anticipated "a timely transfer of the property." That announcement lent us standing on the property and allowed us to quietly begin implementing the fundraising strategy Kristen DeBoer was helping us develop.

The town's faith in us was great news, of course, and helped sustain our energy while we addressed the many negotiating points needing to be resolved before a "timely" transfer could take place. At the time, the questions and conditions that our joint proposal prompted felt onerous and somewhat deflating. Seen in retrospect, however, they were entirely justified. Had the members of the review committee and the staff of the Department of Planning and Land Management been less vigilant and not held us to high standards, the Trust might have become mired in a partnership agreement that consumed our resources and compromised our vision. As it turned out, throughout the arduous process of responding to the town's strict terms and conditions, we took steps to strengthen our infrastructure, engage expert advice, and solidify our alliances with other local institutions. The lengthy process also gave us the time we needed to examine our planned partnership with Bay Trust more closely—and uncover serious drawbacks to such an arrangement.

XXVII
TAKING ON THE TASK

Nothing can bring you peace but yourself.

—Ralph Waldo Emerson

One of the first things the Thoreau Farm Trust did in the fall of 2003 to build strength and viability was to complete our course in Nonprofits 101 by hiring our first executive director. A few grant makers had told us they would not consider us for an award, no matter how worthy our cause, until we had become more professional in our operation. Common wisdom held that organizations run by volunteers could not sustain the leadership and momentum necessary to complete a long-term project. We also realized that, as committed as we all were to this project, we were busy people who had been at this for a long time. We needed a coxswain to keep us all pulling together. So as we moved toward crafting a partnership with Bay Trust, negotiating with the Town of Concord on a purchase-and-sale agreement, overseeing historic restoration plans, and implementing an ambitious fundraising drive, we made one of our best decisions yet: we hired Molly Eberle to keep us on course. A longtime Concord resident, Eberle was a respected development professional and dedicated town volunteer, known for her hard work, wide-ranging talents, and unmatched organizational skills. She seemed to know everyone in Concord and was well acquainted with all the town officials we were working with. We knew Eberle was the perfect match for us, and to our delight, she agreed to sign on as our part-time executive director beginning that fall.

Another key decision came as a result of the town's objection to our choice of design architect Richard Wills, president of Royal Barry Wills Associates. Wills's firm had been very successful at designing historic reproductions, but the town's representatives did not believe he was qualified to plan for and design the complex, nuanced restoration that the Thoreau birth house required. Carol Kowalski, a knowledgeable member of Marcia Rasmussen's planning staff, offered us a list of historic architects the town would accept to lead the design effort. With the expert help of board member Barbara Lambert, we chose two of these to interview that fall: Lawrence Sorli, an independent architect from the neighboring town of Carlisle, and William Finch of Finch and Rose, from the North Shore town of Beverly.

Sorli and Finch each toured the house and then sat for separate interviews at Joe Mullin's office complex at Clock Tower Place in Maynard. Sorli had extensive experience as a design architect and project manager and had spent ten years working as a historic architect for the National Park Service. At the time of his interview, he had been working as an independent contractor and had been chosen to complete several important historic preservation projects, both as a design architect and project manager. Finch ran a preservation design and consulting firm with his wife, Carol Rose, and had an excellent reputation as a historic materials conservator. He had also spent several years as a historic architect for the Massachusetts Historical Commission. Both were well versed in the Department of the Interior's Standards for Treatment of Historic Properties and capable of offering us valuable advice about how to proceed with restoration planning that would not remove the house from consideration for listing on the National Register of Historic Places.

Luckily, we never had to make the difficult choice between Larry Sorli and Bill Finch. They were both excited by what they had seen of the house and asked if they could present us with a joint proposal to work together. Their enthusiasm, which we welcomed along with their joint proposal, marked a turning point in our own attitude toward the restoration project. Sorli and Finch had looked through the deterioration that was so distressing to our untrained eyes and seen the treasure beneath it. They might very well have been channeling Thoreau himself, who famously wrote in his journal, "The question is not what you look at, but what you see."

All three of the people we engaged in our work that year were in it for the cause, not for the money. Molly Eberle accepted an inordinately modest salary for her extraordinary work, and Larry Sorli and Bill Finch agreed to start with a small project and accept payment when we could afford to make it. They were all clearly smitten with the project, and their generosity went a long way toward allowing us to move ahead within our limited means, acquired through board member donations and a small number of annual gifts from other loyal supporters.

Our first contract with Sorli and Finch covered an initial phase of the restoration project. They would evaluate the house, propose a restoration and an "adaptive re-use" plan, and engage with the Massachusetts Historical Commission on our behalf to facilitate a listing on the National Register. They promised to complete this first scope of work by Nov. 30. The confidence and enthusiasm these two projected reinvigorated us all, and we finally felt we were on the right path to determining exactly what should be done to bring Thoreau's birth house back to life.

With Molly Eberle on board, we proceeded through our negotiations with the town, which ranged from word changes in our developing agreement to important site plan details and deed restrictions. We would be allowed to secure permitting approvals from the appropriate town boards during the negotiation stage, which meant we would be poised to begin stabilization work immediately upon signing a purchase-and-sale agreement. Most of the initial negotiating points would run through numerous iterations before they became final the following spring, but a few of the most important early conditions would stand. The most important of these—and the one that would occupy the Thoreau Farm Trust for the next several years—was that the town would convey title to the house and two acres of land for $1 only after we had procured funds and pledges totaling $800,000, the estimated cost of a complete restoration of the house.

We did not balk at that requirement, believing it to be based on sound judgment. Instead, we enlisted our new executive director to help us get started on a systematic fundraising campaign. The strategy drawn up by our consultant Kristen DeBoer called for a long-term fundraising goal of $2.15 million and included house restoration, barn construction, landscaping, design consultants, educational programming, startup costs, administration and overhead, and the initiation of an endowment. In light of that enormous figure, the $800,000 required for taking title seemed manageable. One of our board members noted that we had only to convince 800 people to give $1,000 each to reach our goal. But—just in case that didn't work—we began exploring grant opportunities. The residents of Concord had stepped up to help purchase the birthplace property, and though many of these early supporters would continue to contribute, we knew we would have to reach well beyond the Concord area for potential major donors. As we shared contacts and drew up our list of possibilities, we encouraged each other to "think big and think far."

Despite the urgent need to raise funds, we knew we could not create fundraising materials or approach foundations, government agencies, and other major donors without a thoughtful plan for how the house would be restored and re-used. We also felt we needed the National Register listing to confirm the value of the property we would be asking others to support. So though we sent out an end-of-year solicitation to early supporters, we relied on Sorli and Finch to help us articulate a plan that we, and the Massachusetts Historical Commission, could embrace.

They did not let us down. In only a few weeks' time, they presented findings that took into account our wishes, the state's guidelines, and their own assessment. They believed we and the house would be best served by opting for an acceptable standard of historic preservation called "restoration and rehabilitation." This treatment would allow any existing 18th-century features, both exterior and interior, to be restored. Since the birth room had barely been touched over time, much of it could be restored to its 1817 appearance under this standard, but reconstruction of a central chimney and rear lean-to would not be allowed. A new addition could be constructed, perhaps to house office space, as long as it did not impart a false sense of history to the house by appearing to have been there in the past. It would have to be distinguished in some way from the 18th-century structure. Sorli and Finch said they were prepared to make the case that the 20th-century alternations carried no historical significance and so could be altered or removed.

Most of us on the Trust board liked this option, but a few members preferred a plan that would include a central chimney and lean-to. So we invited Sorli and Finch to meet at the house with a group of us and representatives from the Massachusetts Historical Commission, including Michael Steinitz. At that gathering, which took place in December, we presented the alternatives and asked for advice on which direction to take. If we had not been sufficiently convinced before, that meeting proved to us the enormous benefit of having Sorli and Finch on our team. Commission representatives enthusiastically supported their restoration/rehabilitation plan and, satisfied that we had engaged the help of excellent preservationists, agreed to recommend to the National Park Service that the house be listed on the National Register of Historic Places, a designation that finally became official in March 2004. Their positive response ended our debate: there would be no replacement of a central chimney or rear lean-to.

We approached the new year with renewed confidence in our ability to meet the challenge the town had given us. We now had a clear plan in mind and an executive director helping us design an informational brochure and implement a fundraising strategy. Bay Trust participated in most of our important decisions throughout the fall and into 2004, including our hiring of Sorli and Finch and our ongoing negotiations with the town. But Joe Mullin and his associates had not been as active as we had imagined they would be, especially on the financial front. Our end-of-year fund drive added $13,000 to our coffers, but Bay Trust responded with a pledge of only $2,500, to be donated when a purchase-and-sale agreement had been signed.

It is quite possible Mullin and his colleagues had been put off by the town's strict conditions. Though the review committee accepted our joint response to the RFP, town officials did not want to work with two entities. As a result, we had come to a joint decision that the Thoreau Farm Trust would become the sole deed holder and Bay Trust would serve in a consulting capacity. But the refusal to allow Bay Trust's chosen architect, Barry Wills, to design the restoration project was likely perceived as a lack of confidence. Bay Trust was a nonprofit arm of the Wellesley Management Group, and Mullin and his colleagues had assumed we would contract with their preferred designer and in-house contractor for the birthplace project. The fact that officials insisted on a town-approved historic architect having the final word on restoration planning and construction decisions would likely complicate the working relationship we would have with Bay Trust's people.

Whatever the reasons, we were beginning to feel a cooling of interest on the part of Bay Trust at the same time that our own interest had been re-ignited. This feeling was heightened when, in March, Bay Trust presented us with a joint venture agreement that we had agreed to negotiate with them. Their proposed draft indicated that the two nonprofits would form a limited liability company (LLC) that Bay Trust would manage, receiving 7.5 percent of any expenditures coming out of the new company to cover its own costs. When the property was conveyed by the town, the new company would hold the title until the project was completed. This last point ran counter to Bay Trust's earlier agreement that the Thoreau Farm Trust would be sole owner.

While the agreement did not seem unreasonable from a business standpoint, it contradicted some of Bay Trust's earlier statements of support, particularly the promise to advance funds for the project. It did not seem to us that the proposal was in the spirit of our earlier understanding. If Bay Trust advanced us the funds to restore the house in the way Mullin had initially said it would, we could satisfy the town's fundraising requirement immediately upon signing a purchase-and-sale document. But that offer of advance funds had receded into deep background.

By this time, we had developed a warm, trusting relationship with Sorli and Finch, who told us they saw no obstacles to carrying on the design and construction project without Bay Trust's help. In the absence of an advance from Bay Trust, which would have accelerated the restoration work, we saw no reason to tie ourselves to the constraints of a partnership. The town would agree to grant us two years to raise the necessary $800,000, and we felt we could meet that challenge with the help of the educational and cultural alliances we had forged. So on April 8, 2004, the Thoreau Farm Trust voted unanimously to disengage from any partnership arrangement with Bay Trust.

Joe Mullin agreed that pursuing our plans for a partnership would not be in the interest of either organization, and we ended our relationship on cordial terms. In a joint letter to Planning Director Marcia Rasmussen, who had overseen the town's Request for Proposals, Mullin and I asked that Bay Trust be removed as a joint designee for the restoration project and that the designation be transferred exclusively to the Thoreau Farm Trust. I had already prepared town officials for this letter, so they were not surprised by the request and, in fact, had already expressed their support for it.

At our Annual Meeting in May 2004, the Trust's board re-elected our four officers, Court Booth, Joe Wheeler, John Mack, and me, and accepted the resignation of Concord Museum Director Désirée Caldwell, who would remain a valuable ally in the years ahead. Other members continuing on the board were Jayne Gordon, Barbara Lambert, Helen Bowdoin, Michael Kellett, Brian Donahue, and Tim Rodgers.

We looked forward to signing a purchase-and-sale agreement with the town within weeks. Once again, we had received the pro bono support of Hale and Dorr to help us review and adapt the intricate language of the multiple drafts, which had taken several months. With the final version now completed, we expected to be on the Board of Selectmen's agenda in June. It was an exciting prospect, but also a daunting one: when we signed that document, we would be doing it on our own.

Gaining Ground expands at Thoreau Farm.

XXVIII
"COME CELEBRATE!"

Celebrate not the Garden of Eden, but your own.

—H.D. Thoreau, Journal

On the evening of June 28, 2004, the Thoreau Farm Trust's board members were invited to attend the Concord Board of Selectmen's meeting. As the local cable station's camera rolled and friends and family looked on, I took the long-awaited step of signing a document that would bind us to the Thoreau birth house for the foreseeable future. Signing on behalf of the town were Selectmen Virginia McIntyre, chair; Anne D. Shapiro; Philip H. Benincasa; Joseph Lenox III; and Margaret B. Briggs.

After all that time and effort, one would think the event itself would have felt anticlimactic. It did not. We were a little giddy at finally reaching this milestone, and we knew we had many more miles to go. It was gratifying to receive the town's blessing at last. It was also clear that town officials were once again taking a leap of faith, and we were once again leaping with them.

By the time we signed the purchase-and-sale agreement, the town had increased the amount of land it was leasing to Gaining Ground. The farm now occupied eighteen of the twenty acres, and our deed would include the remaining two. The purchase price for the house and the two acres would be $1. As agreed, we would not take title to the property until we had demonstrated that we had raised $800,000 for the complete restoration/rehabilitation of the historic house, and we would have two years to complete that requirement. In the meantime, we would work on gaining all the permitting approvals for our site plan and construction design, and we would pay to insure the property throughout the two years we were raising the funds to restore it.

Having succeeded in our wish to sign our agreement with the town before July 12, Thoreau's 187th birthday, we were ready to celebrate. *The Concord Journal* and *The Boston Globe* printed lengthy features on the purchase-and-sale news, which served to remind readers of the long history of the preservation effort.

Selectmen agreed to join us on July 12 for a signing celebration at the birth house, which would correspond with the Thoreau Society's Annual Gathering. Besides sending out press releases to publicize the event and announcing it to Thoreau Society members, the Trust mailed printed invitations to all past donors of the project, including those who had contributed to the original purchase. We also invited past board members and selectmen, our neighbors on and near Virginia Road, staff members from the Town of Concord, Bay Trust associates, and representatives from other historical sites around town. As our list of invitees lengthened, we were struck by the large number of people who had become involved in the preservation project in the previous nine years. It was inspiring to recall the partnerships that had started it all, and we were buoyed by the large number of early adopters who had remained engaged in the effort and the dozens who had joined them in the intervening time.

The event drew about seventy-five enthusiasts, many of whom had not been to the house before. Selectman Anne Shapiro told the crowd she and fellow board members were proud of the work that had already been done to save the historic property. "Many Concord citizens and others answered the needs of the property," she said. "I'm thrilled and humbled by the efforts of our citizens."

The Trust's Joe Wheeler evoked the memory of his mother, Concord historian and journalist Ruth Wheeler, who had taken an active interest in the house that had been moved from the Virginia Road site where she was raising her own family. "She was interested in preserving this historic house but didn't think it was possible," said Wheeler. "Now, I think we've found the formula."

One of the guests at the party was Mark Thoreau, who had traveled from London, England. A distant relative of Henry David—third cousin five times removed—he had just been interviewed by the BBC about his famous cousin and pronounced the plan to restore the birthplace "absolutely brilliant."

We at the Thoreau Farm Trust took advantage of the opportunity to outline our plans for the property. These included a Phase I restoration/rehabilitation project—our first priority—which would involve restoring the exterior of the house to its appearance at the time it was moved in 1878; restoring the birth room to its 1817 appearance; and rehabilitating the rest of the interior for re-use, with all the existing historic fabric preserved. When additional funds had been raised beyond what was needed for the restoration/rehabilitation project, the next two phases would involve implementing educational programming on Thoreau-related subjects and agricultural history, and constructing a modest barn for limited use by students and teachers.

The joyful comments, full of possibility and promise, helped soothe the sight of the house's peeling paint and crumbling interior. After the brief remarks were done, we all savored slices of cake that proclaimed, "Happy Birthday, Henry!"

A Celebration!

The Thoreau Farm Trust
and
The Town of Concord

Invite you to join us to celebrate
the signing of a Purchase & Sale Agreement

Monday, July 12, 2004
(Henry David Thoreau's birthday)
4:00 p.m.
the Thoreau Birth House
341 Virginia Road, Concord, MA

Come share in the good news and hear
the Thoreau Farm Trust's plans for rehabilitation and
restoration of this historic property now listed on the
National Register of Historic Places.

www.thoreaufarm.org

One of Nicholas Reed's landscape designs.

XXIX

"THE REAL WORK HAS NOW BEGUN"

As a cure for worrying, work is better than whiskey.

—Ralph Waldo Emerson

Once the celebrations had ended, the Thoreau Farm Trust board turned to face the challenge of raising $800,000 in two years, that is, by June 2006. We were ten volunteers aided in our efforts by a ten-hour-per-week executive director. We had lost two partners since our incorporation in 1998, both of which were forced in the end to yield to the multiple demands of their respective organizations. Each of these, EDCO and Bay Trust, Inc., had offered valuable assistance that helped shape our plans for the house and carry on worthwhile negotiations with the Town of Concord. But neither was able to stay the course.

On the one hand, our ability to make our own decisions would allow the Trust to act nimbly to surmount or circumvent obstacles. We would be able to set or change direction with a single vote. On the other hand, though we may not have had the institutional demands that EDCO and Bay Trust had to consider, we felt a strong responsibility to the people who had helped save the property and to the town officials and staff who had expended so much time and patience to bring us to this point. Selectman Anne Shapiro had said at the July 12 celebration that she was "thrilled and humbled." We were experiencing the very same emotions, along with a feeling that would accompany us through the next several years and often wake us in the night: anxiety. We did not want to let anyone down.

Luckily, we were the grateful beneficiaries of support from many quarters. In late summer, we enlisted the help of Concord resident Ellen Foley Rice, who had worked as a development professional for Harvard's Kennedy School of Government and was currently raising her family and serving as a consultant and community volunteer. Rice agreed to work closely with Executive Director Molly Eberle on our fundraising materials and the implementation of our strategy. We also instituted an Advisory Board composed of local educators, historians, environmentalists, neighbors, historic house lovers, and Gaining

Ground representatives, many of whom had been active in the effort to save the property from development. The first members of the Advisory Board included landscape architect J. Walter Brain; educator Susan Curtin; writer Stona Fitch, president of Gaining Ground's board; historian Anne McCarthy Forbes; teacher and neighbor Heidi Kaiter; Concord resident and historic house enthusiast Linda Painter; Minute Man National Park re-enactor D. Michael Ryan; and library archivist and historian Leslie Perrin Wilson. Finally, we designated our erstwhile colleagues—Joe Valentine, Al Lima, Theresa Cohen, Jack Green, and Désirée Caldwell—as Board Members Emeriti to honor their past efforts on behalf of the birth house and recognize their continuing interest in the work. There was both truth and irony in our message to these former board members informing them of the purchase-and-sale agreement. "After seven years of effort, the *real* work has now begun," we wrote to each of them. I can only hope they smiled.

Architects Larry Sorli and Bill Finch became active members of our growing team and influenced every major decision we made over the next several months. They continued to examine the house to determine how much original fabric remained, and each time they reported their findings to us, they seemed more excited about what they had found and what they hoped to do to bring the house alive again. Sorli brought in a landscape designer, Nicholas Reed, whom we hired to help us imagine what the revived house could look like on the land immediately around it and how it could be integrated smoothly into the farm atmosphere of the entire property. The result of many discussions and drafts, Reed's final rendering served as an evocative illustration for the four-color fundraising brochure we were developing. Like a photo of your more ideal self on the refrigerator door, his landscape designs allowed us to see what the ruined house could become, and that helped us stay focused on our goal.

After receiving an anonymous gift of $25,000 to launch our capital campaign following the July 12 celebration, the Thoreau Farm Trust recorded assets of $39,325.33 in the fall of 2004. Our expenses at that point were minimal, and we were working with a projected annual operating budget of $21,000, which included a $5,000 contingency for unexpected needs. Our executive director worked from home, and our outlay included a small salary, the cost of insuring the property, and minor expenses to cover office supplies, events, fundraising materials, and mailings. Our strategy for staying solvent involved using income from annual fund donations for operational needs and reserving capital grants and gifts—those designated for the restoration and rehabilitation of the house—for the design work by Sorli, Finch, and Reed, and the future construction project.

To help build advocacy for the house and support for our capital campaign, we decided to reach out to a group we had not previously engaged: owners of historic properties. Concord alone boasted approximately 175 antique houses built before 1850. Thoreau Farm Trust board member John Mack and his wife, Lorna, lived in one of the oldest of these, the circa 1650 Thomas Dane House on Lexington Road. The Macks offered to host a house tour and reception, so we made their warm, welcoming home the center of our first major cultivation event. Held on Oct. 3, the afternoon began next door to the Macks' home, at the Concord Art Association. Upstairs in one of the gallery spaces, Bill Finch gave an illustrated talk on some of the original historic elements he and Larry Sorli had found in the Thoreau birth house. The sixty-five guests, old-house aficionados all, appeared mesmerized. Even those of us from the Trust, who were more aware of the architects' meticulous examination of the house's structure, found the amount of historic fabric that still existed in the house surprising—in the best possible way. It was becoming clearer and clearer to us that the town had saved something truly precious. Finch's talk was slated to last about twenty minutes but was prolonged far beyond that. The questions just kept on coming.

The audience for that event also responded enthusiastically to the news that the Thoreau Society had begun discussions with us about relocating their headquarters to a portion of the rehabilitated birth house. Not only would the Society provide regular income for the house's upkeep in the form of rent, but its executive director and members would become on-site partners with the Trust in designing educational programs. It would be an ideal situation for both organizations and would fulfill the promise to the property's original donors that education—about Thoreau and his legacy as well as the history of agriculture—would become a major activity at the site. As we had expected, the more concrete our plans, the more interest they inspired, and we were gratified by the spontaneous applause that followed the announcement.

Our efforts to get the word out about the Thoreau Farm Trust's plans for the restored and rehabilitated birth house and the urgency of our fundraising deadline started to show results in the final months of 2004. We received more than $21,000 from our end-of-year annual appeal letter, enough to cover our year's projected operating budget.

Our capital campaign was on its way, with $42,663 in donations. An endowment fund was also begun in our name, seeded by an anonymous donor who had invested $100,000 in a charitable gift annuity through the Greater Lowell Community Foundation. The Trust was designated as the beneficiary of annual income from the annuity for the purposes designated by its board of directors. The small endowment fund was an important development for the Trust. Though it generated only about $5,000 in annual income, it signaled an understanding of our long-term commitment and our sense of fiscal responsibility. It would obviously be a long time before we had raised sufficient funds to accomplish even our short-term goals, but the presence of a budding endowment served to remind everyone that we were putting down roots.

XXX

HOW MANY BALLS CAN WE KEEP IN THE AIR?

It is not enough to be industrious; so are the ants.
What are you industrious about?

—H.D. Thoreau, letter to H.D.O. Blake

At the start of 2005, we were already six months into our two-year quest to find $800,000. By that time, we had mastered the art of juggling. Many of us had to bring our A-games to our day jobs, and even our few retirees were involved in a number of time-consuming community activities. But the demands of the Trust's work required unusual dexterity. We had to begin a systematic capital campaign. To do so, we needed a clear idea of what the house and grounds would look like. So we worked simultaneously on fundraising plans and a site plan design.

Ellen Foley Rice, our fundraising consultant, gave us an "I-needed-that" whack in the head in March 2005 when she pointed out, in a detailed strategy document, the differences between a traditional capital campaign and our own. The Trust had no time for a feasibility study, no current short list identifying our best leadership prospects, and a very short timeline that had already been reduced to sixteen months. We would have to combine the early phase of a traditional campaign (preparation of materials, timeline, and specific goals) and the quiet phase (solicitation of board and leadership gifts). Once we had raised at least 50 percent of the funds, we could go public with a wider appeal. Rice estimated that, to meet our deadline of June 30, 2006, we would have to have raised that 50 percent by the end of October, a most ambitious goal.

At the same time, our architects and landscape designer were meeting regularly with us to determine a workable site plan that we could share at events and in our case statement. We had drafted language for the brochure, and selected a variety of photographs and drawings to illustrate it, but it still contained a placeholder for the landscape rendering. In particular, we had to decide whether or not to build a new ell, an addition that must remain architecturally distinct from the historic portion of the house to satisfy the Massachusetts Historical Commission's requirements. The new structure would accommodate rental space, accessible bathrooms, and possibly an elevator to the upstairs birth room.

We were also in frequent discussions with the town's Planning Department about the location of a permanent, half-moon driveway to the west of the house that the Trust would share with Gaining Ground, whose heavy farm vehicles demanded a more solid surface than the packed, earthen driveway they had been using. This might seem like a mundane concern, but it was not. The Trust was determined to establish a cooperative working relationship with Gaining Ground, but we realized as well that the needs of the two organizations were not always complementary. We wanted visitors to the house to arrive at a welcoming place that was easy to find and pleasant to view. Sharing the proposed driveway with a working farm meant asking our visitors arriving from the west, that is, from Concord Center, to enter the property before they could see the house and travel along a circuitous path frequently rutted by truck wheels. It was not ideal, and we hoped to resume discussions once the house was reopened for use. But at the time, we felt it best to accept the town's plan. Among other considerations, there were safety issues related to the number of entrances and exits we should open on a winding, well-traveled road, and we did not want to cause undue complications over aesthetics.

Yet we *were*, in fact, concerned about aesthetics. The town's staff did its best with the time they had to prevent the property from becoming overrun. But the Trust decided to host a spring cleanup day in early April to help out. Board members and their spouses and children were joined by neighbors, including several from the new Elm Brook housing development across the road, and other friends of the project, as we raked up winterkill and debris, and weeded the still thriving rhubarb patch. When we saw how many people came to help and how much they enjoyed being at the house and working to spiff it up a bit, we realized we should plan more participatory events that would highlight the special feel of the property. The interior was still in a pitiful state, but just being around the grounds seemed to buoy people's spirits, and that helped lift our own.

A bit later in April, the Trust signed a rental agreement with the Thoreau Society. In 1995, after the closing of the Thoreau Lyceum, the Society had moved its offices to the newly created Thoreau Institute in Lincoln. Then in 2003, the offices were moved back to Concord, to a small house owned by the National Park Service, while the Society's extensive Thoreau collections remained in the climate-controlled archives of the Institute, where they continue to be made available by appointment to scholars, teachers, and students.

The Society's executive director at the time was Jayne Gordon, also a founding member of the Thoreau Farm Trust. Once the Trust had succeeded in securing a purchase-and-sale agreement for the birth house, Gordon began speaking with the Society's board members—who had once considered trying to purchase the house for the Society—about moving its offices there, and they had voted in favor of the idea in January. Gordon and I had been in conversation ever since, and on April 11, we issued a joint press release announcing the plans to share habitation of the birthplace, the Trust as owner and the Society as tenant.

"We are delighted to announce this development," wrote Gordon. "Our members all over the country and in so many other nations have come to recognize the importance of having our headquarters in this very special place." On the Trust's behalf, I called the arrangement "a perfect fit for us," adding, "the Society will provide a quiet but significant presence at the house while adding enormous educational value to our whole enterprise." We offered the Society space upstairs, on the western side of the house, but we were still in the throes of deciding whether or not to build an ell at the rear that would make the house more comfortable for our tenants.

Meanwhile, we continued our effort to present our project to potential funders with the help of new and old friends. One of our newest friends, Linda Painter, had joined our Advisory Board after attending the event for antique-house lovers the previous fall. She and her husband, Whit, owned an 18th-century home and barn on Monument Street, which they agreed to open for a reception and tour on April 24. A small but enthusiastic group of interested residents attended the gathering in the Painters' cozy front room, listened to a lively presentation by architect Larry Sorli, and offered excellent advice about how we could continue to spread the word about what we were doing. Little by little, event by event, our advocacy group was widening its reach.

One objective that gained strength in the spring of 2005 was our desire to make the restoration/rehabilitation project "green." We had always believed it would be important to honor Thoreau's legacy by considering the environmental impact of what we were creating. Now that restoration plans were under way, it was time to act on that belief. Larry Sorli and Bill Finch were agreeable to the idea, but they warned us against doing anything that would compromise the original features they were uncovering in their ongoing investigations. The realization that we would need to find a workable balance between "green" and historic brought to light an unanticipated way the house could carry meaning into the future. It could become a model for owners of historic properties seeking ways to lighten their environmental impact while retaining the timeless beauty that had drawn them to their houses in the first place. To help us advance this idea, we turned to the Concord Green Team.

The Green Team is a group of local volunteers with professional expertise in sustainable building and other environmental practices. Town officials enlist the team's advice on new municipal facilities and other matters. The group's website features a portrait of Thoreau next to an invitation: "Have a low-impact living question? Want to reduce your carbon footprint? Ask Henry." Visitors to the site can click on the link—and they do—and receive answers to their questions. The Green Team's stated goals are "to ensure consideration of energy and resource conservation, as well as other sustainable practices, in all town projects."

As we had hoped, Green Team members were happy to meet with us and offered many valuable suggestions over the next several years. We had drawn up a one-page outline of our objectives, entitled "What Distinguishes This Project," which highlighted our educational programs encompassing Thoreauvian principles and agricultural history, and our plan for a community meeting room. With the Green Team's help, we were able to add language reflecting the Trust's commitment to environmentally sensitive design practices. The team, led by our liaison Andy Proulx, would continue to provide advice to our architects, who evaluated their suggestions and incorporated into their plans as many as they could without destroying historic fabric. This meaningful collaboration became just one more partnership in the many that had propelled the project forward from the start—and without which it never could have advanced as far as it had.

Two underground concrete tanks on the west side of the house
provide a gray water system.

Joe Wheeler (left) and Larry Sorli remove linoleum from the house.

Richard Fahlander dismantles a baseboard heater from
Thoreau's birth room.

Nancy McJennett scrapes off peeling
wallpaper from the kitchen.

XXXI

"NOT YET READY FOR *HOUSE BEAUTIFUL*"

*The invariable mark of wisdom is
to see the miraculous in the common.*

—Ralph Waldo Emerson

The start of our new fiscal year, July 1, 2005, marked the halfway point in our tight, two-year fundraising requirement. Besides not having the time for a traditional capital campaign, we found ourselves weathering a difficult philanthropic climate. Public funds were scarce throughout the country, and nonprofits were competing for many of the same dollars. Local residents had already been asked to contribute to the property when the town purchased it in 1997, and they were now being solicited for a number of other worthy projects, including a renovation of the much-loved Concord Free Public Library. So, in our first year of fundraising, we had not seen the hoped-for rush to contribute. On July 13, our treasurer reported just over $49,000 in capital gifts. The good news was that we were having no trouble meeting our lean operating budget and staying solvent for the work ahead.

The disappointing capital gift figure was a bit deceptive, because it didn't reflect the work we had done throughout the past year to raise awareness and solicit gifts we hoped would materialize in the near future. Our energy remained high and was boosted by the addition of three new board members. At our Annual Meeting in June, we welcomed to the board Richard Fahlander, Ellen Foley Rice, and our executive director, Molly Eberle. Fahlander had been my colleague at *The Concord Journal* during the years we covered the property acquisition and was currently working as an event planner and fundraiser for the Wellness Center in Wellesley, Massachusetts. Rice had been our fundraising consultant and expressed a desire to volunteer her services in a more general way moving forward. And Eberle, who had been putting in many more hours than the ten per week for which she had contracted, wanted to move out of her staff position and become part of the citizens' group that was leading the effort. None of the sitting board members—Joe Wheeler, Court

Booth, John Mack, Barbara Lambert, Helen Bowdoin, Brian Donahue, Tim Rodgers, Jayne Gordon, Michael Kellett, and I—chose to step away, so our lucky number was raised to thirteen. All three new members had already been involved with the Trust's work in some capacity. As it had done with so many of us, the project had grabbed them and wouldn't let go. Fahlander brought to our work his gifts as a writer, event planner, intrepid handyman, and creative thinker. Foley brought her fundraising acumen, which had already guided us through the early stages of our effort. And Eberle continued to bring her organizational skills, gift for clarity, and wide-ranging community connections to everything we did.

Eberle's move to the board created an opening for a new executive director. We received several excellent responses to our ads, but by far the best came from a young woman named Nancy Tevnan Grohol. Grohol held a master's degree in management from Brandeis University and had served as a development officer at the American Textile History Museum in Lowell, Massachusetts, and most recently, at the USS Constitution Museum in Charlestown. Besides this relevant work with nonprofit historical organizations, Grohol had also been a volunteer with three community agencies in the Greater Lowell area and had served on the board of directors of SuitAbility, an agency serving women seeking employment. We were immediately taken with Grohol's fresh energy and enthusiasm for the project and were delighted when she accepted a 20-hour-per-week position as our new executive director, beginning in mid-July. In a move that we would come to know as characteristic of her, Grohol asked to take home books about Thoreau and all the Trust's file folders so she could learn as much as possible before her official start date.

One of the reasons our own energy never flagged during that summer of 2005 was that we remained in perpetual motion. Our illustrated case statement, entitled "A New Life For Thoreau Farm," was completed and printed in June, with a landscape drawing minus the ell, which we were still debating. It contained a brief history of the property, a description of its significance, a detailed explanation of our plans for the house, and a presentation of our financial need. We were very proud of the brochure, which had been beautifully designed, at a significantly reduced rate, by the talented graphic artist Irene Chu. We sent it around to town officials and, from then on, used it in all our initial communications with potential funders and interested parties.

During that same month, board member John Mack worked with Molly Eberle and other board volunteers to deliver gifts of Thoreau Farm rhubarb to the homes of major donors to the project, along with our new brochure and a note of gratitude for their past support. It was an idea worthy of Henry himself, who loved to go a-berry picking with local children and deliver gifts of the land to his friends throughout town. The whimsical nature of the gift delighted those who received it, and more than one returned the favor with a freshly made pie.

My own favorite activity of that busy summer, but only in retrospect, was our massive cleanup of the house's interior, which happened on June 25, one of the hottest, most humid days of the summer. That morning, with temperatures already reaching ninety degrees, eleven volunteers donned our gloves and masks, picked up our tools and cleaning supplies, and got to work. By noon, we had lifted off layers of soiled linoleum, removed electric heating vents, scraped peeling paint, hauled out rusty appliances (some of which had to be thrown down from a rear upstairs window), and mowed the high grass. At the end of our workday, we had filled the dumpster the Department of Public Works had graciously supplied. As I wrote in an op-ed piece for the July 14 *Concord Journal*, "The place might not be ready for *House Beautiful* just yet, but we will feel better now about showing people in and helping them get to know this special place, the story of its agricultural past, and the rich promise of its future."

Historic architect Larry Sorli on cleanup day 2005.

A week later, after dusting ourselves off and cooling down a bit, a number of us set up and staffed a table at Picnic in the Park, Concord's annual July 4 celebration held at Emerson Field. Filled with materials about our birthplace project, our table drew a good number of passersby and even some unexpected donations to the cause. One town resident dipped into her purse, extracted her checkbook, and handed us a $1,000 gift and her best wishes for success. That was a day we would remember.

Then, on July 10, we hosted a Community Open House to coincide with the Thoreau Society's Annual Gathering in town. Between servings of Thoreau birthday cake and lemonade, we took visitors on tours of the house, a few at a time, informing them along the way of our plans for the spaces. As usual, the slow, careful trip up the damaged stairs to the second floor produced an intake of breath as people entered the birth room. I recognized this response from my own first visit back in 1996. The power of the room to stir those who enter continues to be a source of wonderment to this day.

From left, Nancy McJennett, Tim Rodgers, Lucille Stott, Joe Wheeler, Jack Nevison, Richard Fahlander, Heidi Kaiter, Sandy Stott, John Mack.

XXXII

THE LOSS OF OUR "BENEVOLENT WARRIOR"

*The year has many seasons more
than are recognized in the almanac.*

—H.D. Thoreau, Journal

Because Nancy Grohol lived out of town, we needed a space in Concord where our new executive director could work in close proximity to the birth house. With the help of board member Court Booth, who could always be counted on to "make some calls," we made an important and lasting connection with the Concord Chamber of Commerce. Beginning in September 2005, the Chamber's executive director, Stephanie Stillman, offered us free of charge an unused space in their offices at 15 Walden Street. "The Chamber's mission is to promote the Concord business community and support tourism," Stillman wrote in a press release at the time. "The Thoreau birthplace will be an outstanding addition to the existing cultural resources of Concord, which attract tourists and customers to the town. We're happy to donate the use of our extra office space to the Thoreau Farm Trust as they move forward with their plans."

Stillman had told us this arrangement would be temporary. But after she had met and begun working with Nancy Grohol, she realized she had found a kindred spirit: an upbeat, generous woman devoted to her job. As it turned out, Grohol would continue to use that office space until several years later when the birth house finally became habitable, and the Concord Chamber of Commerce would become one of our greatest allies in advocating for support among local businesses and foundations. The Chamber's generosity also allowed us to continue working with a lean operating budget, even though we had doubled the hours of our executive director.

Grohol wasted no time in getting up to speed on the history of the house and the Trust's work up to that point. By the time she took over her job, she had also reread *Walden* and excerpts from Thoreau's journals. She was a natural front woman for the birth house, because her love of Thoreau and enthusiasm for the project were entirely genuine. She forged warm relationships with everyone she met, and her can-do spirit infused us all with energy for the steep fundraising slope we needed to climb. Within a few weeks of her tenure, she had scheduled two open houses at the birthplace, a community gathering on Sept. 18, and a family-oriented pumpkin party on Oct. 16. These events were intended to put as many people as possible in contact with the house and allow them to feel its draw. She also engaged board members Fahlander and Rice to work on finding a local craftsman who would create a sign for the front lawn so the house's significance would be recognized by passersby.

Of course, Grohol's primary focus was on fundraising. She spent most of her time researching and writing grant applications and working with the board to identify and meet with individuals and business owners who might be interested in lending financial support.

Larry Sorli and Bill Finch completed their meticulous study of the birth house in mid-September and began drafting a master plan for the restoration/rehabilitation process. They promised us a schematic design by Jan. 1 and continued to lobby for the construction of a new addition, in the form of an ell at the rear of the house. Sorli, in particular, believed we would want to construct such an addition at some point and felt it would be better to do it while work on the rest of the house was under way. Still divided, the board chose to wait for more information about the cost of the ell and how the house might function without it.

Because we were now opening the house to visitors and potential donors, we worked together to draft a set of questions and answers about its history, the story of its acquisition, and our plans for its re-use in order to provide consistent and accurate information. Since he joined the board, Tim Rodgers had been working on creating and enhancing a Thoreau Farm Trust website, and we put the polished version of our Q & A on the site, which had begun to attract a number of visitors.

Absent from our Sept. 26 board meeting was one of our more tireless workers, who had braved those 90-plus temperatures to help clear out the house in late June. John Mack was visiting England with his wife, Lorna, that night and, the following day, he died suddenly in London. It was devastating news. At 81, John was one of the most vital, energetic, fiercely committed men any of us had ever known, and he had more than once roused us to action on behalf of the Thoreau birthplace. Anna Winter Rasmussen, founder of the Concord nonprofit Save Our Heritage and a generous supporter of our birthplace efforts through her family foundation, was one of John and Lorna's dear friends. In a note to Joe Wheeler, Rasmussen captured our own grieving sentiments when she wrote, "What a profoundly sad loss. My heart is breaking, as I remember the warmth of his smile. He was the most benevolent warrior I think I have ever known. He never shied away from the frontline of battle, but he always fought with kindness and optimism in his heart. We should take a page from his book and remember to live every day with the same zest and determination that was indeed his hallmark."

After service in World War II and a highly successful career as a marketing executive for Welch's Foods and the Gillette Corporation, John had become president of Carter Products in New York City. On retiring to Concord, he immediately became active in community service and was known as a generous, tenacious advocate of worthy causes. From then on, to our great sadness, we would honor him as a Trustee in Memoriam.

John Mack's death was hard on us, especially our founding president, Joe Wheeler, who had brought his friend and contemporary

John Mack

onto the board and spent a great deal of time working with him on strategy. But we soon took heart, realizing the one thing John would not want us to do was stop working. That would get his dander up, for sure. So we kept on moving. Our two open houses were well attended and generated high spirits. Nancy Grohol's husband, John, worked at the time for the Segway Corporation and offered visitors at both events a chance to ride a Segway around the property as part of their tour. In October, local farmer Steve Verrill offered us all the pumpkins we could load onto a pickup truck for our family pumpkin party, which fell happily on a crisp, colorful autumn afternoon The sight of youngsters carving pumpkins in the front yard and kicking a soccer ball around the lawn gave us all a new appreciation for what this place could mean to future generations, and several children wanted to hear all about the story of the Henry who had been born there.

More young people arrived at the house on Nov. 3, this time to do some work. Concord Cub Scout Pack 133's Den 3 troop, with leader Court Booth in tow, turned up with rakes in hand and spent the day clearing the lawns of leaves. In the process, the scouts learned something about the house's history from our resident birthplace historian, Joe Wheeler. "Passing our history on to young people is essential if we want to continue to preserve the things that are important to us and make us who we are," said Wheeler to *The Concord Journal* after the event. "Thoreau and his ideas have inspired millions of people around the globe over the last century and a half, and he was born in this very simple farmhouse right here in Concord."

Scout Matty Teitleman put it this way: "The house should be saved. It's important because Thoreau was born here, and he wrote good books." Young Dylan Booth added for emphasis, "The house needs to be fixed. If you just touch the walls, they fall apart."

Court Booth pointed out that the Boy Scout philosophy had benefited from Thoreau's influence. "The Hornaday Award, given annually by the Boy Scouts, is the oldest conservation award given in America and encourages Boy Scouts everywhere to take responsibility for our planet's future by promoting conservation," he said.

The year 2005, so busy and so fraught, ended nonetheless on a very positive note. On Dec. 12, at our final board meeting of the year, we learned that the Trust was the beneficiary of a $100,000 bequest from John Mack's estate, as a contribution to our capital campaign. It was stunning news and left us speechless for a good, long moment before we could express our gratitude for John's amazing generosity. The following day, Nancy Grohol and I were scheduled to meet with Anna Winter Rasmussen of Save Our Heritage, at her invitation. We assumed she wanted to hear news about our latest plans for the birth house. But before we could begin, she slid an envelope across the conference table toward us. It contained a check for $100,000, a gift from her family's foundation. "I offer this in honor of John Mack," Rasmussen told us. "I know of his gift, and would like to match it in his memory."

What an astonishing two days it had been. We had begun the calendar year with just over $42,600 in our capital fund. By Dec. 11 we had nearly doubled that amount to reach $84,400. Then, on Dec. 13, we were suddenly in possession of $284,400. It was a heady moment. Though we were still far from our goal, with only six months left to raise the remainder, we could not help but feel encouraged—and deeply grateful. Our "benevolent warrior" had not left the fray, after all.

XXXIII

"WE'RE PLEASED TO INFORM YOU…"

We aim above the mark to hit the mark.

—Ralph Waldo Emerson

When the Thoreau Farm Trust convened its first meeting of 2006, on Jan. 18, we were facing six months of hard work. At that point, we had received capital gifts and pledges totaling $285,224, still more than half a million dollars short of our $800,000 goal. With our June 30 deadline in mind, we were working on a variety of fundraising initiatives. Nancy Grohol had sent out several grant proposals, which she enhanced, when possible, with personal contact that lent a face and personality to our requests. I had been invited to speak at gatherings of business owners, and we had begun to visit potential donors individually to make our case. We also planned a number of community events for spring and summer to raise awareness of our project. These included participation in Concord's annual Patriots Day Parade on April 19, the Earth Day Parade on April 29, a Green Team event at the house to teach about sustainable restoration practices, a walk-through of the house with board member and historian Jayne Gordon on May 19, Picnic in the Park on July 4, an open house for Thoreau Society members on July 6, and our annual family-oriented "Happy Birthday, Henry" celebration to be held that year on July 9. It was going to be a busy six months.

On the restoration front, we were also homing in on a definitive plan for the house. Architect Larry Sorli presented us with updated design plans he and Bill Finch had prepared, including the ell-shaped addition that we had finally voted to approve. Whenever Sorli and Finch presented their newest plans, we were struck by the creative way they met code requirements without compromising the historic integrity of the house they had come to love. As the project progressed, their initial designs would be changed and adapted, but many of their early ideas carried through. The addition, for example, would contain a wide staircase to the second floor that would allow a second entrance to the birth room. The original entry to the room opened off the landing at the front of the house, which contained a great many fragile historic features. A new entry, which could be used for most public visits, would allow the older entry to be used only on special occasions, protecting the historic fabric. The ell would also house two downstairs accessible bathrooms, which the Green Team would help equip, and supplemental upstairs office space for use by the Thoreau Society.

Our approval of the new ell kept open the possibility that we would install an elevator, our biggest remaining decision. If we decided against an elevator, we would have to seek a waiver of the second-floor access required by the Americans with Disabilities Act. We believed we could secure such a waiver, especially since the Thoreau Society agreed that a disabled employee would be allowed to work on the fully accessible first floor. But though we worried about our ability to fund a more expensive project, we were uncomfortable with the prospect of denying disabled visitors access to Thoreau's birth room and the magic of that experience. Ultimately, the elevator would make its way into our final plans.

One of our most successful events that year was held on March 5 at October Farm, the 18th-century Concord home of Reinier (Rein) and Nancy Beeuwkes. The Beeuwkeses were both active in community work, and Rein had once pointed out to me that the oldest portion of their home was built circa 1740, about the same time as Thoreau's birthplace. It was not the first time the Beeuwkeses had hosted benefit events, which always drew large crowds to their beautifully maintained historic house and impressive gardens. Still, it was a rare privilege to enjoy the splendor of October Farm, named by famed ornithologist William Brewster, who had purchased the property in 1898. So we were not surprised when our Sunday talk and reception drew more than fifty people on an unusually balmy late-winter afternoon. We introduced our project to the guests, and board member Brian Donahue gave an informative talk, enlivened with projected images, on the history of farming in Concord. Larry Sorli was there to explain the preliminary design plan, and Rein Beeuwkes himself gave an eloquent tribute to the property and our work on its behalf and urged those present to support it.

After the presentations, Rein called me over to talk. He had noticed, he said, that those of us from the Thoreau Farm Trust tended to present the project and expect people to respond out of enthusiasm for what they had seen and learned. After all, hadn't we ourselves done that? But people needed to be asked, he said. Don't be shy. I realized that we had, in fact, been a bit hesitant to come right out and ask for support. We had always expected that the aura of the house, the worthiness of our goals, and the popularity of Thoreau would excite others to sign on. That had happened occasionally, but we were still far from our fundraising goal. Maybe Rein was correct that we were depending too much on the power of suggestion and not enough on the power of persuasion. It was a good lesson to ponder and would influence our actions thereafter.

One immediate result of this interaction at October Farm was to start our board talking about applying for a grant from Concord's nine-member Community Preservation Committee. At the 2004 Annual Town Meeting, and subsequently in November of that year at the polls, Concord voters had approved the adoption of the Community Preservation Act. The law, enacted by the Commonwealth of Massachusetts in 2000 and now adopted by 173 cities and towns, allows municipalities to add a surcharge on residential and commercial real estate tax bills to fund the acquisition and preservation of land for open space and recreational use; acquisition and preservation of historic buildings and landscapes; and creation and support of affordable housing. Once a city or town votes to approve the surcharge, which Concord set at 1.5 percent of the assessed value of real estate holdings beyond the first $100,000, the state distributes annual matching funds representing a formula-based percentage of what the community has raised locally. In Concord, the local CPA committee considers applications in the fall and presents its funding recommendations to the Annual Town Meeting the following spring.

The CPA was adopted in Concord the same year that the Thoreau Farm Trust signed its purchase-and-sale agreement with the town. The applications for the first round of CPA grants were due in the fall of 2005. Our board discussed applying but had decided against asking the town for funding help at that time. When Town Meeting voted overwhelmingly to purchase the Breen property in 1997, residents were told no additional municipal dollars would be spent on the Thoreau birth house. Selectmen put out a call for citizens to step forward and form a nonprofit to raise funds for the restoration and re-use of the house, which is when—and why—the Thoreau Farm Trust was born. But in 1997, the Community Preservation Act did not exist, even at the state level, and it would not become part of Concord's preservation ethos until eight years later. Several people who knew of our project and our funding needs, including former selectmen involved in the original purchase, told us they were puzzled by our reticence. The money was now being set aside every year for the very purpose we were pursuing, with a generous match from the state. Why not see if the town's CPA committee would consider our application?

After several discussions throughout the spring and an informal meeting with former Selectman Sally Schnitzer, the board voted to apply for a grant from the Community Preservation Fund, in the amount of $200,000, for use on the restoration of the birth house. We were receiving very positive responses from the town officials from whom we were soliciting advice, which encouraged us to begin preparing our application, with the expert help of Executive Director Nancy Grohol, for submission by the Sept. 29 deadline.

If the Community Preservation Committee approved our application, we assumed it would do so on the condition that we had demonstrated our ability to raise the remaining $600,000 needed to restore the house. By June 2006, we were closing in on half that amount in capital gifts and pledges. But it was clear we would not meet the July 1 deadline set by the town in the purchase-and-sale agreement. Momentum had built, and we believed we were on our way to success, but we hadn't received the single, transformative gift that would have put us over the top. We simply had to keep plugging. Perhaps anticipating this situation, the town's attorney had included in the purchase-and-sale document a provision granting the Trust an extension of up to one year if the additional time was "necessary to accomplish fundraising goals." At our Annual Meeting in early June, we agreed to seek that extension.

In requesting the extra time later that month, I informed town officials of our progress to that point, indicated our intention to apply for CPA funding, and requested a year's extension to fulfill our goal. The optimism we expressed in asking for the extension was not forced. In the second year of our capital fundraising effort, we had raised nearly five times what we had in the first year. We had held several well-received events at the house, including educational gatherings on green architecture and historic restoration, and in the process had already established ourselves as de facto proprietors. And in the Thoreau Society, we had found a tenant that would not only provide regular income but also contribute to future programming.

We clearly hadn't been passive during this fundraising period, and town officials rewarded our good-faith efforts by granting us the year's extension.

Our Annual Meeting that year ushered in a few changes to our Thoreau Farm Trust board. We were joined by Lorna Mack, an active member of the Thoreau Society who was often called upon by the Princeton University Press to translate Thoreau's nearly illegible handwriting—which she had the uncanny ability to decipher—for their scholarly editions of his complete works. The widow of our former board member John Mack, Lorna wished to advance the work he had begun, and we were very happy to welcome her into our midst. "The restoration of the Thoreau birth house was a cause near and dear to my husband's heart," she told *The Concord Journal* at the time. "I am pleased to be a part of the Thoreau Farm Trust's board and to help bring the project to a successful completion in John's memory."

Also joining us was Dr. Lawrence Buell, an author and distinguished professor of English at Harvard University. Jayne Gordon, one of our founding members, stepped off the board because of the demands of her new position at the Massachusetts Historical Society in Boston but remained one of our closest allies and advisors. Remaining members were Molly Eberle, as vice president; Court Booth, as treasurer; Joe Wheeler, as clerk/secretary; Brian Donahue, Richard Fahlander, Michael Kellett, Barbara Lambert, Ellen Foley Rice, and Tim Rodgers. I agreed to serve as president for another year.

While Nancy Grohol worked on our Community Preservation Act grant application, Larry Sorli reported that the estimated cost of the project was rising. Inflation had bumped up construction prices since the first estimate had been made, and he believed a more realistic cost estimate for the restoration/rehabilitation project was $900,000, a full $100,000 above his earlier figure. The Historic Structure Report he and Bill Finch had prepared revealed a good deal more historic fabric, both exterior and interior, than they had originally thought was present. In fact, Sorli said, to his knowledge the birth house was one of only two historic homes in Concord with that many original features, the other being the early-18th-century Col. Barrett House, owned by the National Park Service. So part of the increase would pay for restoration beyond what was initially planned, and he had added landscaping costs as well. The board agreed that the new figure was reasonable, in light of inflation and new information. Though it would not affect our purchase-and-sale agreement, which still set the amount to be raised for ownership at $800,000, we included the higher figure in our CPA grant application to provide full disclosure and submitted it for consideration in late September. The funding committee would review applications during October and November and decide by the end of December which projects it would recommend for funding at the 2007 Town Meeting the following spring.

After a busy spring and summer of community events, both in town and at the house, the Trust launched the public phase of our capital campaign in October with another round of events—and a piece of very big news: acclaimed poet and former United States Poet Laureate Robert Pinsky had agreed to lend his support to our cause by becoming honorary chairman of the campaign. Pinsky, a professor of English at Boston University and the author of several award-winning books of poetry, translation, and literary criticism, had written a potent introduction to the 2004 Princeton University Press edition of Thoreau's *Cape Cod* and, as a great admirer of Thoreau, was happy to become the public voice of the campaign. "Henry David Thoreau remains enduringly central to our memory and imagination," he said at the time. "His influence, which has extended to Gandhi and Tolstoy, seems deeply related to his home ground. His home, and our ability to preserve it, epitomizes the notion of 'heritage' on a direct, sensible scale that is in the Thoreau spirit."

To kick off the campaign, we hosted three events that coincided with National Book Month, which Concord celebrated with an annual Festival of Authors in October. Founded in 1993 by Rob Mitchell, an author-event coordinator for the Harvard Bookstore in Cambridge, the month-long festival welcomed both celebrated and emerging writers to Concord each year and soon grew so large in scope and audience that its venues had expanded to include capacious auditoriums in the city of Lowell. In 1995, one of the festival's opening night speakers was a soon-to-be-senator from Illinois, Barack Obama, on tour for the publication of his first book, *Dreams From My Father.*

Our first author event that year was a children's workshop and book signing by D.B. Johnson, author and illustrator of *Henry Hikes to Fitchburg, Henry Builds a Cabin, Henry Works,* and *Henry Climbs a Mountain,* all of which the Concord Bookshop has always had trouble keeping on its shelves. As usual when we held events for families, we were amazed at the pleasure children took in being at the house. One of the several dozen who came that day—it was billed as a *Boston Globe* Pick of the Week—even arrived dressed jauntily as Henry.

The second event, also previewed prominently in *The Boston Globe*, was held on a weekday evening and featured movie producer Micheal Flaherty. Flaherty is co-founder of Walden Media, the production company that has produced such movies as *The Chronicles of Narnia, The Lion, the Witch, and the Wardrobe,* and *Charlotte's Web.* Flaherty screened scenes from some of his films and shared with the audience the ways Thoreau's belief in simplicity and connection to the natural world had influenced his work as an educator and children's filmmaker.

The final October event, held at the Concord Art Association, presented the premiere screening of a video production by naturalist Dick Walton and photographer John Huehnergard, entitled *Henry David Thoreau Speaking for Nature.* A visual celebration of Thoreau's natural history explorations, the production offered lyrical images of the local landscapes he knew so intimately. Though we could host only outdoor gatherings at the house itself at that point and had to rely on other venues for two of the three October events, our participation in the Concord Festival of Authors served to establish the Thoreau birthplace as a community-centered resource with a great deal to offer.

It seemed the Town of Concord felt the same. On Dec. 20, we received one of those wonderful "We're pleased to inform you" letters that can only mean good news. The Community Preservation Committee had voted to recommend to the 2007 Town Meeting that the Thoreau Farm Trust be awarded a CPA grant in the amount of $200,000 for the restoration and rehabilitation of the Thoreau birth house. There were, of course, conditions. As we expected, if approved by Town Meeting, the dispersal of funds would be contingent on the Trust's receipt of all necessary permitting and our demonstrated ability to fund the entire project.

The news lifted us to a high we hadn't experienced since that day in 1997 when Town Meeting had voted overwhelmingly to purchase the Breen property. Confident of a positive vote, we now considered ourselves three-quarters of the way toward our goal. It was a satisfying end to what had been a busy and productive year.

As Bill Finch and Lary Sorli studied the birth house, they used blowups from this historical photograph, taken by Alfred Hosmer around 1896, to guide their future restoration of the trim elements and window frames.

XXXIV
CLEARING THE WAY

Success treads on every right step.

—Ralph Waldo Emerson

On Jan. 1, 2007, the Town of Concord began its tenth year as owner of Thoreau Farm. No one had imagined so much time would pass with the historic house in "mothballs" and the town still responsible for keeping it standing. It is disconcerting to imagine today the devastation the house would have suffered had the Thoreau Farm Trust not become a big brother to the project. Our work at the site and behind the scenes felt natural at the time, as did our cooperative relationship with town officials. In retrospect, the town's willingness to share information, exchange ideas, and accept help with caretaking, and our board members' readiness to offer knowledge, resources, event planning, and elbow grease, seem like plotlines in stories that begin with, "Once upon a time...." It was all the more extraordinary because, since the very beginning, the cause had remained community-based. Though we received support from our state legislators and outside agencies from time to time when we requested their advocacy, Concord's officials and citizens had relied essentially on each other. Certainly, no one knew back in 1997 how long amassing funds to restore the house would take—and at what personal cost. As board member Court Booth has said, "What kept us going, I think, was collective ignorance!"

Still, the key word was "collective." When the Trust applied for a grant from the Massachusetts Cultural Council early in 2007, a long process shepherded expertly by Nancy Grohol, we were gratified by the letters of support sent to the Council from Concord committees and agencies. Their words reminded us of the distance we had traveled from the days when we would be asked, "So, why should we care about the Thoreau birthplace?" Whether from inside or outside Concord, the letters sent on our behalf that winter reflected all the work the Trust had done over the past decade to highlight the significance of the birthplace and promote our vision for the house as a place that would honor the past while pointing toward the future.

Our project had benefited from the time it needed to mature and mellow. The comments from our public advocates indicated it was now ready to decant.

In her letter of support, Dr. Barbara Lynn-Davis, chair of the Concord Historical Commission, wrote, "Concord's historic resources are embodiments of our American heritage, contribute to the health of our local economy, and increase the quality of life in our town.... The Thoreau Farm Trust's plan for this house has earned the support of the local community and is worthy of funding."

Stephanie Stillman, executive director of the Concord Chamber of Commerce, was more specific: "I have been impressed with the professionalism of the [Thoreau Farm Trust] and their unrelenting dedication to the restoration effort," she wrote. "In addition, the Trust has worked very hard to become part of the community fabric through their own public events, support of community activities, and development of relationships with other historic and cultural organizations. I have no doubt they will be successful in their endeavor."

As early as the spring of 2005, we had received from the National Trust for Historic Preservation (NTHP) one of only thirteen nationally competitive grants awarded that year to fund pre-development work at the house. In their letter to the Cultural Council two years later, the NTHP commended the Town of Concord for its "commitment and foresight" in purchasing the property and for its "partnership with the Thoreau Farm Trust to ensure the house's restoration, interpretation, and re-use." The letter also expressed a strong belief in the cultural importance of the birth house and in "the Thoreau Farm Trust's capacity as a steward of the property."

In an interesting aside, NTHP's field representative Rebecca Williams noted that more than 118.1 million Americans visit heritage destinations every year, over half the nation's adult population. "Henry David Thoreau is an American icon, and the restoration of his house will enrich the experience of tourists and residents alike," wrote Williams. "It has been an unofficial tourist destination since at least the 1800s, but only now, through the work of the Thoreau Farm Trust, will it be open to the public."

State Representative Cory Atkins, chair of the House Science and Technology Caucus, told the Cultural Council she was particularly impressed with the Thoreau Farm Trust's "innovative goal of integrating green building techniques" that would save energy and enhance sustainability. "When renovations are completed," she wrote, "the Thoreau birth house can serve as an example of how to integrate energy-saving technologies into a building project while protecting the historical integrity of the structure. It will be an excellent model for future renovation projects around the Commonwealth. ... As a symbol of Concord's legacy—and of its future in an age of green buildings—the Thoreau birth house is an important landmark that deserves our best efforts at preservation."

Since the Trust had tried hard to present the birthplace as a living memorial to Thoreau's genius, and not a museum, Atkins's reference to its future promise felt especially satisfying. State Senator Susan Fargo ventured even farther in this direction when she remarked in her letter that "the Trust's proposal is just as much about the future as it is about the past."

The one surprising note appeared in a letter of support written by Concord Town Manager Christopher Whelan. After offering his enthusiastic approval of our plans for the house, he informed the Cultural Council that the town planned to transfer title to the Trust in June or July, implying that he believed we could raise the necessary funds by that time—with the Council's help, of course. But he was also implying that he believed Town Meeting would approve the Community Preservation grant, a decision that was still more than a month away.

Town Planner Marcia Rasmussen also appeared optimistic. She told us she would allow us to proceed with some site work at the house that spring while it was still in town hands. Larry Sorli was scoping out engineering and construction firms for us, and his warm rapport with those he had worked with in the past brought rewards in the form of deep discounts for Thoreau's birthplace. To save money, we continued to use our own workforce, enhanced with spouses and friends. When Sorli told us the airless, cobweb-draped attic, with its untrustworthy floorboards and blackened corncob insulation, needed to be cleaned out, we showed up. A dusty job it was, but we enjoyed the chance to take our enthusiasm for the house, quite literally, to the rafters.

Despite the confidence emanating from town officials, the Trust's board knew from experience not to take Town Meeting approval for granted. We continued to plan public events and support those held in the community, including participating in a town-wide Global Warming Symposium held in late March. We were still receiving prominent coverage and editorial support from our local *Concord Journal.* And on April 22, the Sunday before Town Meeting was to convene, *The Boston Globe* published a long article about the birthplace, with the headline, "Thoreau project close to key goal." The article stressed the critical need to begin shoring up the deteriorating structure, and Nancy Grohol was quoted as saying the Trust was hoping not to lose another construction season.

On May 4, shortly after the close of Town Meeting, the Trust was happy and relieved to receive official confirmation that our Community Preservation Act grant request had been approved with no opposition. We would not be able to draw on the $200,000 fund until construction on the house had begun, so the grant remained contingent on our ability to raise all the funds needed for the restoration/rehabilitation project. But it brought us within about $146,000 of our goal. In fact, if we counted the funds we had received over the years toward our operating expenses, we had already exceeded $800,000 in total fundraising. We were not the only ones to appreciate that fact. As he had done in his letter to the Massachusetts Cultural Council, Town Manager Christopher Whelan indicated to us directly that he would be willing to recommend transferring title to the property to us in advance of our reaching our capital goal, if we were willing to go ahead. It was clear the town was beyond ready to shift responsibility for the house's welfare to another owner, and there was no doubt, given the structural dilapidation, that sooner would be better.

It was, of course, the moment we had been waiting for. But we curbed our glee and proceeded cautiously on the way to a decision. There was a long list of details to consider. If we signaled our readiness to accept ownership earlier than expected, we would need to accelerate all our activity, including our architectural design work, the hiring of a contractor, and the town permitting processes, while simultaneously sustaining our fundraising efforts. An early ownership date would only increase the urgency of those efforts and raise the stakes for success, since we would be taking on the responsibility for the project without the necessary completion funds in hand. Yet construction costs would just continue to rise as more time passed, and we had secured enough money to fund the most important work on the house. So after long consideration, we voted unanimously to answer the town manager's offer with a definite "Yes." If the town was willing to commit to us, we were ready to commit to Thoreau Farm.

The

🍂 THOREAU FARM TRUST 🍂

welcomes

ROBERT PINSKY

U.S. Poet Laureate
1997-2000

SUNDAY, JUNE 10
ELIZABETH B. HALL CHAPEL
CONCORD ACADEMY
CONCORD, MASSACHUSETTS

XXXV

ONE GREAT POET HONORS ANOTHER

My life has been the poem I would have writ,
But I could not both live and utter it.

—H.D. Thoreau

It would take months to complete the documents sealing our ownership agreement with the town. We knew that. But what remained were the formalities, and we did not want to keep the good news to ourselves. Poet Robert Pinsky, who had signed on as the honorary chairman of the Trust's capital campaign the previous year, agreed to offer a talk and poetry reading to help promote our cause and celebrate our impending ownership of the birth house. That event, held on June 10, 2007, in the Elizabeth B. Hall Chapel at Concord Academy, remains one of the highlights—perhaps *the* highlight—of the Thoreau Farm Trust's first decade.

Thoreau wrote in his journal, on Dec. 9, 1859, "The prosaic mind sees things badly, or with the bodily sense; but the poet sees them clad in beauty, with the spiritual sense." Anyone visiting the birthplace that summer, 190 years after Thoreau was born, might respond only to what could be seen with the eye: peeling paint and a crumbling interior. That day, Robert Pinsky captured the spirit of the place and clad it in the beauty of his words.

With a packed crowd of about 250 people looking on from the chapel's lower pews and upper balcony benches, Pinsky introduced himself as the great-great-great grandson of Henry David Thoreau. "A typical American is made of wisps and bits from here and there," he said. "If I want to have a right to the patriotic feeling of calling myself a 'descendant' of Thoreau ..., then I have to take care of our history. On this project, you've got it right."

Referring to the crazy-quilt nature of our work, he said, "[T]he ability to improvise, to patch something together out of bits and pieces, is something I admire about the New England spirit."

One of the Trust's more whimsical initiatives that spring, spearheaded by board member Richard Fahlander, had been the launching of a haiku contest on our website, which fellow board member Tim Rodgers had developed into an informative and interactive resource. We called the contest "Haiku for Henry," and stated that the winning poems would be read at the Robert Pinsky event and published in the program. To our amazement, we received more than 150 entries. Here are the four that appeared in the day's program:

"Untitled"

Probe a silent place

Of lichen, logs, and hummus

Where the sidewalk ends.

—Toni Giarnese

"July 12, 1817"

Today I know light,

Soft sounds, warm breeze. Today no

Need to simplify.

—Caroline Ellis

"For Henry"

Though you fathered none

How vast your seed's dispersal

Entire earth your heir.

—Margo Van Kuren

"A Tolerable Planet"

Bare hands gently place

Compost 'round roots from a friend

Three lives are enriched.

—Jim Meehan

Capping off an extraordinary day, a number of invited guests gathered at a reception for Pinsky at the 255 Main Street home of Sarah and Kenneth Lazarus, across the street from the Concord Academy campus. The stately home, known in Thoreauvian circles as "the Yellow House," was the last Thoreau family dwelling, which they purchased in 1850. The family used a rear ell, no longer there, to mix the graphite formula for their thriving pencil-making business. Henry died in its front room on May 6, 1862, at the age of 44. As we gathered there, most for the first time because the private residence was not open to the public, the atmosphere was decidedly subdued. We all noticed, in particular, that Robert Pinsky appeared moved in a way he had not perhaps anticipated. For this moment—at least not yet—he could find no words.

Welcome to the Thoreau Farm Trust's

CONCORD BARN TOUR

SUNDAY, SEPTEMBER 30, 2007
1 – 4:30 P.M.

EVENT SPONSORED BY

This program is your admission ticket.
Please present it at each site.

XXXVI

A YEAR AS BROAD AS A BARN DOOR

While one hour lapses I am conversing in George Minott's barn while the sun is
disappearing from the prospect of its wide door, upon pigeons and raccoons, and corn and
potatoes, and snuffing the odor of new hay, and the wholesome breath of the cow.

—H.D.T., Journal

On July 9, 2007, eight members of the Thoreau Farm Trust appeared before the Board of Selectmen to request title to the birth house. Representing the Trust, I asked selectmen to consider our success at raising $700,000 toward the original $800,000 requirement, plus more than $100,000 in operating funds. The burst of applause that followed the presentation meant all eight of us could start breathing again.

"In my mind, [transferring the deed to the Trust] will enhance the ability to raise the remaining funds," said chair Peggy Briggs. The subsequent vote was unanimous, and Selectman Stan Black, an architect himself aware of the reality of inflation, urged us to "spend the money as fast as you can."

Throughout the rest of that summer, yet again with the pro bono help of Hale and Dorr, we negotiated an amended purchase-and-sale agreement, which lowered the amount of capital funds to be raised to $700,000. We also worked with the town on a series of protective restrictions, easements, and covenants governing the property transfer, none of which conflicted with our earlier understanding of how the property would be conveyed, restored, or used. The purchase price remained eminently affordable at $1, and the town retained right of first refusal if the Thoreau Farm Trust needed to resell the property at any point. If that should happen, the Trust would be allowed to sell only to an appropriate government agency or a nonprofit with a similar mission.

During the months of frequent exchanges and emendations, the Trust kept up a busy schedule of events, appearances, and grant writing. At our Annual Meeting in mid-June, we had welcomed Nancy

McJennett, Kevin Foley, and Melita Teichert to the board, all Concord residents, active professionals, and experienced community volunteers. McJennett had worked in book design and marketing and was a former School Committee member; Foley was a building contractor with an avid interest in helping us with useful contacts; and Teichert had a great deal of experience in marketing and fundraising. Founding board member Michael Kellett, busy with his duties at RESTORE, moved from the Board of Directors to the Advisory Board. His final contribution as a director was characteristically meaningful: he sought and would soon receive the participation of noted author and environmental activist Bill McKibben on our board.

Our grant request to the Massachusetts Cultural Council, which had elicited such fervent tributes from our public supporters, was rejected this time around for lack of a detailed programming plan. It was an important reminder that many foundations like to fund programs more than buildings, and board members agreed it was time to develop this aspect of our project before resubmitting the grant request in the following round. We did receive a second award from the National Trust for Historic Places, however, and the responses from several other grant makers left us hopeful for more success, especially since we could now be treated as owners of the property. Besides the hard work and articulate representation of our mission and goals by Nancy Grohol, the expertise of board members such as Brian Donahue and Barbara Lambert helped sustain our outreach and keep it compelling.

We again participated in the annual July 4 Picnic in the Park, held a Thoreau Society birthday picnic for Henry on July 12, and hosted an open house for the entire community on July 15, all events that had become part of a Thoreau Farm tradition. Board member Court Booth remained our liaison to the Concord Historical Collaborative, informing us of events and initiatives at other sites in town and keeping our own project alive in the minds of local historians and educators.

One of our most fruitful relationships, given our inability to host large gatherings inside the unrestored birth house, had been forged with the Concord Art Association, which had twice offered us space in its airy, light-filled upstairs gallery for birthplace-themed events. The Association's executive director, Lili Ott, also happened to be a historic barn preservationist and served on the state's Preserve Mass

Barns Task Force. She believed the Thoreau Farm Trust would be an ideal choice to organize the town's first barn tour as one of our signature events. We had always been committed to using Thoreau Farm as a way to honor the town's agricultural tradition, but we knew such a large undertaking as a town-wide barn tour would demand a great deal of organizational wizardry. Luckily, our in-house wizard, Nancy Grohol, was eager to take on the challenge. She set the date for our "Evolution of Barns Tour," Sept. 30, to coincide with the town's annual farm market weekend in the town center.

Sponsored by Welch's Foods, our event served as a small fundraising vehicle as well. We charged $12 for advance tickets and $15 at the "door," which was actually a table set up in front of the birthplace, where the self-guided tour began. Local historian Anne McCarthy Forbes, who served on our Advisory Board and had written the successful nomination for the birth house's listing on the National Register of Historic Places, graciously offered to prepare the text for the day's illustrated program brochure. Her commentary included a brief history of the New England barn and detailed descriptions of the six participating Concord barns, which dated from 1701 to 1903. With the help of about three dozen volunteers, some stationed at the barns, some at the birth house, we welcomed more than 200 visitors, double the number we had expected. The enthusiastic response from all who attended, and their request for more such events in the future, showed us there was indeed a demand for programs on agricultural history and practices, as we had suspected.

While we awaited our official closing date with the town, architect Larry Sorli, who had begun doing exploratory work at the site, kept us apprised of his findings. To offer an idea of the details involved in the crafting of a finely parsed restoration/rehabilitation project, here are the bullet points from just one of Sorli's reports, which he presented at a board meeting on Aug. 29, 2007:

- About 4 feet of the main beam under the second floor has water rot, and that piece will be replaced.

- The west chimney post has carpenter ants, but isn't too damaged and can be epoxied and kept.

- Removed a few stones from the foundation and discovered a deeper crawl space than expected.

- Also found the "summer beam," whose original sill on the back of the house is rotten.

- Opened up the left side sill; the sheathing is all later construction, and all needs replacing.

- Drew up preliminary drawings of the window frame; will bring to meeting actual samples of window trim and header; trim will be easy to reproduce; will consult with my contact at Architectural Components about whether to construct a solid or hollow header.

- Discovered that the front door is an unusual $38\frac{1}{2}$ inches wide.

- The corner quoin boards have been incised to look like blocks but are really all one board.

- All 20th-century exterior features and most likely all the sheathing will be stripped; will probably replace it with clear pine treated with borates, then paint.

- Recommend enlisting corporate sponsors for "green" heating and other environmentally sensitive materials and systems.

I was among those whose learning curve on such matters was actually a vertical line. But Sorli was clearly a poet-architect who could look at a seemingly prosaic list of details and clad it in his own brand of beauty. His love of the work was infectious, and I learned to share his joy and trust his judgment, even if I didn't always grasp the nuances of all he was saying. Over time, I learned a great deal from him and came to appreciate the many stories an old home can tell us if we listen closely. To this day, I think of Larry Sorli as our House Whisperer.

Thoreau loved Concord always, but especially when it "[blazed"] with all the glories of October." In his life-affirming essay, "Autumnal Tints," written shortly before his death in 1862, he exulted in the vividness of the "painted" season and in the "joy and exhilaration which these colored leaves excite." So when 145 years later, the

Thoreau Farm Trust took title to the birth house—at last—at 10 a.m. on Tuesday, October 30, 2007, at the Town House on Monument Square, we celebrated along with Nature who, Thoreau proclaimed, "holds her annual fair in October."

Falling on a workday morning, the momentous event was shared by only a handful of board members and could not lead to extended revelry. So the few who were free that morning satisfied the urge to revel with pancakes—and perhaps an extra splash of maple syrup.

From left: Molly Eberle, Eben Hansel, Esq. (from Hale and Dorr), Court Booth, Nancy McJennett, Lucille Stott, and Nancy Grohol the day that the Thoreau Farm Trust took title to the birthplace of Thoreau.

Labor of Love, Epic of Restoration

A feature article on the restoration of the birthplace appeared in *Northbridge Magazine* in 2008 with this arresting image of the house at dusk, photographed by Brian Smith.

XXXVII

THE *REAL* REAL WORK BEGINS

*Drive a nail home and clinch it so faithfully that you can wake up
in the night and think of your work with satisfaction…. Every nail driven
should be as another rivet in the machine of the universe; you are carrying on the work.*

—H.D. Thoreau, *Walden*

When we walked away from the Concord Town House with our title to the birthplace in hand, there was no way to pause and take a breather from the months of work that had brought us there. Instead, we had to reset our odometers at zero and start the next leg of our journey—the two-year period encompassing 2008 and 2009—toward the day when the house would be restored and rehabilitated and ready to begin its new life.

Our meeting notes from the period following the property transfer are laden with decisions to make, tasks to fulfill, contacts to make, permission to secure and—of course—money to be raised. Richard Fahlander headed our Building Committee, which also included Kevin Foley and Barbara Lambert, and all three were in frequent communication with Larry Sorli, who had hired local carpenter Ben Gifford to help with the work and arranged with Grodin Construction to be our general contractor. But Sorli had developed such a close kinship with the house that he chose to do a good deal of the hands-on work himself. With the structural report and restoration/rehabilitation plan completed, historical materials conservator Bill Finch had finished his portion of the work but would remain in the wings as an advisor.

We had been granted a building permit, which allowed Sorli and his colleagues to work on-site, securing the exterior windows and clapboards in anticipation of the coming winter weather, repairing what they could of the interior fixtures, and removing everything not worth saving. By the spring of 2008, the interior would be largely gutted down to its sturdiest elements in preparation for the restoration and rehabilitation to begin.

Our plans at that point still included the construction of a barn. The original house would be returned to its two-over-two configuration. The downstairs "west parlor" would be reserved for office space for the Thoreau Farm Trust, and the "east parlor" for community gatherings. The upstairs "west chamber" would be part of the Thoreau Society's rental space, which would extend into the new addition, and the "east chamber," Thoreau's birth room, would be open for public visits. None of these spaces was large enough for gatherings of more than thirty people, so the barn was meant to welcome larger groups, students and teachers on a visit to Concord and the general public to programs and lectures for all ages. We planned to expand our use of "green" construction materials in the barn, where there would be no concern about destroying historic fabric. But in retaining our plans for a barn, we had not counted on the Wall Street crash that would occur in the fall of 2008. Devastating for so many, the deep recession that followed reduced public funding and put a great deal of discretionary personal spending on hold. We were fortunate enough to continue securing the necessary funding for the birth house itself, which had risen to $1 million, but our hopes to raise additional funds for a barn began to wither.

In their place, more pressing concerns cropped up: what kind of septic system and insulation to install; what types of plumbing, electrical, and HVAC systems to use; what kind of flooring to put down; what to do about an elevator. Several of us shared middle-of-the night moments of anxiety when we wondered if we were up to the task of owning such a precious property. What if we made the wrong decisions? What if something happened to the still-vulnerable house while it was in our care? But by day, in our more serene moments, we realized our most important decisions had been spot on: we had an executive director whose excellent research skills would guide us to the right choices, and we had engaged trusted partners who shared our goals and were committed to best practices.

Amid the nagging details, some of the romance returned early in the spring of 2008 when a number of us were interviewed by a glossy new quarterly, *NorthBridge Magazine*, serving the upscale towns of Concord, Carlisle, and Lexington. Entitled "Labor of Love: Epic of Restoration" ("epic" sounded just right to us), the resulting article appeared in the Spring 2008 inaugural issue and was compelling to view and read. Writer Peter Golden began with fantastical prose that would have fit neatly into a scenario for *Mission Impossible*:

Out of the dust and disorder, a human figure emerges—a jagged assortment of saw blades clutched in a gloved hand, dusty clothing virtually indistinguishable from an aged hearth area barely visible in the shadows.

This is Larry Sorli, one of the area's leading preservation architects and an expert in colonial structures. No tweed coat and shiny shoes are in evidence; hands-on is the order of the day.

Sorli and Concord native Ben Gifford, a carpenter on the project, are locked in a battle with all the degrading forces of nature, struggling to overcome three centuries of use, bugs, and weather.

They have a mission: to stabilize, restore, and make habitable this house, the birthplace of a seminal figure in the creation of the American experience, Henry David Thoreau.

Golden managed to capture the sweat and strain of the work in progress while hinting at the underlying beauty—and uneniable aura—of the place:

The front door gapes open, revealing a small entryway and paneled staircase. But where the hallway floor should be, there is nothing save empty space. A support beam stabs into the air above a shallow cellar hole.

Somewhere in the gloom of the unlit interior the tink-tink-tink of a masonry hammer can be heard. The musty smell of earth and disuse dominates the senses.

Stressing the public-private collaboration that saved the birthplace and led to the revivification project, Golden acknowledged the challenges he was witnessing as he toured the debris-strewn construction site:

Restoration is what Larry Sorli is all about, but now he pauses to chat while Gifford doggedly works to replace a rotted casement window in the cellar. How this story will resolve itself remains to be seen. But if good will, force of personality, and the intentions of Thoreau Farm Trust members are any indication, these two—along with a skilled team of allied restoration specialists, including Nick Reed, an historic landscape architect, and Bill Finch, an historic materials conservator—will accomplish the one thing needed to bring the old house back to life: a miracle!

Golden developed a deeper understanding of the project and its goals as he spoke with those closest to the work, including Bill Finch, who told him, "We'll try to present the birth room with its 19th-century appearance, but we'll use the 18th-century materials that were in place when Thoreau was born."

Very few would have Golden's experience of seeing "the bones" of the house during its period of deconstruction. Despite its interior gloom, "weathered exterior, and thicket-choked yard," the house did not fail to impress him in the end: "The craftsmanship and period features of the home rivet the eye. Exposed floor beams are sufficiently massive to frame a stout sailing ship and the elegant central stairway, probably a late-18th-century enhancement, is still rock solid."

In a way we all appreciated, Golden wrote of Thoreau himself as we hoped to embody him in his birth house. Describing Henry's life as "modest, abstemious, and humble," Golden added, "Like many in the 19th century, Thoreau's life was cut short by tuberculosis, but his legacy lives on. Other lights have shone as brightly in Concord, but none with such an enduring glow."

Shortly after Golden's article appeared, at our Annual Meeting in June 2008, the Trust board elected its four officers: Molly Eberle, as vice president; Nancy McJennett, as clerk/secretary; Joe Wheeler, as treasurer; and me as president. Returning for the new fiscal year were, Court Booth, Lawrence Buell, Brian Donahue, Richard Fahlander, Kevin Foley, Barbara Lambert, Lorna Mack, Ellen Foley Rice, Tim Rodgers, and Melita Teichert, and we were pleased to welcome new member Valarie Kinkade, a Concord resident and experienced archaeologist and museum professional.

By that time, we had surpassed our original goal of $800,000 in capital funds and were on our way to raising an additional $200,000. Despite the grim economic climate, our ownership of the property and our success at reaching our initial fundraising goal had helped build confidence and support. And our work to sharpen our interpretive goals boosted our appeal to the Massachusetts Cultural Council, which granted us an award in our second-round attempt.

With her intelligence, perseverance, organizational talent, and steady hand, Nancy Grohol, was at the heart of our successes. Not only did she manage the details of the construction project with our architects and contractors and guide the board in our decision-making, she also shouldered much of the burden of our event planning. That fall, again in conjunction with Lili Ott at the Concord Art Association, Grohol coordinated our second barn tour, this one entitled "The Art of the Barn." Promoted by a specially designed calendar featuring paintings of signature Concord barns, the event once again began at the birth house and dispersed visitors on self-guided tours around town. As we had hoped, it drew another large crowd of eager participants, and once again brought old and new friends into the action as volunteers and guides.

Since the fall of 2006, in keeping with Henry David Thoreau's literary legacy, the Trust had become a fixture in the annual Concord Festival of Authors. Our 2008 events, held on Oct. 30 and Nov. 2 at the Concord Art Association, featured two very different creative endeavors. The first gathering celebrated the launch of a new journal of nature, art, and inquiry entitled *Wild Apples*, after Thoreau's 1862 essay by that name. The four young editors, poets Susan Edwards Richmond and Sophie Wadsworth, artist-writer Kathryn Liebowitz, and artist-poet Linda Hoffman, read from their first issue, which combined poetry and prose with visual art in the service of environmental awareness and social justice. For our second event, we welcomed photographer Dan Tobyne, whose arresting color photography illustrated a new edition of Thoreau's *Cape Cod*. Tobyne told the audience about his decision to "walk the walk," retracing Thoreau's steps to discover what could still be seen of the Cape Cod he had admired and produce images that corresponded to passages from the original text.

One of the Trust's most recent additions, noted author-activist Bill McKibben, became an honorary member of our board earlier in the year, having accepted an invitation from former board member Michael Kellett. McKibben had grown up in neighboring Lexington and was teaching at Middlebury College. "I've spent the year editing *American Earth*, an anthology of American environmental writing for the Library of America," said McKibben at the time. "It begins with Thoreau, because that is where American environmentalism begins. And so it seems appropriate to join the effort to save the place where Thoreau began."

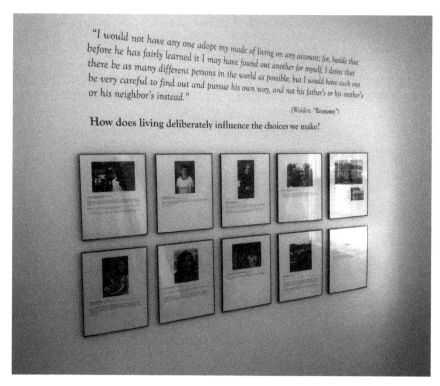

A wall leading up to Thoreau's birth room features stories of everyday people in their efforts to live deliberately.

XXXVIII
A BIRTHPLACE OF IDEAS

Though I do not believe that a plant will spring up where no seed has been,
I have great faith in a seed. Convince me that you have a seed there,
and I am prepared to expect wonders.

—H.D. Thoreau, *Faith in a Seed*

With construction under way, and the house expected to become habitable by the end of 2009, the Thoreau Farm Trust board turned to the task of crafting what we hoped would become the perfect housewarming gift: an identity. Though we had done our best to articulate our vision and distinguish our purpose and activities from those of other local organizations and sites, we were concerned that the long dormant birth house would fail to emerge as distinctive. We were especially determined to avoid the misperception that it was to become a museum house, complete with period furnishings and costumed guides. Our intention had always been to keep the house simple and to use it in ways that would propel Thoreau's ideas into the future. But our earlier discussions about goals for our programming had felt a bit premature and, for obvious reasons, theoretical. Now, the house was ours and the future was here. We wanted to keep the "enduring glow" of Thoreau's flame alive, but we needed help to determine how this *particular* place could do that best.

So, in May 2008, we engaged the services of strategic planning consultant Laura Roberts, our first choice among a number of candidates who had responded to our call for help. Roberts was a proven, highly recommended professional, and her deliberate methods—intended to slow thinking down to a pace that would yield clear vision and measurable goals over the long term—fit our needs perfectly. Working with Roberts was like dipping a photographic negative into developing fluid and watching it gradually emerge as a sharply defined image. She was our fixer.

During the months we worked with Roberts, from May 2008 to October 2009, we came to view all our communications and programming, even those events that could not be held inside the house's gutted interior, as part of a cohesive whole. Our discussions even informed our construction decisions, especially those involving handicap access and "green" practices, both of which we began to view as moral imperatives. It was a fruitful period for us, and a productive way to use some of our time and energy as the meticulous restoration and rehabilitation project slowly advanced.

In the summer and fall of 2008, in the spirit of collaboration that had always been the hallmark of this project, our board members and executive director divided up into teams of two and visited the heads of a number of community and regional organizations. We were seeking information about their mission, goals, and programming priorities in order to deepen our understanding of the historical and cultural environment within which the birth house would take its place. Among those we approached, all of them enthusiastic about welcoming us to the tribe, were administrators of the Concord Free Public Library, the Concord Museum, the National Park Service, Walden Pond State Reservation, the Walden Woods Project, Orchard House, Emerson House, The Old Manse, Gaining Ground, Massachusetts Audubon Society, the Concord Historical Commission, the Massachusetts Historical Commission, the Concord Climate Action Network, and the Fruitlands Museum. One of our reasons for conducting these outreach meetings was to assure other local organizations that we had no intention of duplicating what they were already doing so well. We enlisted their help in identifying a niche for the birthplace that had not already been filled elsewhere. In the process, we benefited from their knowledge and experience and learned a great deal about the inner workings of small nonprofits and the strength they each derived from being part of a team of non-rivals.

From these conversations, two suggestions stood out: the need for education about the history of agriculture, which people felt had largely been ignored, and the wish for a place that students and teachers could gather to discuss and process their visit to the town's other treasures, an idea that had been planted in the early days, during the Seefurth era. Our own vision, which had drawn many of us to the project, involved presenting the lesser-known aspects of Thoreau's life and work: his close connection to his family and community.

With these ideas in mind, we met several times with members of our Advisory Board and other invited guests to brainstorm about what we felt the house represented and what it could teach. Roberts had instructed us to share our ideas openly and freely, without worrying about being quashed, so the sessions were often long and rambling. But these lively exchanges had a purpose. The many arrows in our quiver were all aiming for the center of the target: the drafting of a formal vision and mission statement for our organization and a set of measurable goals that would inform our interpretative model. Roberts would take these statements and help us develop them into a strategic plan.

Without question, the most challenging work of that period involved distilling all our ideas—disparate and sometimes unrealistic as they were—into a clear, concise message. By October 2008, we had reached consensus on the following statements:

VISION:

The Thoreau Farm Trust believes Henry David Thoreau's extraordinary insights and ideas about life, nature, and social justice are as relevant today as they were during his lifetime. We will make his Concord birthplace a source of inspiration for living deliberately, practicing simplicity, and exploring positive change.

MISSION:

The Thoreau Farm Trust is dedicated to protecting Henry David Thoreau's birthplace for future generations as an education center, community resource, and place of pilgrimage.

GOALS:

Educational programming will focus on

• environmental sustainability;

• local agriculture past and present; and,

• Thoreau as a community activist and family man.

Community groups will be invited to use the house for small-group activities and educational programming befitting the site.

Thoreau's birth room will be open to the public. Materials about his life and work and the history of the property will be available to visitors.

Even more significant than these central tenets, however, was a memorable moment of epiphany that surprised and delighted us. As soon as we heard the words, we knew they were exactly right, and it is a testament to the cohesiveness of the team that there is no record of who said them first: the house at Thoreau Farm would become a "Birthplace of Ideas."

We embraced the designation because we believed it honored the house's role in Thoreau's life and, at the same time, allowed it to serve as an inspirational starting point, inviting learning, reflection, and action by forward-thinking people. Thoreau, we knew, had professed "great faith in a seed." This would be a place where seeds of good ideas on a wide variety of contemporary issues could be planted in the hope that some, at least, would take root and thrive.

By the end of 2008, though we were only at the midpoint of our strategic planning process, our discussions had taken us a long way toward shaping an interpretive approach to the house and reaching our most important decisions concerning the house's rehabilitation. We would install an elevator in the new addition to allow full accessibility to the second-floor birth room, an expensive feature but one that had gained our full support. With the help of Nancy Grohol and the Green Team, we had also identified a number of environmentally friendly materials and technologies that would make the restored and rehabilitated house as "green" as possible without compromising its historic integrity or busting our tight budget. We decided on low-VOC (volatile organic compound) paint, stains, and adhesives; recycled materials for the roof and siding; FSC (Forest Stewardship Council)-approved wood; and new insulation. We would also use Clivus Multrum composting toilets with a gray water system, and a low-temperature pump that would heat and cool the house without fossil fuels. Though we couldn't afford it at the time, we held out hope that, one day, perhaps with some form of energy subsidy or in-kind donation, we would install solar panels as well. These "green" practices would benefit the environment and reduce long-term operating costs, but they would also serve to enhance our educational programming, becoming teaching tools for lessons on sustainable restoration techniques.

XXXIX
FINAL PREPARATIONS

And there I sat, long, long ago, waiting for the world to know me.

—Nathaniel Hawthorne

As we honed our mission and shepherded the construction project throughout 2009, the Trust could not afford to spend all its time on detail work and introspection. We had to continue our outreach, fundraising, and event planning, all of which became more challenging during the hard-hat phase of the project. Not everyone visiting the birthplace during that period met the chaos and detritus with writer Peter Golden's imaginative gaze. Our task was to imagine for them.

When we hosted events off-site in 2009, we mounted large-format images from the birth house's past as well as informative renderings, drawn by landscape architect Nicholas Reed, of what it would soon become. At every event, we also distributed copies of our plans for the house, which were becoming more specific as time went on. We actually saw no loss of interest on the part of the public during this period, something that kept us striving for new ways to present the future to audiences of the day.

One of our goals for the events was to create opportunities for multigenerational groups to engage with the messages we believed the house could convey. On March 9, in keeping with our goal of educating people about agricultural practices, we hosted a screening of the Peabody Award-winning film *King Corn* at Concord Academy's Performing Arts Center. The feature documentary, released the previous year, was conceived by two Yale classmates, Ian Cheney and Curt Ellis, who had an intriguing idea. They would move to Iowa and, mimicking the practices of many commercial farmers in the U.S., plant corn using powerful herbicides and genetically modified seeds. They would then follow the harvested corn, the most highly subsidized crop in the country and the one most involved in sustaining our "fast-food nation," as it made its way through the food chain. It was a provocative subject, made more compelling by the presence of

Ian Cheney at the screening, and attracted a wide range of audience members, from farmers to food activists.

Then on June 14, we were fortunate to welcome Concord resident Gregory Maguire, author of *Wicked*, to a special event at the house for invited guests, all of whom had supported the project with their time, ideas, or personal resources. Though the house was not yet officially open for visits, we wanted to give these folks an early-bird tour of the work in progress. Under a tent in pouring rain, Maguire's undiminished good humor took me back to the day I visited his home for an interview, when I was still editor of *The Concord Journal*. I happened to arrive at the end of a photographic session by *The Boston Globe* and was ushered toward the backyard, where I found Maguire perched in the branches of a sprawling crabapple tree, ready for a final shot. His sense of whimsy on that very wet afternoon was a great gift to us all. After touring the house with Thoreau Farm Trust's anointed historian, Joe Wheeler, Maguire became a loyal fan of the project and a vocal supporter of the cause.

Leading up to our Annual Meeting that June, I had informed the board that I would be stepping down as president, a role I had held for six years following the five formative years of leadership by our founding president, Joe Wheeler. So, to kick off FY10—the grand opening year—the board put the presidency in the able hands of Nancy McJennett. Molly Eberle remained as vice president, new board member Sally Long, a marketing professional and wife of departing board member Tim Rodgers, agreed to be clerk, and I remained on the Executive Committee as treasurer. Remaining members were Joe Wheeler, Deborah Bier, Lawrence Buell, Court Booth, Brian Donahue, Richard Fahlander, Kevin Foley, Valarie Kinkade, Lorna Mack, Ellen Foley Rice, and Melita Teichert.

With Nancy Grohol leading our crew along, we took part, once again, in Concord's July 4 Picnic in the Park, which always drew a large family crowd, and welcomed visitors to the birth house lawn later that month, first for the Thoreau Society gathering, and a few days later for our community-wide birthday celebration for Henry, both of which had become popular annual events.

Our contributions to the Concord Festival of Authors that year highlighted two themes we hoped to explore at the birth house: sustainable living and the preservation of wilderness. Linda Booth

Sweeney, author of *Connected Wisdom: Living Stories About Living Systems*, offered a workshop at the birth house for parents and children, designed to help families find kid-friendly ways to teach responsible living practices through storytelling. A few days later, photographer Dan Tobyne returned for the second year in a row, this time to the birthplace, to discuss the images he had gathered for his new illustrated edition of Thoreau's famous paean to wildness, *The Maine Woods*.

Looking ahead to the day when such activities at the house would become more frequent and visitors would at last walk through the restored front door in anticipation of an informative visit, we continued to consolidate our ideas and meld them into a coherent experience we could now all envision. Laura Roberts led our board in several more discussion sessions, prompting us to imagine our potential audience; consider the relationship between the house and the farmland on which it stood; design our interpretive materials; and build an effective business model. By the fall of 2009, we had become more sanguine about our ability to manage the complex functions of a healthy nonprofit. The expertise of our board members, advisors, and consultants had served us well to that point, and we continued to enjoy a good relationship with town staff and the warm support of friends and neighbors.

Despite our growing confidence, we knew we must keep our programming goals modest. Our hoped-for barn would not be part of our official opening the following year and was no longer visible on the far horizon. So interior gatherings would need to fit into the small interior spaces, while in warm-weather months we could expand to the outdoors. We decided to build our interpretative materials around a few of Thoreau's key ideas—simplicity, sustainability, social justice—and his influence on later thinkers, such as Gandhi and Martin Luther King Jr. We would add a kitchen garden near the entrance, designed and managed by board member and gardener extraordinaire Deborah Bier, filled with heirloom plantings redolent of Thoreau's mother's childhood years living on the farm. Finally, we would ask visitors how they themselves were weaving Thoreau's principles into their own lives and invite them to leave messages behind to share with others. The house began to take shape in our minds as an interactive space, where visitors—both local and far-flung—could reflect on what it means to "live deliberately."

To help us in this preparatory work, we were gratified to receive grants from the Massachusetts Humanities Fund and the Sudbury Foundation for interpretive planning and the development of materials. At one point that fall, Laura Roberts convened a "scholars meeting" that included current and former board members Lawrence Buell, Brian Donahue, and Jayne Gordon, and the Thoreau Society's executive director, Michael Frederick—an impressive brain trust, indeed.

Anticipating the impending tenancy of the Thoreau Society, which would move its headquarters to the house in early October, we were in frequent conversation with Frederick, who had been serving as the Society's liaison to the Trust's board. In a bit of bureaucratic déjà vu, we negotiated a lease with the pro bono help of an attorney friend, and Larry Sorli designed the office spaces to accommodate the Society's needs. We had also been in conversation with Gaining Ground, whose board had expressed interest in renting a space in the house, and we had agreed to cede some of the west parlor—the downstairs space the Trust would use for its own office—for use by Gaining Ground's staff. This arrangement with Gaining Ground would not only bring in additional income for the house's upkeep, it would also strengthen the bond between the two primary residents of Thoreau Farm. To help manage the day-to-day issues that might arise with tenants inhabiting the house, we engaged Ben Gifford, who had been working with Larry Sorli on the construction project, to serve as a caretaker.

Major construction on the house was completed by the end of September and the exterior scaffolding removed. Though finish work on the interior spaces was still in progress, the house had become what we had hoped: a pleasing hybrid of the historic and the functional. The minutes of the Trust's board meeting that month show a good deal of sober work having been accomplished, but they also hint at our giddy mood that evening. Clerk Sally Long included "dragonfly" as one of our attendees, later reporting, "A dragonfly dropped in on the meeting, sat next to Sally, was fully present for a few minutes, and then proceeded to transition to the next life—time of death/departure was called at 8:18 p.m. Sad but true." The minutes also recorded a unanimous vote approving the following resolution: as soon as the Trust was set to inhabit the house, we would carry Nancy Grohol over the threshold.

XL

A NEW LIFE FOR THOREAU FARM

In the final months before the Thoreau birthplace would open to the public in June 2010, the Trust put the finishing touches on an identity for the house. After a great many drafts and revisions, we chose a logo we hoped would evoke the literary and agricultural significance of the birth house and announce its place in Thoreau's life. We also hoped our chosen logo would reflect Thoreau's bond with his hometown and the fertile ground on which he was born, as reflected in a journal entry from Nov. 20, 1858: "If a man is rich and strong anywhere, it must be on his native soil. Here I have been these forty years learning the language of these fields that I may the better express myself."

After many months of construction and high-level discussions and strategic planning, it was now time for us to allow Thoreau's birth house to better express *itself*.

So we put preparation to paper and designed interpretive panels that would be displayed throughout the house, allowing visitors to appreciate its long history and benefit from its inspirational value. I recall this creative work as one of the most enjoyable tasks board members, advisors, and executive director accomplished as a team.

By January 2010, both our tenants were settled in and pronounced themselves happy with the space and atmosphere. This was good news, since Larry Sorli remained at work completing interior carpentry and painting, and the driveway and landscaping were still in rough shape.

In February, although we had been receiving small grants for interpretive work, the Trust found itself $40,000 short of the funding needed to complete all the work that would make the house welcoming for our first visitors that spring. A board member and a Thoreau

Society member each offered interest-free loans of $10,000, and we decided to borrow the remaining $20,000 from a local bank. We had hoped to avoid debt but were grateful that the amount was small and the debt service manageable.

By March, we were starting to get the word out that the house would be opening soon. A Boy Scout troop planned to conduct an Eagle Scout project on the site that spring, helping us with the house garden and environmentally conscious practices like composting and rainwater collection for watering. A program for girls had been booked for three weeks in the summer, and a tour group from Texas had scheduled a visit for September. We were on our way.

Our June Annual Meeting saw the departure of Lorna Mack, who was leaving Concord to live permanently on Cape Cod. As happened with other directors emeriti, she would continue to stay interested and involved in the project. All other board members, including officers, remained the same for another year.

Also noted at that meeting was the news that "Larry is leaving." Larry Sorli, who had by now become a fixture of the house in our minds, had completed all the work except for installing gutters and doing a bit of touch-up painting. We could not, of course, really let him go, nor did he want to distance himself from the house. We knew he would continue to serve as a trusted friend and advisor, which he remains to this day. Besides attending many of our events once the house had opened, he planned to write the formal Historic Structure Report that would include every step of the restoration/rehabilitation process and include a trove of photographic evidence of the work. As promised, we would donate the volume to the town so that it could be preserved forever in the Special Collections of the Concord Free Public Library. That month's minutes to the contrary, Larry was not leaving.

We had decided to host two openings. The first was held on Sunday, June 13, for special invited guests. The second involved a weekend of activities on June 26 and 27, for the general public. The two-day event was designed to highlight our schedule moving forward, when we would be open to the public on weekends through Columbus Day.

All three opening days included guided tours of the house, which was now decorated with our interpretive panels. The first of these, displayed in the foyer, was meant to set the tone for a meaningful visit:

> Thoreau Farm believes Henry David Thoreau's extraordinary insights and ideas about life, nature, and social responsibility are as relevant today as they were during his lifetime. We hope you will find his birthplace a source of inspiration for living deliberately, practicing simplicity, and exploring new ideas for positive change.

> As you visit Thoreau Farm, we encourage you to reflect on how you can live deliberately and make choices that have a positive impact on yourself, others, and the social and physical worlds we inhabit.

Also in the foyer was a plaque honoring the generous friends who had given more than $1,000 to the restoration and rehabilitation of the birth house.

At the bottom of the wide staircase leading up to the birth room we installed a narrow counter equipped with paper, pencils, and pushpins, above which was hung a large corkboard that would soon be dotted with the reflections and responses left behind by visitors.

On the landing halfway to the second floor, we placed photographs and commentaries from local people who had been influenced by Thoreau's life and work. We wanted very much for this to be the people's house, not a place reserved for scholars or specialists of any kind, so we chose to devote this prominent wall to a revolving collection of personal stories from those who might consider themselves "just folks."

The birth room, which had retained much of its original fabric, including its pine floor and 18th-century fireplace, became home to most of the illustrated panels, which contained quotations from Thoreau, his contemporaries, and some of his famous disciples.

The downstairs community room, in the original east parlor, was decorated with the remaining panels, featuring historic photographs of the property and information about its long life. This room also contained hearth bricks that had been recycled from the second-to-last Thoreau family home in Concord, called the Texas House because of its location on Texas Street (later Belknap Street). This house no longer exists.

In welcoming our "VIP" guests on the first opening day, Trust President Nancy McJennett, told guests, "Thoreau has come home":

> Of the Concord cohort of Transcendental writers, he is the only native son, and the only one who has not been graced with a house dedicated to him. Until today. Today, Henry David Thoreau has a home in the place he was born.

After thanking all those who had worked over the course of fifteen years—the number astounds even today—to save, preserve, and restore the house, McJennett added:

> I like to think that, were [Thoreau] here today, he would appreciate that we did not create a museum or a shrine to his memory. He would find a practical and lively mix of small offices for the Thoreau Farm Trust, Gaining Ground, and the Thoreau Society and a handy meeting room, open to the community. Were he to enter the room where he was born, I think he would smile at the simplicity and quiet of that contemplative place.

Our later opening weekend was considered "official" but cannot honestly be described as "grand." The turnout on both days was sparse. We were disappointed but philosophical. We had not booked a noted speaker for either day, preferring to open the house as simply as we would run it. And many community members had attended one of our past events over the past few years and, we hoped, had already begun to think of the birthplace as their own. But we were encouraged by the enthusiastic response to the house's new look and interior presentation and by the warm welcome given to our guest musicians, Jackson Gillman, who offered a concert of "Nature in Action, Story and Song," and folk singers Dillon Bustin and Evan Harlan, who performed "Songs from Walden Pond."

We were also pleased with the wide-ranging media coverage our opening weekend enjoyed. In particular, a *Boston Globe* article by Jay Atkinson, published on June 27, featured numerous photographs of the house and interviews with several key figures. Its opening encapsulated the years of work and care that had brought us to that place:

Beyond his most famous role as a "self-appointed inspector of snow-storms and rain-storms," the writer Henry David Thoreau was a classic Yankee do-it-yourselfer, a genuine jack-of-all-trades. The Concord native and author of *Walden* was an accomplished historian, surveyor, naturalist, humorist, and engineer as well as the prototypical environmentalist and a pretty fair hand at carpentry, masonry, and small-plot farming. It's therefore fitting that many of these skills were required to preserve his birthplace.

The exterior of the original house had been repainted white to correspond to its appearance at the time of its move in 1878, and the new addition painted red to distinguish it visually from the historic structure. Explaining that decision, Sorli told Atkinson, "We didn't want to do false history [by] adding characteristics the house had back at the old site."

Sorli pointed out that the first- and second-floor window frames had been made of original old-growth white pine but had been replaced in the early 20th century. The preservation guidelines provided by the Secretary of the Interior allowed us to restore those frames to resemble the windows that were present in 1878, the year the house was moved farther east on the farm. "We're showing the evolution of the house," he said.

He also described some of the green materials and technology he had used for the project, including the Enviroshake roof tiles on the historic house that resemble traditional wood shakes but were made of 95 perent post-consumer recycled material. He pointed to the stone wall lining the border of the property, which had been recycled from local farms, and mentioned the low-temperature heat pump, and the composting toilets and wheelchair ramps in the addition.

Most striking to visitors was the birth room, which we had decided to keep partially unrestored to highlight its historic features. The original wide pine floors remained, and Sorli had left several "view ports," on the walls and ceiling, which afforded a glimpse of the layers of material that had been added to the house over its almost 300-year history. One showed a swatch of the wallpaper that had once covered the bedroom walls, and another the hand-split wood laths and hand-wrought nails in the ceiling. "If you strip it all off," Sorli told Atkinson, "it's gone forever."

For the opening, we placed only two benches in the center of the room, leaving the rest of the space for groups to explore the historic elements. Later, we would add furnishings that allowed the birth room to be used as a writing retreat: a replica of Thoreau's desk, made for us and donated by John Grohol, Nancy's husband; two armchairs for journaling and reflection; a table, chairs, and an oriental rug; and a few floor lamps for soft lighting in the darker seasons.

To decide on the color of the birth room walls, our historic materials conservator Bill Finch had analyzed tiny paint chips through a high-powered microscope. Originally a brilliant blue-green, known as verdigris, the color was later changed to pea green, which Sorli and Finch chose for the restoration.

Robert Pinsky, our honorary campaign chair and loyal supporter, added his own flinty comments to the *Globe* article, offering perhaps the most succinct and apt summary of what we had chosen not to do at the house. Describing Thoreau as "a hippie intellectual," Pinsky said he couldn't imagine him as a "literal preservationist." In Pinsky's opinion, Thoreau would not have wanted his birth house to be "preserved in moral formaldehyde."

In refusing to turn the birthplace into a museum house, neither had we. *The American Heritage Guide [to] Historic Houses of America* tells us that much of the work of preservation is intent on honoring what the past has contributed to the present. But those of us who fought to preserve the birthplace had always been intent on fostering what Henry Thoreau can contribute to the future.

Thoreau's birth room was sparsely furnished on opening day (above) but today contains a replica of his desk, a work table, and comfortable chairs for reflection and journaling. Besides being open to visitors, it is offered as a writer's retreat.

224

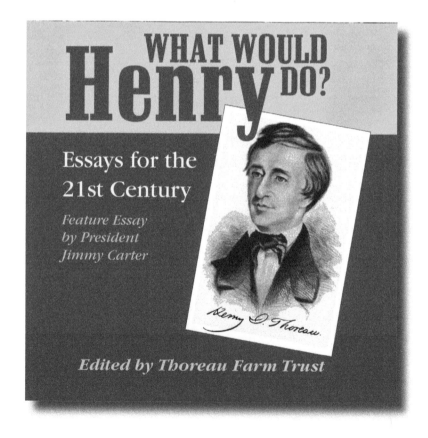

EPILOGUE: 2010–2018

We're so happy to share Thoreau's forward-thinking ideas about life, nature and civic responsibility with visitors and encourage deliberate living in the 21st century. Thanks to all of you who supported this dream.
—Thoreau Farm Facebook message, Dec. 31, 2010

The idea to write this story was conceived on Henry David Thoreau's 200th birthday. At that bicentennial moment, July 12, 2017, the birthplace stood out as unique among all the many Thoreau-related sites in Concord. Hundreds of people strolled the lawns and gardens, toured the house, listened to music and testimonials, and shared stories. Some told of Thoreau's importance to them. Others recalled a time when the house was in no shape to welcome visitors as graciously, and sturdily, as it was doing that day.

The U.S. Postal Service had recently issued a new stamp honoring Thoreau's life and work, which had been released ceremoniously on May 23, 2017, at Walden Pond. Noting the break in tradition—the Postal Service has a longstanding custom of issuing commemorative stamps at birthplace sites if they are available—Thoreau Farm Trust's executive director, Margaret Carroll-Bergman, made a call. That earlier siting of the stamp's release was, she was told, an unfortunate mistake, and the Postal Service wanted to rectify it. As a result, they created a new, illustrated postmark, indicating its origination point as Thoreau Farm Station, Concord MA 01742, and dated July 12, 2017. Postal workers set up shop at the house that day and distributed the new Thoreau stamps and specially postmarked envelopes to scores of visitors willing to wait in line half an hour or more to secure these collector's items. The postmaster would later tell Carroll-Bergman that the commemorative stamp event at the birth house had drawn, by far, more people than any such event he had experienced in the past.

The day also featured the launch of a new book, edited and published by the Thoreau Farm Trust, entitled *What Would Henry Do?: Essays for the 21st Century.* "Dedicated to the residents of Concord and to the Town of Concord, our partners in preserving the birthplace of Henry David Thoreau," the collection includes essays by forty-one authors, artists, scholars, educators, historians, and environmentalists, and features a lead commentary by former President Jimmy Carter. True to the mission of the Trust, the book's contributors focus on the present and future, not the past, and the wide-ranging backgrounds and experiences of the writers testify to Thoreau's continuing relevance among some of the century's liveliest thinkers.

Gone was the day when, before our very first Thoreau Farm Trust birthday celebration in 2004 (and just in time to correct the error), the local baker had decorated the huge green and white sheet cake we had ordered with the words, "Happy Birthday, Harry!" No, on this bicentennial day, it was clear that the HENRY David Thoreau birthplace had come into its own. "It's wonderful to see an appreciation of Thoreau on this day," said the Trust's first president, Joe Wheeler, when he addressed the crowd. "As the new 'forever' stamp declares, Thoreau will continue to live well long after his 200th birthday."

In an essay she wrote for *The Public Humanist*, published on Aug. 9, 2010, just a couple of weeks after the official opening of the birth house, then Executive Director Nancy Grohol expressed the thoughts of the entire Thoreau Farm Trust board when she said, "Those of us who had spearheaded this effort were focused for so long on this goal that it almost surprised us to see it become a reality. At that point, we asked ourselves, 'What next?'"

The question did not spring from bewilderment. We had, in fact, been pondering "What next?" for a long time. The issue was more one of choice. What should we do first?

The year before, our strategic planning consultant had asked us to answer the question, "How do you see Thoreau Farm in ten years?" Our collective imaginings led us to an active, welcoming "meetinghouse for ideas," a rustic farmhouse where "reflection would be cultivated as the main crop," an unstructured experience where visitors would be invited to "pause, look, and see," and a birth room that could be used as a "serene writing retreat." We saw walking trails, a house garden, picnic tables, energy-efficient solar panels, and perhaps even sheep or goats. We hoped the house would become a place where community members could gather and discuss important issues of sustainability and social justice, and we especially dreamed of young people engaging with the house and land as they made their own journeys toward self-awareness and social responsibility. We saw ourselves as collaborators with our birthplace partners, Gaining Ground and the Thoreau Society, as well as with the wider historical collaborative. As an organization, we hoped to remain "a thriving nonprofit with the expertise and the means to keep Thoreau Farm forever lively, inviting, and meaningful."

Except for the sheep and goats, Thoreau Farm in 2018, twenty years after the Thoreau Farm Trust was incorporated, looks very much as we had imagined it would. It has remained simple and largely unadorned; its house gardens enhance the dooryard and complement the active Gaining Ground farm; the birth room has been turned into a place of quiet reflection and offered as a writer's retreat; and the downstairs community room is the site of regular public gatherings. The Thoreau Society has become a true partner, inhabiting the upstairs quarters and collaborating on events and programming. And Gaining Ground's staff shares the downstairs office space with the Trust and interacts daily with its executive director, tour guides, and volunteers. Though the birth house is open officially only on weekends from May to October, if someone is working at the house, no visitor is turned away.

During the eight years since it opened, the birth house has welcomed authors, artists, musicians, filmmakers, educators, historians, environmentalists, gardeners, farmers, and a variety of youth groups. Small panel discussions and talks are held in the community room, and larger groups gather outdoors. Noted author Terry Tempest Williams visited the house in 2016 as a special guest of the Thoreau Society and was visibly moved during her time in the birth room. An equally enthusiastic, though perhaps more surprising visitor was Frank Serpico, the legendary New York City crime fighter and eponymous subject of a best-selling book and popular film. Serpico, at 83, is now an animal and civil rights activist and was the executive producer of the 2018 documentary *Citizen Clark: A Life of Principle*, based on the life of Ramsey Clark as seen through a Thoreauvian lens. Young Edward Emerson wrote that his friend Henry Thoreau, "[o]ur Concord genius of the wood, was a master of the flute." Clearly aware of that affinity, Serpico spent his time in Henry's birth room playing his own flute and reflecting on all that Thoreau had meant to him, thoughts he would weave into a poetic contribution to the *What Would Henry Do?* essay collection.

In February 2015, architect Larry Sorli and architectural historian Anne McCarthy Forbes completed their 170-page Historic Structure Report of the Wheeler-Minot Farmhouse/Henry David Thoreau Birth House. It includes a complete history of the property's ownership, a detailed description of the structure and its evolution, details and photographic records of the restoration/rehabilitation project, and recommendations for the preservation and maintenance of the house moving forward. The report is an essential resource for anyone interested in a comprehensive explanation of all that was done to resurrect the house while honoring its previous lives. It now resides in the Special Collections of the Concord Free Public Library.

Another significant milestone was reached in June 2016, when twenty-four solar panels were installed behind the house, a goal set during the rehabilitation process when Concord's Green Team had helped the Trust find ways to make the house as "green" as possible. The installation of the solar array met the Trust's final objective in making the house sustainable. The panels generate 8,000 kilowatt hours of electricity annually, significantly reducing the Trust's electric bill. What had made the work affordable at last was a generous gift from a board member, and the support of Solect Energy Development, which provided the installation for free. In addition to Solect's donation, Canadian Solar contributed panels for the ground-mount system and Yaskawa–Solectria Solar donated the inverter. In keeping with the tradition of the entire birthplace effort, the solar installation was yet another example of the key partnerships that have continued to move the project forward.

Back in June 2011, a year after the official opening of the house, an era ended when we said goodbye to Nancy Grohol, who had been the Trust's untiring executive director during six challenging years. She had shepherded us—and the birth house—through all our negotiations with the Town of Concord and had created systems and practices that had turned us into a smoothly running operation. She had also forged numerous relationships with other agencies and organizations, which would continue to serve us well.

Our celebration of Grohol's service was heartfelt and sad. But we knew we would be able to call on her experience, wisdom, and common sense as we moved into the next phase of our work. A year after Grohol's departure, when the Thoreau Farm Trust received a 2012 Historic Preservation Award from the Massachusetts Historical Commission, we celebrated her work once again, along with that of Larry Sorli and Bill Finch.

In announcing the preservation award, Secretary of State William Galvin outlined the reasons the Thoreau Farm Trust's project deserved to be honored and ended with these final comments:

> The property's rich heritage presents many opportunities for programming related to New England history, architecture, and agriculture, as well as Thoreau-specific topics, such as literature, philosophy, natural history, and conservation.

> The restoration of the Wheeler-Minot House/Thoreau Birthplace allows this building to function as an educational resource, ensuring that it will continue to inspire and inform future generations.

Galvin's remarks are gratifying in their acknowledgment of the historical significance of the birth house and their ratification of the Trust's decisions on restoration, rehabilitation, and re-use.

To succeed Nancy Grohol in 2011, we welcomed Patricia Hohl, an experienced nonprofit administrator and program manager as our third executive director. We had fashioned a new job description that emphasized the creation and oversight of educational programming, and Hohl came to us with the experience to fill that role.

During her one-year tenure, Hohl introduced two innovations that had been discussed in previous years but had finally found their time. She launched a Thoreau Farm Trust blog, entitled "The Roost," a name inspired by Thoreau's comment in *Walden*: "I do not propose to write an ode to dejection, but to brag as lustily as chanticleer in the morning, standing on his roost, if only to wake my neighbors up."

Today, the blog continues to welcome a wide range of contributors offering musings on nature and social issues in brief essays and photographs. It can be reached through the Thoreau Farm Trust's website: thoreaufarm.org.

Hohl also engaged the services of TourSphere Media to help the board develop an illustrated script for a smartphone app that would allow visitors to take a self-guided tour of the house. In writing the script, which took several months of drafting and revising, we found that we were deepening our knowledge of the history and restoration of the house, which enhanced the value of the project. We were dismayed, however, when we had completed our work and tuned in to a beta version of the voiced narration. The professional narrator had mispronounced Thoreau's name throughout the tour. We had all been well schooled in the correct pronunciation—reported by the family's contemporaries—which places the accent on the first syllable, as in "thorough." The French style of placing the stress on the final syllable has been in popular misuse for a century and a half and continues to be widely heard. But we couldn't let the birthplace perpetuate the error, so we instructed the company to rerecord the entire script, delaying the process even further. Ultimately, the app proved useful, but because it required a hefty fee to maintain accessibility, the Trust chose to let the subscription lapse.

In fact, the months following the birthplace opening, while featuring well-attended events and gaining recognition for the house, were dominated by two concerns: the Trust's need to transition from a preservation-centered group to a programming innovator; and our need to husband our funds in order to remain solvent while completing the final touches on the birth house and meeting our debt service. In the process of spending money on programming and other new initiatives in order to grow our audience and attract support from grant funders, we soon realized we were risking our long-term financial viability.

In June 2012, facing pessimistic financial projections, we chose to sever our relationship with Patricia Hohl and ask Nancy Grohol if she would be willing to return and help refocus our efforts and replenish our coffers. For the next three years, until June 2015, Grohol once again devoted herself to the birthplace in the role of executive director, and it came as no surprise that by the time she rode off into the sunset for the second time, the Thoreau Farm Trust was strong, solvent, and raring to go.

Grohol's efforts, combined with a reinvigorated board willing to share the administrative workload during that period, set us up to attract an outstanding new executive director, Margaret Carroll-Bergman, who joined the Thoreau Farm Trust in the early fall of 2015. "We are confident Margaret will enable us to move our mission forward, especially as we participate in the upcoming events to mark Henry David's 200th birthday in 2017," said the Trust's new president, Ken Lizotte, who had recently joined the board and taken over the presidency earlier that year.

Both Carroll-Bergman and Lizotte brought vitality, talent, and fresh ideas to the Trust's team at an important moment in the organization's life. Carroll-Bergman had been publisher of *Provincetown Arts*, a literary and arts magazine; editor and associate publisher of the *Nantucket Independent* newspaper; a regional editor for America Online's Patch Media; and a public relations and outreach coordinator for The Trustees of Reservations. She also had experience in social media, fundraising, and business management, and many contacts throughout the region.

Ken Lizotte is the founder and chief imaginative officer (CIO) of emerson consulting group, inc., a Concord firm that helps business experts, companies, executives, law firms, and professional services develop and advance their innovative ideas through the publication of books and articles and public speaking opportunities. He is the author of seven books, including *The Expert's Edge* (McGraw-Hill).

Along with Joe Wheeler, Nancy McJennett, Molly Eberle, Court Booth, Deborah Bier, Lawrence Buell, Jack Maguire, Peter Alden, and a long list of supportive advisors and former board members, Carroll-Bergman and Lizotte have raised the profile of the birthplace and made possible the extraordinary event that marked Thoreau's 200th birthday.

When we were painting our mind portrait of what Thoreau Farm would look like ten years after it opened, we sketched in an adjacent barn. We had no money to build it, and we were unwilling to launch another capital campaign effort so close to the last. But our dream still held. We vowed to keep the barn in our long-range plans in the hope that one day we would build an accommodating space for students and teachers to gather and for speakers to interact with audiences of up to 100 people. In talking to several of those who helped save and preserve the birthplace, including Larry Sorli, it is clear that hope for a barn is still alive.

Another forward-thinking idea had excited our board members and a number of our friends and supporters for at least two years following the opening of the house. At the time, it seemed manageable, if too expensive to attempt immediately. Because Thoreau Farm was not located in an area frequented by Concord's visitors, and since so many Thoreau enthusiasts loved nothing better than to shoulder a backpack and lace on walking shoes, why not build a trail that would link the birth house with the National Park Service's Battle Road Trail, a few miles away as the crow flies? This idea had already been floated in the early 1990s by members of the Thoreau Country Conservation Alliance but had failed to gain traction. Flying was, unfortunately, the only easy way to make the trip. A human saunterer would need to cross town wetlands, private property, and federal- and town-owned uplands to reach the Battle Road Trail. It appeared so simple on a map but dauntingly complicated on the ground. A Concord Girl Scout troop approached us with an offer to draw up plans for a trail that would trace a path from behind the Elm Brook housing development across the street to the Battle Road. The Trust's Advisory Board member, J. Walter Brain, himself an amateur mapmaker who had originally proposed such a trail, suggested that we think even bigger. Why not create a walking path from the birth house to Walden Pond?

Talks and plans for a trail, including cost estimates that began to rise precipitously as more and more obstacles emerged, occupied our board meetings for several years. Our two "trail liaisons," former board members Helen Bowdoin and Valarie Kinkade, arranged for the drawing of conceptual plans and convened talks with the National Park Service, the Town of Concord, our Virginia Road neighbors, and several trail advocates throughout the region. Gradually, however, despite the excitement the trail generated among scouts and other young people, it became clear we did not have the resources to address all the practical concerns, nor did we have unequivocal support from the National Park Service. Eight years later, the trail has yet to be built. If it were ever to become a reality, it would add one more public-private collaboration to the birthplace story, and the opportunity for hands-on work could attract a whole new generation to the house.

When I asked Margaret Carroll-Bergman during the writing of this account what she felt to be the Thoreau Farm Trust's greatest need moving forward, she did not hesitate. "An endowment," she replied. "We absolutely must build the funds to maintain the house and keep it looking as good as it did when it opened. With a house that was built in the early eighteenth century, that is never easy."

Carroll-Bergman's answer reflects the final hope we had put forth during the days when we were imagining what the birthplace would look like in the future. We had said we hoped in ten years to have "the means to keep Thoreau Farm forever lively, inviting, and meaningful." The only way to ensure the fulfillment of the "forever" part of that wish is in the form of an endowment. As hard as it is to attract financial contributions for preservation, restoration, and educational programming, it is much more difficult to persuade donors to help build something as intangible as an endowment, even though endowment is what keeps everything else in place. So looking ahead, Carroll-Bergman considers maintaining Thoreau's birthplace for future generations to be the Trust's top priority.

In 1848, Thoreau wrote to his friend H.G.O. Blake, "The heavens are as deep as our aspirations are high." It seems fitting, then, that despite the saving of the property and the revitalization of the house, the vision for Thoreau's birthplace remains aspirational as the Thoreau Farm Trust turns twenty—and counting.

What would Henry do? I think Henry would reach into his pocket for his journal, thumb through his notes for the writing of *Walden*, and urge the Thoreau Farm Trust and its ever-growing family of friends to advance confidently in the direction of their dreams.

A National Endowment for the Humanities teacher conference at
Thoreau Farm Trust, July 2017.

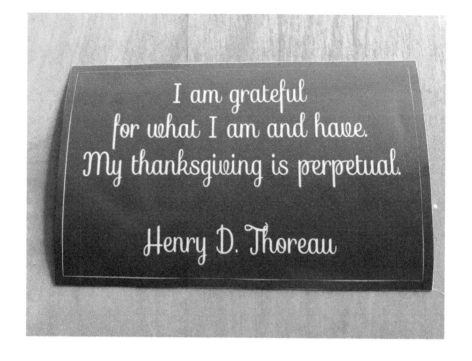

AFTERWORD

If you have been to the top of Mount Washington, let me ask, what did you find there? ...
Going up there and being blown on is nothing. ... It is after we get home that we really go
over the mountain, if ever. What did the mountain say? What did the mountain do?

—H.D.T., letter to friend Harrison Blake

For Thoreau, venturing into challenging territory was a sterile exercise if it did not bear the fruit of wisdom, a taste of what it means to lead a fuller life. Reflecting on what he had seen and heard was, for Thoreau, the necessary complement to seeing and hearing it. One of my hopes for telling this story was to explore what saving Thoreau's birthplace has meant to those who were blown about, rather roughly at times, during the long rescue effort.

"The project presented a great opportunity for me professionally, but it quickly evolved into a more personal mission," recalls Nancy Grohol. "The more I learned about Henry, the more he began to permeate all aspects of my life, and the inspiration he brought to so many became a tremendous motivator for me. The importance of the birthplace to so many people near and far was uplifting and often kept me going despite how overwhelming and daunting the project could be at times. When the house finally opened, knowing that I had played a part in saving the house for all the Thoreauvians to come was the ultimate reward."

For Larry Sorli, the experience became a fascinating detective story that kept offering up clues to century-old secrets. Sorli, a self-described Thoreau lover who joined the Thoreau Society at the age of 15, has left his personal mark on every room. "Most architects don't know how to pick up a hammer," he said with a laugh, as he recalled his hands-on work beside Bill Finch and Ben Gifford. "The Thoreau birthplace became the highlight of my career," he said, "mainly because I was given so much freedom by the Thoreau Farm Trust to take control of nearly all aspects of the restoration and rehabilitation project."

Former Selectman Sally Schnitzer, who worked hard to keep the effort focused on Thoreau and his legacy, said, "I am left with the thought that what has evolved on the property is quite true to the original vision. It's a thoughtful, collaborative farm, with kids and adults engaged in learning, reflection, and productive work. It has remained simple in appearance and spirit. And it honors Thoreau, the town of Concord, the Breen family, and Nathaniel Seefurth's ideals. It is certainly a testament to those who stuck with it for so many years."

Town Planner Marcia Rasmussen acknowledges her surprise—and occasional dismay—at the length of time the town owned the property before it was permanently adopted, restored, and re-used. But Rasmussen says she remains convinced that the time and care that went into saving and reviving the house and farm reflect "Concord's best side." Calling the effort "one of the most remarkable town projects" she has been involved with in a more-than-thirty-year career, Rasmussen says she was especially impressed by the willingness of people of different minds to compromise in order to reach shared goals. "It was an extraordinary community-building experience."

The early advocates who spoke to me about their involvement—including Doris Smith, Helen Bowdoin, Joe Valentine, Michael Kellett, Joe Wheeler, Court Booth, and Jack Green—all pointed to others who, they believed, had done more than they. During these conversations, I never failed to ask leading questions about the impact of the experience on people's lives and work. What had the house said to them? What had it done? What I heard in response, over and over, was not deep philosophical insight but something much more buoyant: joy. The delight everyone expressed at recalling the shared struggle and positive result emerged as the lasting effect, outliving disagreements, frustrations, and fatigue. It was better than any other lesson I could have hoped for.

I have been continually surprised by the stir of emotion that accompanied so many of my conversations. Those unexpected feelings became the perfect bookend to the long-ago moment I first set foot in the room where Thoreau was born.

Today, many visitors leave their own thoughts behind before ending their time at the birthplace. In the summer of 2018, the bulletin board held these responses, among many others, to the question, "How do you choose to live deliberately?":

By enjoying the "moment," and every moment, with joy and purpose—trying!!

I gather wild berries and other edible wild plants and mushrooms and share with family, friends, and other folks interested in connecting to nature via their taste buds.

I try not to judge but to understand. It's hard work.

I run with my dog off-leash through the woods observing flora and fauna, reflecting each night on the wonder I live in.

I am educating myself about where the food I eat comes from and making choices about what I eat based on what I learn.

Trying to learn even better what "deliberately" means.

Every time I'm in the house, I read all the notes on the board. They've become as meaningful a part of my visit as time alone in the birth room, confirming for me Thoreau's ability to prompt people not just to think, but to act. He believed that society's hope rests with the individual, and in the eight years since the house opened to the public, each individual visitor has been encouraged to imagine leading a more considered life. Thoreau wasn't above preaching—and nagging—but he never prescribed a way of life that would be right for everyone, certainly not a cabin in the woods. Instead, he urged each of us to find our own path. It is heartening to see that, for many, that path leads to the modest farmhouse where Thoreau was born. The notes visitors leave behind are the truest testament to what the place continues to say, continues to do. They are the best evidence we have that, in restoring the house, the Thoreau Farm did indeed make it over the mountain.

APPENDIX A
TOWN OF CONCORD
1997 ANNUAL TOWN MEETING
APRIL 28, 29, 30 and MAY 5
LAND ACQUISITION – THOREAU BIRTHPLACE
ARTICLE 35.
Upon a MOTION duly made and seconded, it was
VOTED BY TWO-THIRDS MARJORITY:

That $960,000 be appropriated to acquire by purchase, eminent domain or otherwise land on Virginia Road identified as Assessor's parcel #4286 consisting of 18 acres more or less, together with the structures thereon, of which 15.9 acres more or less of such parcel shall be for conservation purposes including passive outdoor recreation as provided by Massachusetts General Laws Chapter 40, §8C and be under the control of the Natural Resources Commission, and the remainder of such parcel shall be for municipal purposes under the control of the Board of Selectmen; that to raise such amount, the Treasurer with the approval of the Board of Selectmen is authorized to borrow $960,000 under Massachusetts General Laws Chapter 44, §7(3); that the Board of Selectmen be authorized to grant, on such terms as they shall determine, conservation or other restrictions on such parcel; that the Natural Resources Commission be authorized to accept grants and/or reimbursements from the Commonwealth of Massachusetts under the Self-Help Act, Massachusetts General Laws Chapter 132A, §11; that the Board of Selectmen be authorized to apply for, accept, expend and borrow in anticipation of federal, state and other aid that may be available for the project, provided that such purchase shall take place only after receipt of written commitments of gifts, grants and reimbursements for such land acquisition amounting to not less than $800,000, as determined by the Board of Selectmen; and that the Town Manager be authorized to enter into long-term lease agreements for farming the 15.9-acre portion of the parcel, and for developing an educational center by a not-for-profit educational institution on the remaining portion of the project.

Two-Thirds Majority Vote

April 30, 1997

True Copy Attest:

Anita S. Tekle

Town Clerk

APPENDIX B

Remarks offered by Selectman Sally Schnitzer on May 19, 1997, at the Concord Town House in celebration of the town's purchase of the Thoreau birthplace:

We are here tonight to celebrate the upcoming acquisition of the Breen Farm on Virginia Road, the acquisition of over eighteen acres of historically important agricultural land and the historic birthplace of Henry David Thoreau. We are also celebrating the creation of an educational center dedicated to Thoreau.

This project has been about partnering. The cooperative efforts of individuals, agencies, organizations, and the Town have brought us to this evening of celebration. We anticipate closing on the Breen property within these last few days of May, thus meeting the June 1 deadline specified in our purchase-and-sale agreement with the Breen family. Each of you has contributed in some way, large or small, and this evening we would like to recognize your efforts.

In my thanks, I am going to start local, and go afield from there, and then finish up again here in Concord, because that is how I have viewed the success of this project. It began right on Virginia Road and grew from there, reaching out to the larger community, and then finishing up with a strong showing of local fundraising.

To the Breens: Your family were stewards of this land for many decades, carrying on the agricultural tradition that dates back to Colonial times. Your father, James, whose lilacs are gracing our reception tonight, and whose rhubarb we are enjoying, farmed the land until the day he died. We thank your family for entering into an agreement with the Town which gave us the time and the window of opportunity to bring this project together. Thanks, too, to your legal counsel, Nathaniel Brown, for his assistance.

Doris Smith, a neighbor on Virginia Road and the founder of the Save the Thoreau Birthplace Foundation, Inc. Your early efforts brought this project to the attention of the Town, and your persistence launched a successful two-year effort to raise the funds to acquire the property.

Also involved in the early stages was the Thoreau Country Conservation Alliance. Under the leadership of Helen Bowdoin, Michael Kellett, and with the efforts of such Concord residents as Grace Perez, Joe Valentine, Joe Wheeler, Peggy Brace, Theresa Cohen, and others, the TCCA worked tirelessly on many aspects of this project, including publicity, research, fundraising, and strategy. TCCA's work with foundations and historic preservation groups led to the anonymous donation of $180,000 from a Boston-area foundation. Your thoughtful and continual presence at the table during this last year has been greatly appreciated.

Courtland Booth. Court seems to know everyone in Concord and found a way to make connections to all. Through his knowledge of the education community, our early conversations with the Education Collaborative bore fruit. Through his involvement with the museums and the Historical Collaborative, we found ways to complement, rather than compete with their programs. And, of course, Court brought real leadership and organization to our fundraising efforts.

Ian Thompson and his staff at Thompson, Habib, and Dennison did a fantastic job with the town-wide mailing, which brought the immediacy of our need to every Concord home. Thanks, especially, to Suzi Westy Gibson and Mike Spencer who managed the many production details.

Brent Maugel, a Concord architect, worked with the Town staff and EDCO on the conceptual site plan work, site survey, and educational center design. His renderings are displayed tonight.

We thank the Concord Program and its benefactor, the Phillips Foundation, for its support of the out-of-pocket expenses associated with fundraising.

The Concord Journal, particularly editor Lucille Daniel and reporters Bryan Davis and Richard Fahlander, offered not only their editorial support, but also clear, accurate, and continuing coverage of our efforts.

Let me now thank our major sources of funds for this project.

Last April, the 1996 Town Meeting directed the Town to explore all options to secure the permanent protection of this property. By late October, we still had not one thin dime. Thus, the receipt of a Self-Help award from the Commonwealth of Massachusetts in October was the first tangible promise of money toward this important project. The Commonwealth's commitment to the preservation of this historically important open space gave the Town a real incentive to move forward. For their efforts in securing this award, I'd like to thank State Senator Susan Fargo, State Representative Pam Resor, Secretary of Environmental Affairs Trudy Coxe, and Director of the Division of Conservation Services Joel Lerner.

Another agency of the Commonwealth became a partner in March, when the Massport board voted to donate $200,000 toward the acquisition of the property, contingent upon a deed restriction or easement being placed on the land to ensure the land would remain open. I would like to thank Peter Blute, executive director and CEO, members of the Massport board, particularly Jim Coule from Littleton, Massport staff, including Richard Walsh, Barbara Paxner, and former staff member Daniel O'Connell.

This project acquired a true sense of mission and direction when, in March, the board of the Education Collaborative for Greater Boston—EDCO—pledged support of the acquisition, contingent on the Town's entering into a long-term lease for the building of an education center dedicated to the study of Thoreau. Our thanks are owed to Jack Green, executive director, the EDCO board, made up of school committee members and superintendents from twenty-one metropolitan school districts, and the Seefurth family, especially the late Nathaniel Seefurth, founder of the Seefurth Fund administered by EDCO, and his widow, Marian Seefurth, who has followed our progress from her home in California.

We received major support from the following local foundations and nonprofit groups:

The Concord Land Conservation Trust. Early this spring, Dan Monahan and I walked the property with members of the Concord Land Conservation Trust, who were impressed with the environmental and agricultural assets of the property, and who pledged a major gift in support of its acquisition. Thank you.

Derry Tanner of the Sudbury Foundation can rarely donate money for land acquisition projects. In this case, however, the educational component of the project and, in particular, its availability to students throughout the metropolitan area and beyond, made it attractive, and a major donation was awarded. Thank you.

A third local group, Historic Concord, Inc., also voted a major gift in support of the project, saluting the Town and its partners for its efforts to protect this important historic site. Historic Concord also agreed to serve as a conduit for the $180,000 contribution by the anonymous Boston foundation. This money will be used to repay monies forwarded by EDCO and to help fund restoration of the house. We thank Historic Concord, Inc. as well as our friends at this major Boston philanthropy.

We also thank the Historical Collaborative, representing museums, the library, and other educational entities in Concord, who pledged financial support of the project.

Finally, we thank the Neil and Anna Rasmussen Foundation for their major contribution. In a letter to me this week, Neil and Anna stated that Concord "is defined by a fragile chain of special places, from the shops to the schools to the many historic sites. Very often we are faced with a struggle to save these places for future generations. It is wonderful when we actually have an opportunity to add another link to this chain…."

A most generous contribution—of $75,000 in appreciated stocks—was donated by an anonymous contributor just when we needed it most. This extraordinary gift, given without expectation of recognition or publicity, put us within reach of our goals just weeks before Town Meeting. To our anonymous donor—whoever you are—our deepest thanks.

Many local businesses have stepped up to the plate to support our efforts. Our first contributor was Middlesex Bank, represented tonight by Sheila Watts. We received a leadership gift from Welch's, down-the-street neighbors on Virginia Road. Our thanks to Jim Callahan and all the folks at Welch's.

Bill Barber at the Cheese Shop matched money contributed in a jar at the counter, and we also thank him for tonight's delicious and appropriately decorated cake. We thank the Thoreau Club for their support, as well as the Colonial Inn and the Cambridge Trust Company. We also thank Kussins, Nashawtuc Architects, the Poplin Supply Company, the Boynton Company, Incorporated, the Federal Saving Bank, Cirrus Technologies, and Thompson, Habib, and Dennison for their generous support.

In a few moments, in our formal Selectmen's meeting, we will, as required by law, accept all gifts over $500. At that time, we will formally thank the many individuals—residents of Concord—who gave contributions. We also thank the many, many families and individuals who gave smaller, but equally significant and important contributions, ranging in size from less than $10 to $499. One of these smaller contributions came from the Green Beans, who ran a lemonade stand last spring and raised $27.05.

One of the larger donations came from the organizers of the "Thoroughly Thoreau Auction" who also raised money last spring. We thank all of you for your financial support and your vote at Town Meeting.

I need also to thank the boards and committees who supported our efforts. The Natural Resources Commission, Planning Board, Historic Districts Commission, Historical Commission—and very importantly, the Finance Committee, whose members gave us advice, encouragement, and wisdom. I would like to thank the other members of the Board of Selectmen, and my predecessor as chairman, Judy Walpole, who remained a major partner in accomplishing this success.

Finally, thank you to our dedicated town staff. One of the "downsides" of partnered projects is the complexity of details. With many partners to satisfy, the details were enormous. From the negotiation of purchase-and-sale agreements, deed restrictions, site plans, surveying, following up on contacts, grant proposals, and much more, this project would never have come together without Town staff. Under the leadership of Town Manager Chris Whelan, the staff handled such details, and I want to thank Chris, Al Lima, Dan Monahan, Marcia Rasmussen, John Minty, Mike Moore, Tony Logalbo, Jay Clausser, Kaari Mai Tari, Laurel Landry, and town counsels Mary Tracy and Norm Cohen for all your hard work.

APPENDIX C

Thoreau Farm Trust Board of Directors: 2011–2018

2011
Nancy McJennett, President
Molly Eberle, Vice President
Sally Long, Clerk
Lucille Stott, Treasurer
Debbie Bier
Court Booth
Lawrence Buell
Brian Donahue
Richard Fahlander
Kevin Foley
Valarie Kinkade
Lorna Mack
Ellen Foley Rice
Melita M. Teichert
Joe Wheeler
Bill McKibben, Honorary Director

2012
Nancy McJennett, President
Molly Eberle, Vice President
Sally Long, Clerk
Lucille Stott, Treasurer
Alida Bailey
Debbie Bier
Court Booth
Lawrence Buell
Brian Donahue
Richard Fahlander
Carla Gates
Dick Walton
Joe Wheeler
Bill McKibben, Honorary Director

2013
Nancy McJennett, President
Ken Lizotte, Vice President
Molly Eberle, Treasurer
Carla Gates, Clerk
Alida Bailey
Debbie Bier
Court Booth
Lawrence Buell
Brian Donahue
Melissa Juchniewicz
Sally Long
Lucille Stott
Dick Walton
Joe Wheeler
Bill McKibben, Honorary Director

2014
Nancy McJennett, President
Ken Lizotte, Vice President
Molly Eberle, Treasurer
Carla Gates, Clerk
Alida Bailey
Debbie Bier
Court Booth

Lawrence Buell
Brian Donahue
Melissa Juchniewicz
Sally Long
Lucille Stott
Dick Walton
Joe Wheeler
Bill McKibben, Honorary Director

2015
Ken Lizotte, President
Nancy McJennett, Vice President
Molly Eberle, Treasurer
Debbie Bier, Director
Courtland Booth, Director
Lawrence Buell, Director
Brian Donahue, Director
Dick Walton, Director
Joe Wheeler, Director
Bill McKibben, Honorary Director

2016
Ken Lizotte, President
Nancy McJennett, Vice President
Molly Eberle, Treasurer
Debbie Bier, Director
Courtland Booth, Director
Lawrence Buell, Director
Brian Donahue, Director
Joseph Wheeler, Director
Bill McKibben, Honorary Director

2017
Ken Lizotte, President
Nancy McJennett, Vice President
Molly Eberle, Treasurer
Debbie Bier, Director
Courtland Booth, Director
Lawrence Buell, Director
Joseph Wheeler, Director
Jack Maguire, Director
Bill McKibben, Honorary Director

2018
Ken Lizotte, President
Nancy McJennett, Clerk
Molly Q. Eberle, Treasurer
Peter Alden
Debbie Bier
Courtland Booth
Lawrence A. Buell
John "Jack" Maguire
Joseph C. Wheeler
Bill McKibben, Honorary Director

PHOTO CREDITS AND PERMISSIONS

Cover photos courtesy of the Thoreau Farm Trust

Title page — Courtesy of the Concord Free Library
Page iii — Courtesy of the Thoreau Farm Trust
Page vii — Courtesy of *The Concord Journal*
Page 22 — Courtesy of the Concord Free Library
Page 38 — Courtesy of *The Concord Journal*
Page 52 — Courtesy of the Concord Free Library
Page 56 — Courtesy of Thomas Seefurth
Page 60 — Courtesy of *The Concord Journal*
Page 72 — Courtesy of *The Concord Journal*
Page 76 — Courtesy of the Thoreau Farm Trust
Page 83 — Courtesy of the Thoreau Farm Trust
Page 98 — Courtesy of the Thoreau Farm Trust
Page 104 — Courtesy of the Thoreau Farm Trust
Page 105 — Courtesy of the Thoreau Farm Trust
Page 106 — Courtesy of the Thoreau Farm Trust
Page 108 — Courtesy of *The Concord Journal*
Page 122 — Courtesy of the Thoreau Farm Trust/Win Wilbur
Page 128 — Courtesy of Bill Finch
Page 134 — Courtesy of Bill Finch
Page 142 — Courtesy of the Town of Concord Department of Planning
and Land Management.
Page 154 — Courtesy of Gaining Ground
Page 157 — Courtesy of the Thoreau Farm Trust
Page 158 — Courtesy of the Thoreau Farm Trust
Page 167 — Courtesy of Lary Sorli
Page 168 — Courtesy of the Thoreau Farm Trust
Page 171 — Courtesy of the Thoreau Farm Trust
Page 172 — Courtesy of the Thoreau Farm Trust
Page 174 — Courtesy of the Thoreau Farm Trust
Page 176 — Courtesy of the Thoreau Farm Trust
Page 177 — Courtesy of the Thoreau Farm Trust
Page 186 — Courtesy of the Concord Free Library
Page 192 — Courtesy of the Thoreau Farm Trust
Page 196 — Courtesy of the Thoreau Farm Trust
Page 201 — Courtesy of the Thoreau Farm Trust
Page 202 — Courtesy of ElmBank Media, LLC/Brian Smith
Page 208 — Courtesy of the Author
Page 223 — Courtesy of Nancy Grohol
Page 224 — Courtesy of the Thoreau Farm Trust
Page 228 — Courtesy of the Thoreau Farm Trust
Page 233 — Courtesy of the Thoreau Farm Trust
Page 234 — Courtesy of the Author
Page 237 — Courtesy of the Author

CPSIA information can be obtained
at www.ICGtesting.com
Printed in the USA
BVHW061511031118
532063BV00005B/9/P